Drupal 8 for Absolute Beginners

James Barnett

Apress®

Drupal 8 for Absolute Beginners

ISBN-13 (pbk): 978-1-4302-6466-8

ISBN-13 (electronic): 978-1-4302-6467-5

Managing Director: Welmoed Spahr
Lead Editor: Ben Renow-Clarke
Technical Reviewer: Massimo Nardone
Editorial Board: Steve Anglin, Mark Beckner, Ewan Buckingham, Gary Cornell, Louise Corrigan, Jim DeWolf, Jonathan Gennick, Jonathan Hassell, Robert Hutchinson, Michelle Lowman, James Markham, Matthew Moodie, Jeff Olson, Jeffrey Pepper, Douglas Pundick, Ben Renow-Clarke, Dominic Shakeshaft, Gwenan Spearing, Matt Wade, Steve Weiss
Coordinating Editor: Mark Powers
Copy Editor: Lori Jacobs
Compositor: SPi Global
Indexer: SPi Global
Artist: SPi Global
Cover Designer: Anna Ishchenko

Distributed to the book trade worldwide by Springer Science+Business Media New York, 233 Spring Street, 6th Floor, New York, NY 10013. Phone 1-800-SPRINGER, fax (201) 348-4505, e-mail orders-ny@springer-sbm.com, or visit www.springeronline.com. Apress Media, LLC is a California LLC and the sole member (owner) is Springer Science + Business Media Finance Inc (SSBM Finance Inc). SSBM Finance Inc is a Delaware corporation.

For information on translations, please e-mail rights@apress.com, or visit www.apress.com.

Apress and friends of ED books may be purchased in bulk for academic, corporate, or promotional use. eBook versions and licenses are also available for most titles. For more information, reference our Special Bulk Sales–eBook Licensing web page at www.apress.com/bulk-sales.

Any source code or other supplementary material referenced by the author in this text is available to readers at www.apress.com. For detailed information about how to locate your book's source code, go to www.apress.com/source-code/.

This is dedicated to my wonderful family, who has supported me while writing this book and throughout all my endeavors. Thank you to Annette, Harry, Greyson, Phoebe, and our parents for their advice and support.

Contents at a Glance

About the Author xv

About the Technical Reviewer xvii

Acknowledgments xix

Introduction xxi

■Chapter 1: Installing Drupal 1

■Chapter 2: Site Building: Building Drupal Sites Without Programming 7

■Chapter 3: Getting Started with HTML 39

■Chapter 4: Creating a Basic Drupal Module with HTML Output 57

■Chapter 5: A CSS Primer for Drupal.. 73

■Chapter 6: Adding CSS to Your Drupal Module 91

■Chapter 7: A JavaScript Primer for Drupal 97

■Chapter 8: Adding JavaScript to Your Drupal Module 119

■Chapter 9: A PHP Primer for Drupal 125

■Chapter 10: Adding PHP-Generated Output to Your Drupal Module.................. 143

■Chapter 11: Creating a Drupal Block Programmatically and Basic
MySQL Usage.. 147

■Chapter 12: Theming Your Site Part 1: Theme Functions and a Twig Primer 167

■Chapter 13: Theming Your Site Part 2: Creating a Custom Theme
and Subtheme.. 189

■Chapter 14: Working with Forms and Creating Custom Forms 205

■**Chapter 15: Using Git to Manage Your Source Code** 227

■**Chapter 16: Advanced MySQL Primer** 249

■**Chapter 17: Linux** 271

■**Chapter 18: Publishing Your Site to a Production Linux Box** 293

■**Appendix A: Other Ways to Install Drupal** 321

■**Appendix B: Basic Linux Commands** 331

Index 333

Contents

About the Author xv

About the Technical Reviewer xvii

Acknowledgments xix

Introduction xxi

■Chapter 1: Installing Drupal 1

Installing Acquia Dev Desktop 1

Installing Drupal 8 1

Configuring Drupal 8 3

Summary 6

■Chapter 2: Site Building: Building Drupal Sites Without Programming 7

Setting a New Site Title and Logo 7

Adding More Users to Your New Drupal site 8

Assigning Roles and Permissions to Site Users 9

Creating a Blog 11

Editing and Customizing Your Blog Post 14

Adding More Fields to Your Blog Node 18

Working with Blocks 19

Working with Views 24

Changing Your Site's Theme 30

Installing a Theme Using Drush (Preferred Method) 30

Installing a Theme from a URL 34

Installing New Add-on Modules 35

    Installing a Module Using Drush (Preferred Method)..35

    Installing a Module from a URL 37

Summary.. 37

Chapter 3: Getting Started with HTML **39**

Creating Your First Web Page 39

Adding Comments to Your HTML.. 44

Working with Images... 44

Creating Lists 46

Creating Tables.. 47

Adding Anchors 48

Creating Forms.. 51

    Text Fields..52

    Password Fields 52

    Radio Buttons 52

    Drop-downs 53

    Text Areas 53

    "Submit" Buttons...53

    All Together Now..54

Using Layout Elements.. 55

Summary.. 56

Chapter 4: Creating a Basic Drupal Module with HTML Output **57**

Working with the Drupal Docroot Directory.. 57

Creating a Basic Drupal Module 58

Looking at the Model, View, Controller Design Pattern.. 63

Showcasing Different HTML Elements Within the Drupal Module................................. 64

Renaming a Module—and How to Create a Module Not Named "hello_world" 71

Summary.. 72

■**Chapter 5: A CSS Primer for Drupal**.. **73**

A Quick Look Back at the Limits of HTML 73

Styling Your Text with an External Style Sheet... 74

Using \<div\> and \<span\> Tags.. 75

Commenting Your CSS... 76

Creating Additional Styles 76

Choosing Between Classes and IDs 78

Working with Conflicting Styles 79

Using Internal Style Sheets 80

Using Inline Styles.. 81

Understanding the Cascade Order 81

Working with Commonly Used CSS Styles 82

    Text Styles 82

    Fonts and Font Sizes 83

    Links 84

    Tables 84

Working with the CSS Box Model.. 88

Summary... 90

■**Chapter 6: Adding CSS to Your Drupal Module** **91**

Using CSS Within Your 91

Summary... 95

■**Chapter 7: A JavaScript Primer for Drupal**... **97**

Getting Started with JavaScript 97

Adding Basic JavaScript to a Web Page.. 99

Installing Firebug... 101

Using Firebug 102

Modifying JavaScript Code.. 104

Working with JavaScript Programming Constructs...**106**

Variables...106

Arrays...108

Objects..108

Booleans...109

Creating JavaScript Events **109**

Using the jQuery Library..**112**

Using the jQuery Library with Events **116**

Summary..**118**

■**Chapter 8: Adding JavaScript to Your Drupal Module** **119**

Adding JavaScript to Your Drupal Module **119**

Summary..**123**

■**Chapter 9: A PHP Primer for Drupal** **125**

Verifying Your Installation of PHP **125**

Serving Up a Hello World Web Page with PHP...**126**

Working with Some Basic PHP Code..**127**

Working with PHP Looping Structures **130**

Using the foreach Loop..130

Using the while Loop 131

Printing to the Screen **132**

Using If, If Else, and Else If Statements **133**

Switch Statements...**134**

Working with Strings..**135**

strlen 135

strpos and stripos..135

Using Functions..**136**

Functions Operating on Arrays **138**

Summary..**141**

■**Chapter 10: Adding PHP-Generated Output to Your Drupal Module**................... **143**

Adding Custom PHP to the hello_world.module File 143

Summary 146

■**Chapter 11: Creating a Drupal Block Programmatically and Basic
MySQL Usage**... **147**

Creating Your First Block Programmatically 147

Learning about the Drupal Database and Using a MySQL Query in a Custom Block ... 152

Using a Query to Display Data in a Custom Programmatically Created Block............. 157

MySQL Primer 161

Wildcard Character in Queries 161

Summary 166

■**Chapter 12: Theming Your Site Part 1: Theme Functions and a Twig Primer** **167**

Theming Output from a Module 167

Using a Theme Function 169

In Depth with Twig: A Twig Primer 178

Twig Variables 179

Summary 187

■**Chapter 13: Theming Your Site Part 2: Creating a Custom Theme
and Subtheme**.. **189**

Creating a Subtheme 189

Creating a New Base Theme 197

Overriding Existing Theme Functions 199

Exploring Other Options for Overriding Theme Functions 201

Summary 204

■**Chapter 14: Working with Forms and Creating Custom Forms** **205**

Using the Form API 205

Creating a Node Programmatically Using a Custom Form 210

Showing a Custom Form in a Block 222

Summary 225

■**Chapter 15: Using Git to Manage Your Source Code** **227**

Introducing Git 227

Installing Git 228

Installing Git on a Mac 228

Installing Git for Windows 228

Installing Git with Linux 230

Creating an Account on Github and Downloading the Book's Code 231

Using Git to Contribute to a Project 234

Creating a Github Repository 234

Navigating Your Github Repository 237

More Great Git Commands 240

Checking Differences Between Branches and HEAD 244

Using a GUI for Git 247

Summary 248

■**Chapter 16: Advanced MySQL Primer** **249**

Creating a New Database 249

Using phpMyAdmin to Create a Database 249

Using the Command Line to Create a Database 250

Creating Tables 251

Using phpMyAdmin to Create a Table 251

Using the Command Line to Create a Table 252

Inserting Data into a Table 254

Updating Tables 257

Deleting Data 260

Creating and Editing Tables in Drupal 261

Creating the Table in the Drupal Module 262

Inserting Data in a Drupal Table 263

Updating and Deleting in Drupal 269

Summary 270

■Chapter 17: Linux **271**

Introduction to Linux on a Mac 271

Connecting to Ubuntu 272

    Connecting to Ubuntu from a Mac 273

Getting to Know Some Common Linux Commands 276

    Navigating Among Directories and Managing Files 276

    Installing LAMP 278

    Adding Security with Permissions 278

    Searching for Specific Files 282

Creating Shell Scripts 282

Editing Files on a Linux Box 284

    Editing Files with Komodo Edit 284

Summary 292

■Chapter 18: Publishing Your Site to a Production Linux Box **293**

Setting Up the Linux Box in the Cloud 293

    Connecting to a New Linux Box Via SSH 297

    Setting Up the LAMP Stack on an Ubuntu Linux Box 299

    Installing git for Version Controlling Your Code Base 300

    Installing Drush 301

Putting Up Your First Web Pages 302

Installing Drupal 303

Getting a URL for Your New Drupal Site 312

Summary 319

■Appendix A: Other Ways to Install Drupal **321**

Installing Drupal with MAMP on a Mac 321

Installing Drupal with XAMPP on a Windows Machine 327

Summary 330

■Appendix B: Basic Linux Commands **331**

Index **333**

About the Author

James Barnett has been an application architect and adjunct lecturer in the Technology, Operations, and Information Management division at Babson College since 2011. Besides teaching, his responsibilities include designing, coding, and releasing tools and web sites for the college, working with Babson's leaders to keep Babson at the forefront of the technology space. James's team released the advanced discussion boards, the new Faculty Portal and Student Portal web sites, as well as other important initiatives for Babson. James has brought Drupal content management system expertise to Babson, a technology that accelerates the development of cutting-edge web platforms for community sites, web portals, and everything else the Web can provide.

James holds a master's degree in Economics and Finance from Brandeis University, as well a BA from Brandeis University. His past work experiences in the technology space include positions at EMC, Fidelity, and IDG and work as a consultant managing all the software technology needs of a startup in Needham, Massachusetts for more than three years. As a technology consultant for many companies, he has been successful in providing programming, database and information management, and system administration expertise.

James's areas of expertise include PHP, MySQL, Oracle, SQL, PL/SQL, Unix/Linux, shell scripting, Apache, JAVA, PERL, XSLT, JSON, XML, Ruby, Ruby on Rails, HTML, CSS, JavaScript, AJAX, network operations skills, information management, load balancers, and front- and back-end web work.

About the Technical Reviewer

Massimo Nardone holds a master of science degree in Computing Science from the University of Salerno, Italy. He worked as a PCI QSA and Senior Lead IT Security/Cloud Architect for many years. Currently, he leads the Security Consulting Team at Hewlett-Packard Finland. With more than 19 years of work experience in SCADA, cloud computing, IT infrastructure, mobile, security, and WWW technology areas for both national and international projects, Massimo has worked as a project manager, software engineer, research engineer, chief security architect, and software specialist. He worked as visiting lecturer and supervisor for exercises at the Networking Laboratory of the Helsinki University of Technology (Helsinki University of Technology TKK became a part of Aalto University) for the course of "Security of Communication Protocols." He holds four international patents (PKI, SIP, SAML, and Proxy areas). This book is dedicated to Pia, Luna, Leo, e Neve, who are the reasons for my being.

Acknowledgments

This book has been a long labor of love. I've really enjoyed the process and am excited to have the book finally get published. I want to first thank my family and friends for all their love and support. I want to thank the Apress team—they have been awesome, and I cannot imagine writing a 100+ page book without a team to support finding all the typos, hard-to-follow paragraphs, and more. Thanks for all your hard work. I hope everyone feels good about the success of publishing this title together. I have enjoyed working on this title and wish everyone well and success in all that is to come.

Introduction

As with anything else you do, it's important to start at the beginning. So . . . what is Drupal? Drupal is an open source project that allows community-shared code to be assembled to quickly make web sites for any purpose. Drupal is used to power web sites for the White House, Warner Brothers, 30% of all universities and colleges (Babson, where I have been working and teaching, is using it extensively now as well), the Louvre, Zynga, PayPal, Chris Rock, The House of Representatives, Led Zeppelin, and many more big-name sites. Using the power of LAMP (Linux, Apache, MySQL, and PHP) technologies and open source, Drupal can accelerate any technology project, web site, or startup to get up and running fast and for a fraction of the cost. Whether you're creating blogs, wikis, corporate home pages, e-commerce sites, or collaborative communities, Drupal can do all of this—and more—very well. And it's free to download and free to use whether you're using Windows or a Mac! If you want to see the impact Drupal is making, check out the site http://buytaert.net/tag/drupal-sites, which exhibits many of the top businesses and organizations that are using and contributing to Drupal.

What You'll Learn in This Book

Drupal 8 for Absolute Beginners will introduce you to everything you need to start your journey toward becoming a great Drupal developer, or just a plain old good web developer. Most of the skills presented are applicable whether your primary content management system is Drupal or WordPress, or whether your primary programming language is Java, Ruby, or PHP. This book will give you the tools you need to continue to grow as a web programmer, whether for a career as a software engineer or just to understand one of the pivotal technologies in the world today.

This book starts off by teaching you how to install Drupal. Then the book teaches you to do some "site building," which is a term in the Drupal community referring to building awesome Drupal sites without needing to program much if at all, just by using community-contributed add-on modules, themes, and core Drupal itself. Finally, you'll learn how to program—you'll learn HTML, CSS, JavaScript, and PHP—and then you'll see how to use that knowledge to further extend and customize Drupal. By the end of this book, if you practice along and work hard, you'll be primed to become a Drupal rock star in an industry hungry for new talent. At a recent education Drupal summit, we voted on groups to break up into, and the largest group by far was the "how to attract and train Drupal talent" discussion group.

This book will help you achieve the following objectives:

- Create web sites using Drupal.

- Use HTML, CSS, and JavaScript to theme Drupal.

- Learn about the LAMP stack.

- Extend and tailor Drupal with the programming skills previously mentioned.

This book will not teach you every bit of HTML, nor will it teach you every bit of CSS, PHP, MYSQL, or Apache. But it will teach you absolutely enough so you will be empowered to easily learn the details on your own. If you know how to make text blue with CSS you can easily use the same concepts to make the text bright purple, and to make the text a bit larger in headers, and so on. My point is, you simply need a primer, and this book is exactly that. If I forget the syntax to float an element to the left, and have text float around that picture on the right, I look it up. But I know how to look it up, I know where to look it up, I have enough of a background that I can read any technical writing and figure out what I need to get done, and I have enough background so that even though I'm usually more of a back-end programmer in my job role, I can easily double as a themer and decorate a page to mimic designs I've been asked to implement for web pages. The point is, this book is a primer, giving you enough, teaching you to fish, and teaching you where to go to get work done. After I've taught you enough so you get the primary concepts for a web technology I'll provide links to info on the rest of the details, links that I often have used and continue to use. Even when you know this stuff, you will use the Internet as your manual to get exact syntax, or to remember how to use a command.

KEEPING UP WITH TECHNOLOGY

Before you take on any new skill, it's important to understand why you're doing it or how that skill might take you further in your career. In the Drupal classes I teach, I've been starting off by showing this great video: `http://youtu.be/nKIu9yen5nc`. This clip is an awesome video from some famous people exposing how important technology skills are today, and the video highlights that those with knowledge of how to program are "rock stars" in today's working world. The future is now, and I hope this video will inspire you to work hard to learn.

I also should call attention to this page on code.org: `http://code.org/stats`. Note that even today there is a tremendous shortfall of programmers—and as of this writing it's expected that there will be 1,000,000 more jobs requiring programming skills than students by 2020. I firmly believe that every young person should learn basic programming skills. Programming is an awesome tool to have in your tool chest and should be as ubiquitous as a hammer or screwdriver. Programming skills fetch the highest-paying salaries for young graduates, as the `http://code.org/stats` page points out.

I love the quote from Einstein, "Strive not to be a success, but rather to be of value." Having deep knowledge of programming I often feel like one of the most useful people in a company boardroom, and the joy of feeling useful, higher wages, and great jobs and companies looking to attract my skills makes it quite a worthwhile endeavor to learn this stuff.

Ready, Set . . . Let's Learn

So. . . get yourself into a good, comfy chair, ideally with your computer in front of you, and let's learn some Drupal. I'm confident that this book will jump-start many careers, and I have evidence of this already, having succeeded in getting internships and jobs for many of my students in the Boston area with some top companies that provide Drupal services. I'm excited to be able to contribute toward helping folks learn the skills to find and maintain great careers in the technology space.

CHAPTER 1

■ ■ ■

Installing Drupal

Drupal 8 is a much awaited release in the Drupal community, finally bringing Drupal into the world of object oriented programming, better configuration management, stricter separation of concerns by introducing TWIG for templating, and much more that will all be covered in later chapters. This chapter walks you through the easiest way to install Drupal and get it up and running: use the Acquia distribution called Acquia Dev Desktop, which is available for both PC and Mac users, on your local machine (your own computer). For additional install methods, see Chapter 18, "Publishing Your Site to a Production Linux Box," which covers installing Drupal within a Linux Ubuntu server, and Appendix A, "Other Ways to Install Drupal," which covers alternatives to Acquia Dev Desktop for installing Drupal on your local machine.

Installing Acquia Dev Desktop

You can download Acquia Dev Desktop 2 from www.acquia.com/downloads. If you use a Mac, choose the dmg version of the installer; if you have a PC, choose the exe version of the installer. After you have downloaded the appropriate version of the installer, double-click the downloaded file and follow the installer instructions.

Installing Drupal 8

After you have run through the Acquia Dev Desktop installer, you'll be prompted to "Start from scratch, I don't have an existing Drupal site." Alternatively, you can start with an existing Drupal site. For the purposes of this chapter, click the link to start from scratch. You'll then see a window prompting you to select a Drupal distribution to start from. Scroll down until you see the Drupal 8 installation, and click the Install button next to it (see Figure 1-1).

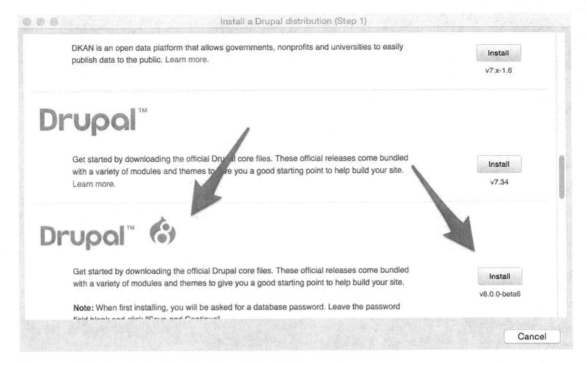

Figure 1-1. *The Acquia Dev Desktop Drupal 8 installation screen*

You'll then see a window similar to the one shown in Figure 1-2. You can accept the default settings and click Finish. However, you may want to change the local site name (the name of your Drupal site) from the default name, because the site name will be featured on the top of every page of your Drupal website by default. Doing so will change the local site URL (uniform resource locator) and database to match the site name you provided.

Local codebase folder:	/Users/jbarnett/Sites/devdesktop/drupal-8.0.0-beta6 Change...
Local site name:	drupal-8-0-0-beta6
Local site URL:	http://drupal-8-0-0-beta6.dd:8083
Use PHP:	Default (5.5.17)
Database:	Create a new database
New database name:	drupal_8_0_0_beta6

< Back   Finish   Cancel

Figure 1-2. *When installing Drupal 8, you can accept the defaults or change the local site name*

Finally, you'll see the window shown in Figure 1-3, which includes a link to where the code lives locally within your file system (the "Local code" link) and a link to view the raw data in the database (the "Local database" link). Most important, however, is the "Local site" link. Clicking this link will take you to your first Drupal 8 site. Acquia (a professional Drupal hosting company) has made it that easy to install Drupal 8 with Acquia Dev Desktop. Go ahead and click the "Local site" link now.

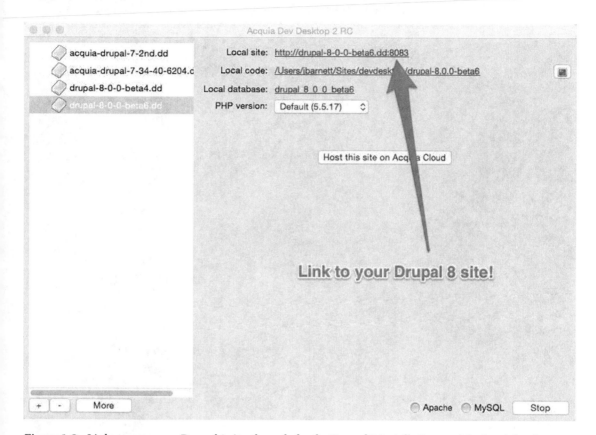

Figure 1-3. *Links to your new Drupal 8 site, the code for the Drupal 8 installation, and the local database*

After clicking the link to your Drupal 8) site, the basic installation process is complete, but you still have some configuration work to do.

Configuring Drupal 8

To begin the configuration process, choose the language you want to use for your Drupal site and then click the Save and continue button.

On the next screen, you can choose the standard installation or the minimal installation. Choose the standard installation and then click Save and continue.

The next screen prompts you for information about the database you'll be using and asks for a database username. The password field is blank, and for now, you can just ignore this setting. This installation of Drupal will live only on your own computer, and you don't need the installation to be secure; accepting the defaults in this case is fine. In a production Drupal installation, you would set up a MySQL database prior to installing Drupal, and you would at that time set up a secure MySQL database username and password combination (see Appendix A for more information). Click the "Save and continue" button.

The final screen, "Configure site" (see Figure 1-4), is where you enter a valid e-mail address for the site, as well as an admin username, password, and e-mail address. In addition, you can choose your default country and time zone settings. Enter that information now. Finally, you can choose to be notified about updates to the Drupal 8 software. When you are finished, click the "Save and continue" button.

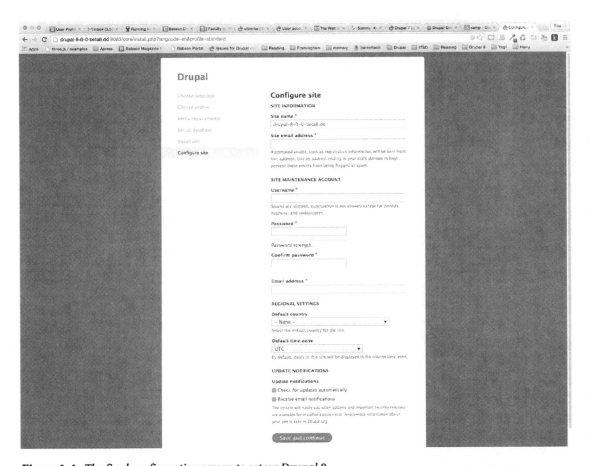

Figure 1-4. *The final configuration screen to set up Drupal 8*

At this point, your Drupal site is set up (see Figure 1-5) and ready for tailoring to your heart's delight. You can change the theme (the look) of your site, change the site's title, create blogs, and more. As easy as it was to set up your first Drupal site on your local computer, you'll soon be crafting your own web site, complete with blogs and all the rest.

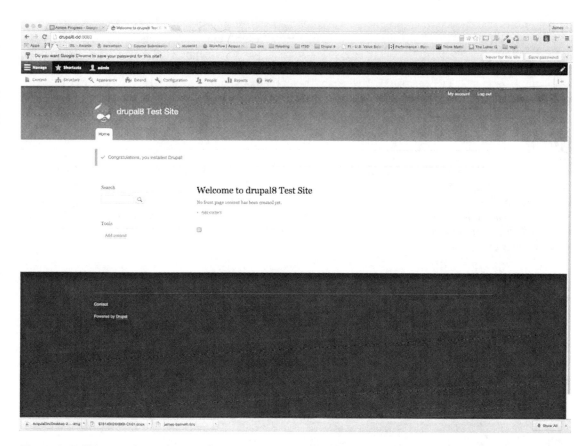

Figure 1-5. *Your new Drupal 8 site after using Acquia Dev Desktop to easily and quickly spin up your first site*

Now that your Drupal 8 site is up and running, you can always bring up the Dev Desktop Control Panel by going to your applications list within a Mac, or within the Start ➤ All Programs area on your PC. The control panel has everything organized for you: it shows you the health of your Apache web server running locally (running on your computer) and the health of your local MySQL database (we'll be diving into the database layer later, but basically it's where all your Drupal back-end data is stored). Within a click or two, the control panel has a way to manage your MySQL database. Through the control panel, you can also spin up another new Drupal site (if you click the plus sign within the lower left-hand corner of the Acquia Dev Desktop control panel).

There are many ways to install the LAMP stack on your computer and to then get Drupal installed (Appendix A goes over a few other options in detail). I usually use MAMP (`www.mamp.info/en/index.html`) and I use it for development on my Mac currently. I've also done well in the past using the Zend Community Edition of the LAMP stack (`www.zend.com/en/products/server/free- edition`). Often you will install Linux, Apache, MySQL, and PHP (LAMP for short) and manually download Drupal; this is a common way for some folks to get started. Also, once you have the LAMP stack installed you can install Drush (the Drupal command-line tool which is awesome) and you can use Drush to install Drupal (`https://www.drupal.org/node/1791676` and `http://www.drush.org/en/master/install/`). I encourage and teach Drush usage in many scenarios throughout this book. I'm going to assume you're using Acquia Dev Desktop right now (for either a PC or the Mac), since you'll be up and running within a few minutes, and then I can give you a quick tour of the many things you can do in Drupal with just a half hour or so of training.

As always I'll refer you to the programmer's handbook for more information: Google. Anything you don't know in the world of Drupal and you can usually, if you're tenacious enough, figure out how to do most anything by googling the problem. But it helps to know the basics so you know what to search for. Throughout this book, I'll be guiding you through the way to learn in the computer science arena. If you have a Mac, try Googling "How to install Drupal MAMP"; you'll find plenty of blogs on how to get it set up. I just tried that Google search for you and sure enough it came up with five YouTube videos on how to set it up on a Mac.

Summary

This chapter walked you through the simplest way to get Drupal up and running on your own PC or Mac: using the Acquia Dev Desktop 2 installation package. Within minutes you should have been able to download and install Acquia Dev Desktop 2 and install and configure Drupal 8. In doing so, you should have been easily able to spin up your own basic Drupal 8 site on your local computer. In Chapter 2, you'll learn to do lots of great things, like creating blogs, creating users, creating views, changing the site's theme, and more.

CHAPTER 2

Site Building: Building Drupal Sites Without Programming

This chapter describes what is known in the Drupal community as "site building," which is the art of making web sites with Drupal without needing to know or write code. And, believe it or not, you *can* use Drupal to do quite a lot as you work to create bust web sites—all without ever writing a singl e line of HTML, JavaScript, or PHP. In fact, using Drupal just as it comes, out of the box, makes it easy to create full web sites with more generic requirements. Let's get started and take a look at the many things you can do in Drupal without programming skills.

Setting a New Site Title and Logo

To personalize your first site, you'll likely want to change the site's title and upload a new logo, as shown in the following steps.

1. In the black admin toolbar at the top of the screen, click the Manage tab, and then click the Configuration tab, which displays below the black admin toolbar. Under the SYSTEM heading, click the Site Information link. On this page you can set the title of the site. You can also enter in a page to replace the default error pages for the site, and you can put in an alternate page to be your site's home page. For now, simply enter your site's title. In this example I use the title "Drupal 8 Web Programming Essentials." Click the "Save configuration" button.

2. To change the default logo, click the Appearance tab in the top admin menu toolbar. Then click the Settings link.

3. Scroll down the page a bit and uncheck the "Use the default logo supplied by the theme" check box. Click "Upload logo image." After you upload your new image, click the "Save configuration" button.

4. Click in the upper left of the site on the "Back to site" link.

In Figure 2-1 you can see the finished product of what my site looks like after I changed the site name and logo.

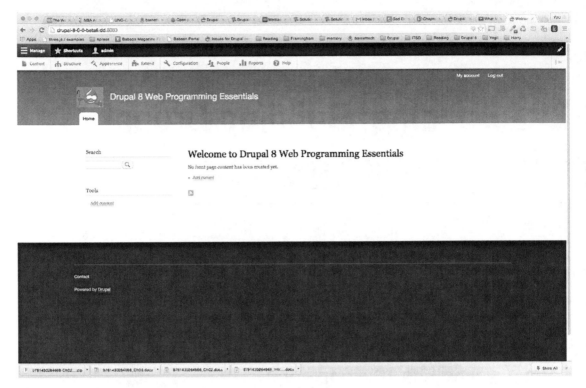

Figure 2-1. *This is what my Drupal site looks like after changing the site name to "Drupal 8 Web Prgramming Essentials" and updating the logo to show a Drupal guy holding some tools*

Now that you've rebranded your site with your own site name and logo, you're ready to move on with building your great new Drupal site.

Adding More Users to Your New Drupal site

In Drupal you can gate your content so only logged-in users—known as "authenticated users"—can see content, or you can allow all "anonymous" non-logged-in users to view your site. You can also have a mix, allowing only certain pages to be viewed by authenticated users while leaving other pages open for even anonymous users to view. The following steps show you how to add more users to your site, so they can log in successfully and access your content.

1. In the admin toolbar at the top of the screen, click the Manage tab and then click the People tab that appears. You'll see a list of users who can log in. Again, these users who can log in to your site are known as "authenticated users." "Anonymous users" are folks who visit your site without logging in. These are key terms in the Drupal world.

■ **Note**   If someone has removed the black admin bar, which is possible, you can always go to the ...admin/ index URL on your Drupal site to see all the available admin options, so if your site is usually www.barnettech.com, for example, you would just go to www.barnettech.com/admin/index. As long as you're logged in as the admin user or a user with administrative privileges, you'll see all the admin links available to you. I often go to the ... admin/index URL and then press CTRL+F (or on a Mac, Cmd+F) to invoke the browser's built-in search capability. Then you could search for the word "people" on the page and you would find the same admin screen links.

2.   In the upper left, notice the "Add user" link. Use the "Add user" link to add an authenticated user or two to your site.

Now that your site has some users, you can assign different permissions to these users.

Assigning Roles and Permissions to Site Users

When you add one or more new users to your site, you'll want to think about what these users should and should not be able to view and do on your site. This section looks at how to group your different users into roles, as well as how to limit their user activity by their role with the help of the Drupal permissions system. Assigning different roles and different permissions within your web site governs what users can do and view on the site.

1.   Navigate to the ...admin/people/permissions URL by clicking the Manage tab and then clicking the People tab. Alternatively, go to ...admin/index and search for "people." See Figure 2-2.

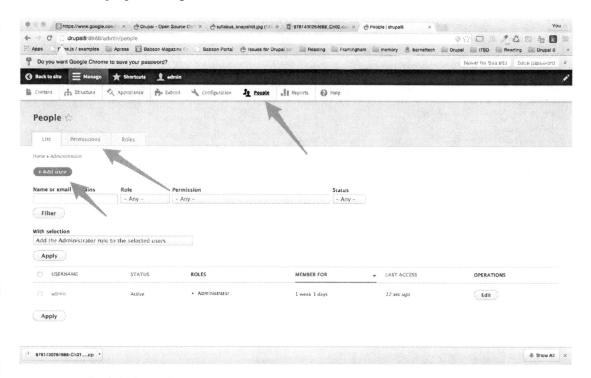

Figure 2-2. *The default People page*

2. Click the Permissions tab. Your screen should resemble Figure 2-3, which
    shows the Permissions page. Browse this permissions list to take a look at the
    type of control you have over content visibility, access to different pages, and
    so on within your site using permissions. Feel free at this point to change the
    permissions users on your site have to act within your site.

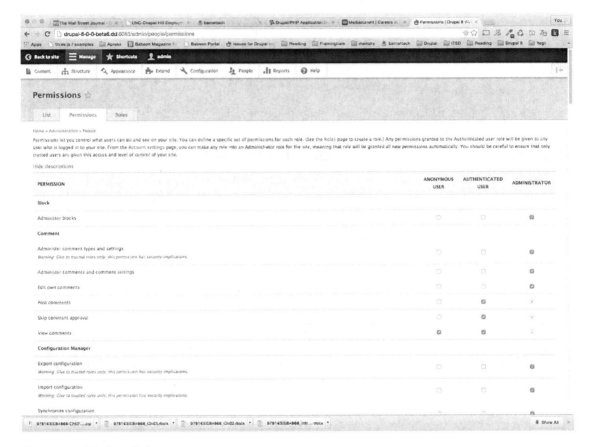

Figure 2-3. *The Permissions page*

If in the list of permissions you locate the "Post comments" permission and select the check box under the heading "ANONYMOUS USER" to the right, then just as you would guess, anonymous users will be able to post comments on your site. I don't recommend allowing the anonymous posting of comments on a live site, however, because your site will be the victim of a lot of spam.

In Figure 2-3, notice the Roles tab, which is next to the Permissions tab. The Roles page lets you control permissions based on a user's role(s). Out of the box, Drupal has an "anonymous" role for handling permissions for non-logged-in users, as well as an "authenticated user" role for all logged-in users. In addition, Drupal offers the "administrator" role, which is a role you can grant to anyone who should be able to administer the Drupal site. In the Roles tab, you can add new roles to be available.

3. To add a role to a user's account, click the List tab (next to the Permissions tab and Roles tab). Find a user you want to edit and click the "Edit" button next to that user's name.

4. Scroll down until you see all the different roles with check boxes next to them. Select each role you would like to grant to the user you selected.

5. Click Save at the bottom of the page.

Now that you've learned about users, roles, and permissions, it's time to learn how to create a basic blog.

Creating a Blog

With the home page set up with a new site name and logo, as well as users and their permissions, you're now going to create a blog to feature on your home page. The recipe for creating a blog in Drupal is easy.

1. If you are logged in as an admin, click the Manage tab and then click the Content tab. Next, click the "Add content" link. Figure 2-4 should help you make sure you're in the right place.

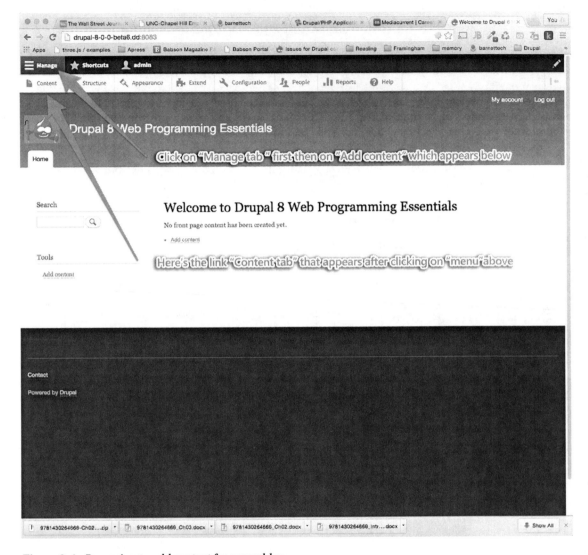

Figure 2-4. *Preparing to add content for a new blog*

2. Click the Article link to create a new article. (The other link is for "Basic page" to create a new basic page. You could click either link, but this example uses the Article link.)

3. Fill out the fields presented to you. You'll need to fill out the title and body fields at a minimum. You might, for example, choose to title your first post "Test First Post." The actual body of you blog might be long or short, but for now try "Here is my blog's body text!"

4. On the right-hand side of the screen, click PROMOTION OPTIONS. You'll see that Promote is set by default (see Figure 2-5). This option will promote this post to show up on your site's home page. Also, notice the check box next to Sticky. This option ensures the items you've marked as "Sticky" will remain at the top of the list when you add subsequent pieces of content to be promoted to the home page of your site. I often use the Sticky feature to keep my "featured" blog articles at the top of my site's home page. For this example, choose to make the current blog post you're creating "Sticky."

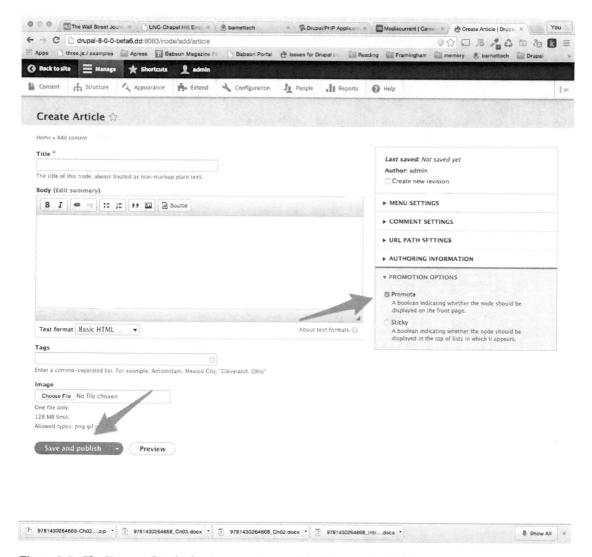

Figure 2-5. *The "Promote" to the front page option and the "Save and publish" button*

5. Click the "Save and publish" button.

■ **Tip** If you want to save the piece of content without publishing it, click the arrow next to the "Save and publish" button. This brings up the option to "Save as unpublished."

---

6. Repeat starting again from step 2 to add more blog entries to your site.

7. When you are finished adding blog entries, click the "Save and publish" button again.

Okay, there you go. Now you know how to create a basic blog or two! Easy, like Sunday morning.

Editing and Customizing Your Blog Post

This section will show you how to edit and customize an existing blog post, modify the blog's title or body fields, turn commenting on and off, and more. If you point your mouse to the upper right of your blog post, you'll see two pencil icons appear. Click the top pencil icon to modify the view that is displaying your list of blog posts (I'll explain what a view is in a bit); click the second pencil icon to edit your blog post (see Figure 2-6). You can choose Quick edit to modify the body of the blog post without leaving the page, which is a pretty cool new feature for Drupal 8. Alternatively, you can click Edit or Delete. In this example, you use the Edit feature, shown in step 1.

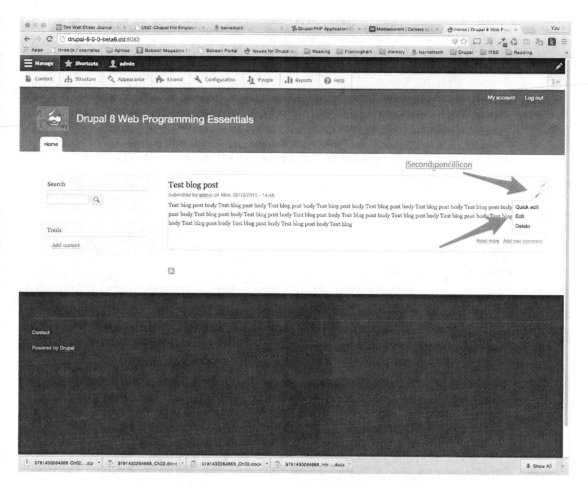

Figure 2-6. *The edit pencil icons appear when you hover your mouse to the right of your blog post title*

■ **Note** In Drupal technical circles, any existing piece of content, like your existing blog post or a Wiki post, is referred to as a "node."

---

1. Click the bottom pencil icon and then click Edit.

2. On the right side of your screen, you'll see a bunch of settings that you can use to change your piece of content, or node. Let's look at the comment settings and authoring information.

3. Click COMMENT SETTINGS. You'll see you can change this setting from Open to Closed, which will turn on (Open) or turn off (Closed) comments for this piece of content. If you were to change this setting to Closed, you would see—after you click "Save and keep published"—that when you view the piece of content, the option to add a new comment is gone (or is present if you chose Open). When you click "Save and keep published," you will leave Edit mode and Drupal will automatically take you back to a screen where you will be viewing the piece of content again. For now, leave this setting to be Open.

▓ **Note**   Nodes can have comments. You will see the term "node" over and over again in your Drupal development work. It is a key concept!

---

4. Click AUTHORING INFORMATION. If you have multiple users in the system, you can change the author of this node (i.e., this article) to be any user of the Drupal site who has a registered account. You can change the "Authored on" time here as well. For now, leave this setting as is.

5. Click PROMOTION OPTIONS. You'll see that you can promote the node to the front page, which forces the node to show up on the home page of your web site. Promote the current blog post you're editing to your site's home page. You'll also see the Sticky option, which I described in the previous section "Creating a Blog." If you select this option for your blog post (your node), then that blog item will stick (stay) at the top of the list of blog articles, if you have multiple blog posts listed on your home page. This option is great for keeping some featured articles/ blog posts at the top of your site. For now, leave this setting as is.

6. Note the "Save and keep published" button at the bottom of the Edit screen (see Figure 2-7). You'll see there is an arrow you can click. If you click this arrow, you have the option to "Save and unpublish" the piece of content. This option used to be alongside the options within Promotion Options in previous versions of Drupal, so if you're a Drupal veteran, make sure to note this interface change.

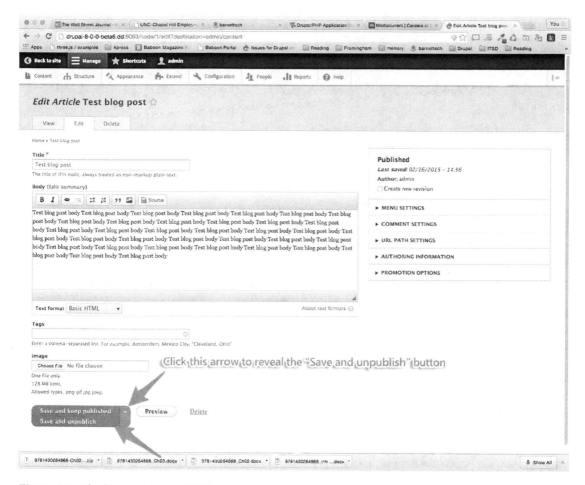

Figure 2-7. The "Save and unpublish" button

■ **Note** If you choose not to publish a piece of content, or node, you can go and find it again by clicking the Manage tab in the admin toolbar and then clicking the Content tab. On the resulting screen, you'll see a list of all content, both published and unpublished. By default, the most recently created items will be at the top of the list.

This exercise demonstrated how to edit an existing piece of content, or node, in Drupal. If you changed the node title or body, updated authoring information, or turned comments on or off, you'll now see your changes reflected on the home page.

Adding More Fields to Your Blog Node

When you create a blog post or any other kind of post, you have a title field and a body field. These fields are available when you install Drupal without your having to do anything. One of the most popular features of Drupal is that through the user interface, you can add more fields. These additional fields are known as "cck fields," and it's the CCK (content construction kit) module that comes with Drupal that allows this functionality.

1. Click the Manage tab in the admin toolbar and then click the Structure tab. (As I said earlier, you can also go to the ...admin/index URL on your web site and find the same admin links.)

2. Click the "Content types" link.

3. Click the "Manage fields" link next to the content type called Article—these are our blogs right now.

You can easily create a new content type by clicking the Manage tab in the top admin toolbar, clicking "Content Types," and then clicking the "Add content type" button. You can call your new content type "blog." You may want to do this to help organize your content more clearly—it certainly would make it more clear for any other editors of your Drupal system because they aren't in your brain and may not realize that the article content type is really where you're putting your blog content. Let me clarify—your site users will not know you used an "article content type" for your blog content, but if you have other admins/editors of the system, making a new "blog," "content type" would help to avoid confusion, because these are the terms they will see in the admin screens.

4. After you click the "Manage fields" link, you'll be able to add fields. Add a field of type "text (formatted, long)." Name the field Metadata. (In this case you're using Metadata as the field name because metadata is a place to collect data about your data. So you would use this field to collect some info from the user about the entered piece of content.)

In the real world—outside this book, that is—you really can name the field anything you want. If you wanted to associate each piece of content with a country, for example, you could create a Country field, and users would fill out a node form field with the country name associated with the node content. Or you could create a Phone Number field and have users associate a node with a phone number. You can create any field that you find useful to add to your node for data collection and to display.

5. Click Save. On the next screen you're asked for the "Allowed number of values." You can just leave it as "1" and then click the "Save field settings" button. On the next screen that displays, you can enter a default value for this field and some help text that will help show users, who will be entering the form, what they should enter for this field. For now, just click "Save settings."

6. Go back to the home page of your site by clicking the "Back to site" link in the upper left corner of your screen.

7. Follow the directions from the section "Creating a Blog" to add a new blog article. You'll see that the new Metadata field is available, ready to fill out.

8. Create the new blog post and click the "Save and publish" button. You'll see the output of the new field in View mode of the blog article (in View mode of the node, not to be confused with Edit mode of the node).

■ **Note**   We have the ability to extend a content type, as was shown here, thanks to the CCK module in Drupal. Most of CCK has moved into Drupal core since Drupal 7, so it wasn't necessary to download the module. Some special field types still require a download of an add-on module. For example, you can add a file field type, which lets you add files to a node, or you can add an image field type. There are all sorts of field types that let you customize Drupal nodes.

You've now learned to add fields to content types to extend Drupal's nodes to collect any kind of information you want to collect from users and display. In the next section, you'll explore Drupal blocks, which allow you to better place content in any region of your Drupal site.

Working with Blocks

Blocks in the Drupal system refer to blocks of content that can be placed in different areas, or "regions," of the site. A block could be placed in the header, the footer, the right sidebar, left sidebar, or any other region that you set up for your site.

For example, you could have a block in the right sidebar with the most recently created comments on the site, an option you can use out of the box. Or you could have a block with the most popular nodes on your site. You could also have a block with some advertisements from your site's sponsors. The footer of your site might have a block with copyright info or links to your company's job boards.

Blocks really can have any type of content you like, and Drupal's block system allows you to easily place these blocks of content into different regions of your site. The following steps contain the easy recipe to place blocks in the Drupal system.

1. In the admin toolbar, click the Manage tab, click the Structure tab, and then, under the "Block layout" heading, click the Block layout tab (see Figure 2-8). These are the different regions on your web site, where you can place blocks.

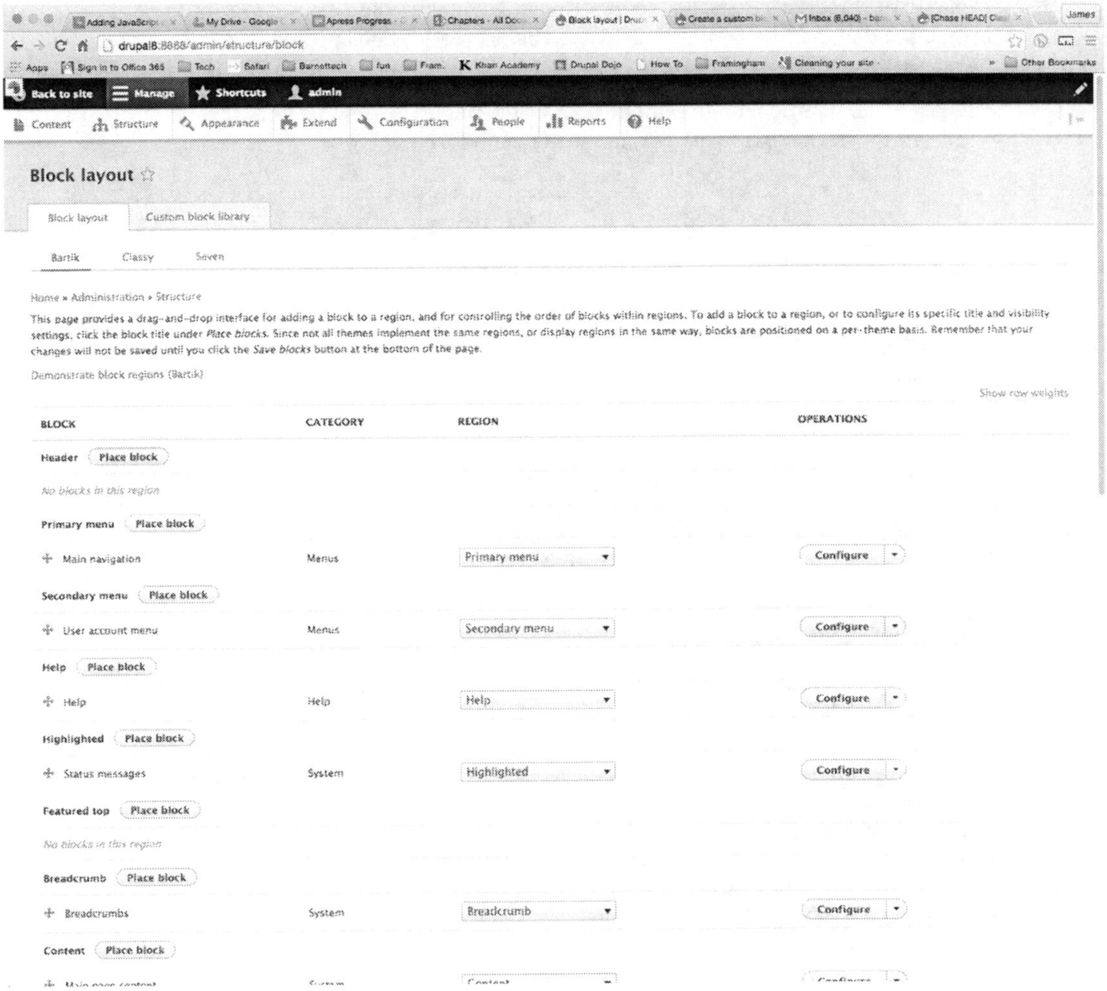

Figure 2-8. *The Block layout screen*

2. Click the "Demonstrate block regions (Bartik)" link. You'll see where on the screen each region exists within your theme.

3. Click the "Exit block region demonstration" link at the top of the screen.

4. Now in whatever region you would like to place a block you can click on "Place block", and then you'll see a list of the existing blocks available (i.e., the blocks that come with Drupal) for placement in the given region. The "Who's online" block displays in a block, users who are currently logged in to your Drupal site. The "Recent content" block shows recently published nodes. The "Recent comments" block shows recent comments users have posted to your site. These blocks all come out of the box with Drupal, and you can place these blocks easily in whatever region(s) on the site you choose. Just click on the "Place block" button next to one of these blocks in the list of blocks. Try this on your own now. You can choose to display the title, or not, and you can restrict which pages the block appears within. When you are finished, click "Save block."

5. Add a block by clicking the "Custom block library" tab at the top of the page, then click on "Add custom block". This will allow you to create your own new block, and you can easily add text or HTML into the block. Type some basic text or HTML in the block body textarea and type in a block description in the textfield, and then click Save. Back on the main block page (as seen in Figure 2-8) you'll see a "Confifigure block" button next to each placed block, clicking this button provides a bunch of options you can change (feel free to play with these options, or you can just leave them alone for now). You can change the title of the block here. You can restrict what pages your block shows up on, you can display the block on just certain pages that are of a certain content type, or you can restrict which roles can view your block (e.g., maybe only site administrators should be able to view a certain block). Chapter 11, "Creating a Drupal Block Programmatically and Basic MySQL Usage," shows you how to programmatically create a block and opens the doors for creating far more complex blocks to enhance your site.

6. To make edits to any custom block you created, remember the Custom Block Library tab in the upper right of the Block layout screen (see Figures 2-10 and 2-11). Within this tab you'll find all your custom blocks made via the graphical user interface (GUI).

7. After you save your changes, go back to your site's home page. If you placed a block in the "sidebar second" (the right sidebar), footer, or whatever region you chose, you'll now see the block show up there. Figure 2-9 shows what this looks like on my site.

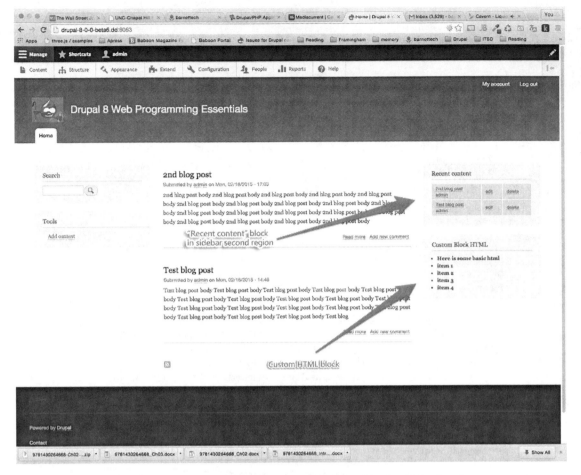

Figure 2-9. The "Recent content" block placed in the "second sidebar" (right sidebar) region

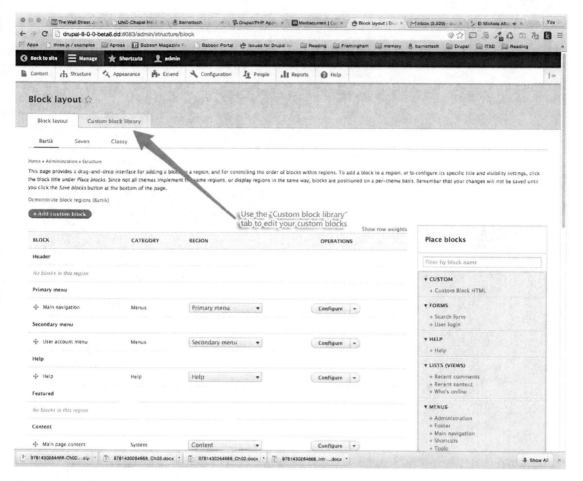

Figure 2-10. *The Custom Block Library*

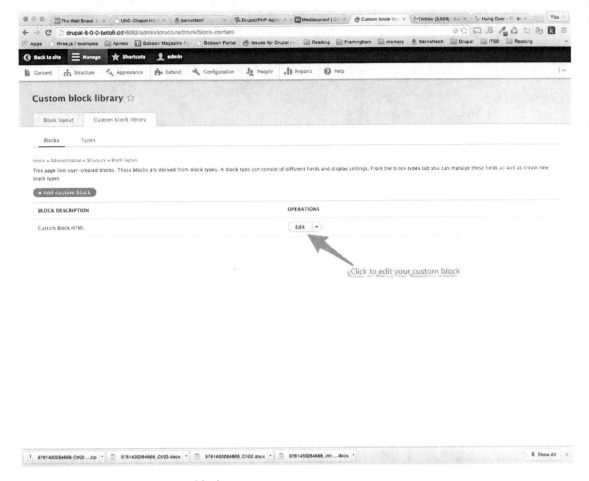

Figure 2-11. *Editing your custom block*

In this section, you used Drupal blocks to place content within your site and display where that content appears. In the following section, you'll use Drupal views to gain more control over the look of your content.

Working with Views

You've now created a blog on your site, but that blog appears as Drupal's default representation of the data. This section looks at Drupal's Views feature, which gives you much more control over exactly how your blog or any other content is displayed. The Views feature is a popular option among site builders.

The Views feature allows you to create varied representations of the content that you've entered into the system by allowing you to alter the view of your nodes and the content you created by using the different content types. Views allows you to create pages with lists of your content items (your nodes), for example, or you can present your node data as a slide show (if you download and install the add-on module Views Slideshow). Views allows you to control the display of your nodes, including what fields are displayed and what fields are not displayed. There are many different ways Views allows you to present your data, and there are many add-on modules that further extend the many different ways to present your data. And, again, the beauty of Views in Drupal is you can do all this without needing to know how to program with HTML, JavaScript, and PHP.

In Drupal 8, the front page is now considered a view. If you are logged in as the admin user, you can hover in the upper right of the main content area of the home page and edit the view (see Figure 2-12).

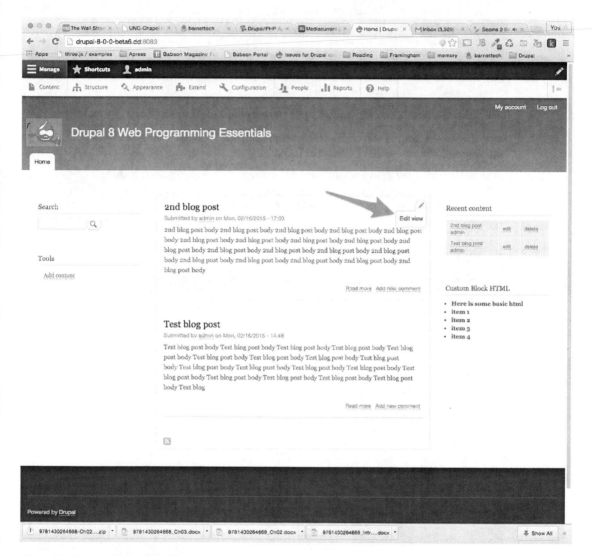

Figure 2-12. *The "Edit view" link*

In this section, you're going to use Views to change the display of your blog data on the home page of your Drupal site. One way to continue would be to just click the "Edit view" link, as shown in Figure 2-12, and make edits to this existing view. But I want to demonstrate how to make a brand-new view should you ever need one, which is likely. The following steps walk you through creating a brand-new view to create a new display of your blog data.

1. Make sure the Views module and the Views UI (user interface) module are enabled; these modules allow you to construct the view(s) through the user interface. Click the Manage tab in the admin menu toolbar; then click the Extend tab. (Alternatively, go to ...admin/index and click the Extend link.) Once on the modules admin page, within the Core section, select, if necessary, to install the Views module and the Views UI module. If these modules are already enabled, continue to step 2. Click "Save configuration" at the bottom to enable these two modules.

2. Click the Manage tab and then click the Structure tab. Click Views. (Alternatively, the link is available at the ...admin/index URL.)

3. Click "Add new view." (You can find and edit any existing view from this page as well.)

4. Name the view whatever you wish—this example will use "bloglist." Then, under Page Settings, click the check box next to "Create a page."

5. There are some other options on the page, but for now just click "Save and edit." You'll see a screen similar to the one shown in Figure 2-13. This page has an overwhelming list of options to construct the view, but this exercise focuses on just a few of these items.

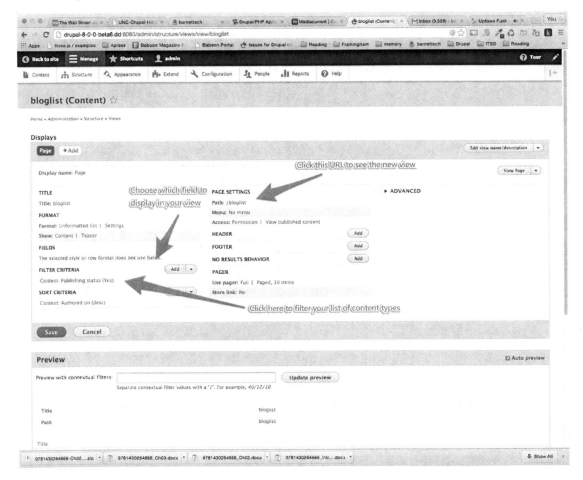

Figure 2-13. *Configuring a view*

6. Click the "Add" button next to FILTER CRITERIA and then click "Content: Type." (There's an option to search, and I usually use it. In this case I searched for "type.") Next, click "Apply (all displays)," choose just Article, and then click "Apply (all displays)" one more time. Now the view will just be showing content of type Article. If you created a content type called "Wikis" or "Blogs," you could just as easily filter to only show data (content) from one of these content types.

7. Now, to allow it so you can just pick certain fields from your Article content type to display, click Settings next to Format and then click the check box next to "Force using fields." Click Apply.

8. Under FORMAT, you'll see "Unformatted list | settings." Click the settings link, choose "Force using fields," and then click the "Apply" button. Click the "Add" button next to Fields, which is now available, and choose the fields you want to display. There are a lot of fields to choose from, and this list can be a bit hard to sift through. But there is a search field at the top of the page, and there are some dropdowns also to help you quickly get to the fields you're interested in. You may decide to show just titles in your display, show just the title and the body, or limit the view to show whatever fields you like from the content type. This option is very useful. For example, if you want to create a view that is not a page, but perhaps it's a block, then you can display just the titles of new content—this might be all that you want to fit into a narrower "new content block." Then you can display the block you create in Views in any region you like using the block system. When you are finished, click "Apply (all displays)" two times.

9. Right now the view you've created is displayed as a Page. To create a version to show in the block system, click the "+Add" button at the top of this Views configuration screen under Displays and then choose Block. Now there will be a block version of the view available for placement in the Drupal blocks system. Figure 2-14 helps you follow along on how to create a block display for your view.

Figure 2-14. *Creating a block using Views*

10. Remember to click the "Save" button. Your created view is not permanently changed until you click the "Save button." Make sure to remember this.

You can show more than one content type in a single view. For example, you can download add-on modules like Views Slideshow (`http://drupal.org/project/views_slideshow`), which even allow you to create slideshows using Views. Or your blog might allow users to input an image using an image field if you've added an image field to the content type, which you've learned to do previously in the earlier recipe for how to add fields to your content type (to your blog). Views will let you select your article content type; then you choose just the image field to display and you follow the recipe outlined in the Views Slideshow add-on module to easily add a slideshow on your site within 15 minutes. (See the `readme` file or documentation on the right-hand side of the preceding link; it will eventually take you here: `http://drupal.org/node/903244`.) Setting up Views Slideshow is beyond the scope of this discussion, but I wanted to give you some sense of the wide array of possibilities Views brings to Drupal site builders.

Take some time to play around with the various views. You can represent your data in a table view, for example. In the GUI, look next to Format and click the hyperlink (the link) next to it—you'll have lots of display options to choose from (Grid, HTML List, Table, Unformatted List, etc.). Notice at the bottom of the screen that there's a live preview of how your view will look.

You can set the URL for your view, under PAGE SETTINGS—in the case of the view I've just created, it shows Path:/bloglist. (Make sure next to Displays you have the Page display type selected and not Block to set the page's path. If Block is selected, simply select Page right next to where it says Block instead.)

After saving my view by clicking the "Save" button at the bottom of the screen, I can then visit my newly created view by going to `http://localhost/bloglist` if I'm developing locally or `http://myurl.domain.com/bloglist` if I've posted this using a full URL (probably not hosting it locally in that case). There are instructions on `drupal.org` on how to now make this view your home page, replacing the default page: `http://drupal.org/node/265172`. You click the Manage tab in the top admin toolbar, click the Configuration tab, and then click "Site information." (Alternatively, at `...admin/index` just look for the "Site information" link). See Figure 2-15, which shows the "Site information" configuration screen. In the FRONT PAGE, "Default front page" text box, type bloglist and then your new bloglist view will also become your site's front page.

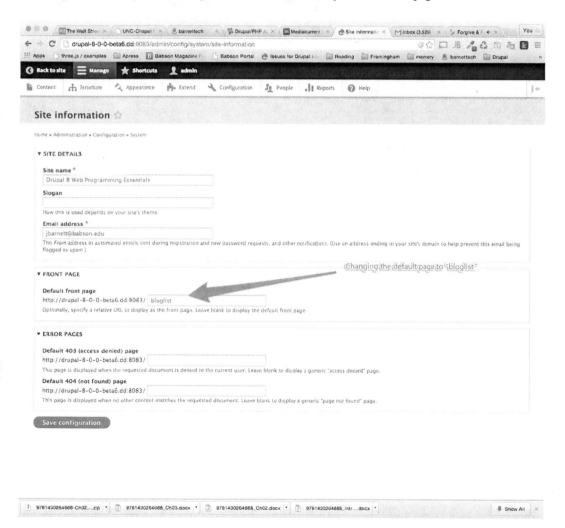

Figure 2-15. *Change your site's home page from the "Site information" configuration screen*

Changing Your Site's Theme

The "theme" is the overall look of your site—the general layout, colors, and graphics that define how your site looks. There are a few different ways to install a theme, to change the overall look of your site. You can install themes by using Drush or by downloading right from a URL (this latter method usually works only if you're developing on your own computer, which allows file transfer protocol (FTP), to work; on a Linux box in the cloud, usually only secure file transfer protocol (SFTP) is enabled. First, this section looks at downloading a theme using Drush, which is the preferred method of installation.

Installing a Theme Using Drush (Preferred Method)

My favorite way to download and install a new theme in Drupal is to use Drush. To use Drush, you'll need to install it. For step-by-step instructions on how to install Drush using Windows or Mac, refer to this book's Appendix.

■ **Note** If you're on a Linux box in the cloud, Drush is very much the easiest way to download another theme to use within Drupal. Otherwise, you have to download the module to your local machine and then SFTP (copy the files over from your computer to another remote computer using an SFTP tool, such as fireFTP) the files over to the Linux box. Drush makes it much easier.

If you're using Windows, open the "Drush command prompt" program (which you can learn to install in this book's Appendix if you don't have it installed already). Once open, type **cd C:\Users\James Barnett\Sites\devdesktop**—be sure to replace my name, "James Barnett," with your Windows username. There you will see all of the folders created for your different Acquia Dev Desktop Drupal sites. Type **cd** and then the name of the folder that houses your Drupal site. If you're unsure of which folder houses your Drupal site, you can always open the Acquia Dev Desktop Control panel and look at the link next to "Local code" which shows which folder houses your site's code base.

Almost the same directions work on a Mac. Open the Terminal program and type **cd /Users/jbarnett/Sites/devdesktop**. This is the location on the Mac file system where you'll find the folders that house your Acquia Dev Desktop Drupal installation(s). Be sure to replace "jbarnett" with own your username.

Now you can issue the following Drush command to download the barnettechetjlb theme, a theme that I've published for this book's release, as shown in Figures 2-16 and 2-17:

```
drush dl barnettechetjlb
```

Figure 2-16. *Using the Drush dl zen command in Windows*

```
● ○ ○                    drupal-8.0.0-beta6 — bash — 129×27
L12-1007:drupal-8.0.0-beta6 jbarnett$ cd /Users/jbarnett/Sites/devdesktop/drupal-8.0.0-beta6
L12-1007:drupal-8.0.0-beta6 jbarnett$ drush dl barnettechetjlb
```

Figure 2-17. *Using the drush dl barnettechetjlb command on a Mac. The directory path in this case is* /Users/jbarnett/Sites/drupal-8.0.0-beta6. *The path shown here is from a live Ubuntu site where I have installed the Drupal filesystem. You'll notice that no matter where you're using Drush or Drupal—on Ubuntu, a Mac, or Windows—the commands are all the same; only the directory path structure differs*

Using this command will download the barnettechetjlb theme from drupal.org (https://drupal.org/project/barnettechetjlb).

■ **Note**   Another example is to download the Busy theme (https://drupal.org/project/busy). To download the Busy theme you would type **drush dl busy** at the sites/default directory.

A trick to know what to put as the name of the project or theme to download is to look at the URL of the project or theme for what follows drupal.org/project/ in the name of the project. In this case, it's "busy" because the URL is www.drupal.org/project/busy, so that is what you type for your Drush command. Sometimes projects with more than one word in the title have a name that has underscores in it—when you type the name into your Drush command, the underscores often replace the spaces between the words that comprise the project's name. I've also seen cases where the spaces between the words of a project name are just removed. If you look at the Corporate Clean theme, they just concatenate the two words and the name to use in Drush is "corporateclean." You can see that in the URL for the project as well https://drupal.org/project/corporateclean.

Now, type the following at the command prompt in your sites/default directory:

```
drush dl corporateclean
```

Once your new theme has been downloaded, you can go to the ...admin/appearance URL of your Drupal web site to enable the new theme and set it as the default theme. On my local machine the URL would be http://localhost:8082/admin/appearance. To navigate there you can also click the Manage tab in the admin toolbar and then click Appearance. Figure 2-18 shows the admin/appearance page.

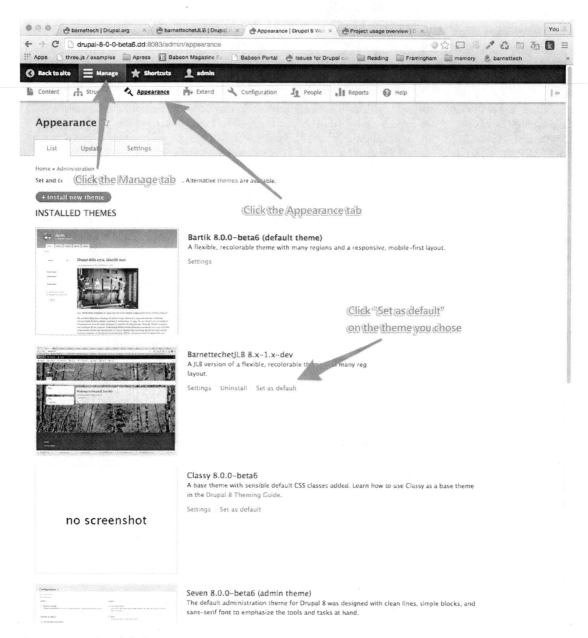

Figure 2-18. *The admin/appearance URL to set the theme for your site*

Installing a Theme from a URL

This section shows you how to download a theme without using Drush, which works well when Drupal is installed on your local machine, because your local machine allows FTP connections. Linux boxes in the cloud require the more secure SFTP to transfer files. (I still prefer using Drush to install themes—and modules—locally.)

There are many alternative ways to install a theme, but in this section you'll install a theme from a URL. This method works best if you're working on a local copy of Drupal on your own computer. If you're on a remote Linux box, this method of installing from a URL will work only if your Linux box supports FTP and not just SFTP—which is unlikely these days because SFTP is more secure, as I said.

■ **Note** If you don't understand the difference between FTP and SFTP, don't worry. Just know that installing from a URL isn't likely to work if you're not working on your own local (personal) machine. FTP and SFTP are just behind-the-scenes ways (protocols) that computers use to transfer files from one computer to another.

The next few steps assume you are working on a copy of Drupal installed on your local machine.

1. Click the Manage tab and then click the Appearance tab in the admin toolbar.

2. Click "Enable and set default" next to any of the theme's you have installed already (a few come with Drupal). Click Save and then go view your home page again. Just like that you can change the look and feel of your site.

You can create your own themes as well, or you can download more themes from the Internet. Drupal.org showcases many themes at the following site: http://drupal.org/project/Themes.

3. Back at the top of the Appearance page, click the "Install new theme" link.

If you don't see the "Install new theme" link at the top of the ...admin/appearance page, go to the ... admin/modules URL of your Drupal site (on my local site it's http://drupal-8-0-0-beta6.dd:8083/admin/ modules). This is the Extend admin menu item you've seen previously by clicking the Manage tab and then clicking Extend in the admin toolbar. Make sure the "Update manager" module has a check mark next to it on this screen; if not click the check box next to this module and then click the "Save configuration" button.

4. Go to the http://drupal.org/project/Themes page and find a theme you like that has a Drupal 8 version. (I like the Business theme.) Under Downloads, locate the tar.gz file, right-click the latest Drupal 8 version, and choose "Copy link address."

5. Back on the ...admin/appearance page of your Drupal site, click "Install new theme." Then click within the "Install from url" field and paste in the link you just copied a second ago by right-clicking and choosing Paste.

6. Click the "Install" button and then choose the option to enable the theme.

7. On the appearance page, choose "Enable and set as default" next to the new theme that was just downloaded.

And there you go. Your Drupal site probably looks awesome already—if you chose a handsome theme.

Installing New Add-on Modules

Recall that modules are like plug-ins that extend Drupal functionality. Modules extend Drupal and add functionality. Although Drupal comes with several modules out of the box, you may have a need for additional modules. For example, you can download modules that will allow you to create slideshows, connect to your Google account, schedule nodes to be released based on a given time and date, and so on. You can find the list of 10,000+ Drupal modules in order of usage at www.drupal.org/project/usage.

Like the processes for installing themes, there are many ways to install new modules. Again, you'll start with the easiest method: installing a module via Drush.

Installing a Module Using Drush (Preferred Method)

Just like you added a theme through Drush, you can add on new modules as well. There are many popular downloadable modules that extend Drupal's functionality. You can find a list, sorted by which modules are most used in the Drupal space, at www.drupal.org/project/usage. So let's say I want to download and install the Layout module, which allows for a responsive (mobile friendly) layout builder to manage the layout of your pages. Its project page is at https://drupal.org/project/layout. (This module almost made it into Drupal 8 core by the way. See https://drupal.org/node/2053879.)

1. Go to a command prompt and navigate to the directory where you have your Drupal installation. Then within that directory, just as you did earlier with downloading a theme using Drush, issue the following command to download the layout module:

    drush dl layout

2. To enable the module, type

    drush en layout

dl stands for download and en stands for enable.

Alternatively, you could use Drush to download the module. Then you could go to the admin/modules URL of your web site, enable the layout module by clicking the check box next to the module, and then clicking "Save configuration" at the bottom of the screen. To navigate there you would click the Menu tab in the admin toolbar, then the Extend tab in the admin toolbar. This would take you to admin/modules, which in Drupal 8 is now called the "Extend" area where you can add on modules to extend Drupal's functionality. See Figure 2-19 for a screenshot of the admin/modules page.

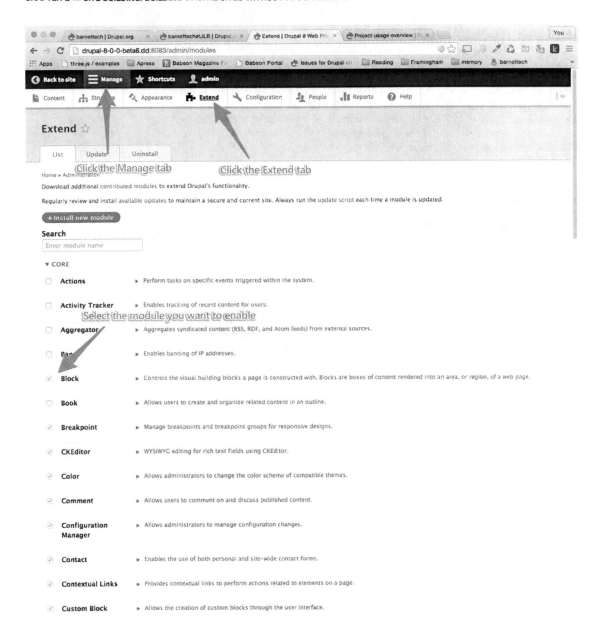

Figure 2-19. *The "Extend" page in Drupal to administer add on modules to extend Drupal functionality*

Installing a Module from a URL

This section looks at installing a module from a URL, just as you did with installing a theme. You'll download the Views Slideshow module this time.

1. Click the Manage tab in the admin toolbar in your Drupal 8 installation; then click Extend (you could also go directly to the `admin/modules` URL). If you don't see the option at the top to "Install new module," make sure the "Update manager" module has a check mark next to it on this screen. If not, click the check box next to this module and then click the "Save configuration" button at the bottom of the screen.

2. Now you should be able to click "Install new module" at the top of this `admin/modules` screen, where you can manage all your Drupal modules.

3. Go to the `http://drupal.org/project/views_slideshow` page.

4. Go to the recommended releases section and right-click the `tar.gz` file next to the Drupal 8 version (just make sure it begins with *8.x*—the rest of the numbers may change if they publish updates to the module). After right-clicking, choose "Copy link address."

5. In the Install from a URL text field, right-click and choose Paste. You'll have pasted in something like the following: `http://ftp.drupal.org/files/projects/views_slideshow-8.x-3.0.tar.gz`. (The URL will vary depending on what project / module you're downloading and which version.)

6. Click "Enable newly added modules."

On the `http://drupal.org/project/views_slideshow` page, look for the "Read documentation" link on the right-hand side of the screen (yes, in a block on the right-hand side of the screen—`drupal.org` is a Drupal site, after all). Read the documentation and play around with your new functionality in Drupal. Note: many modules have documentation from a link on their project page on `drupal.org` on the right-hand side of the screen. All modules have a `README.txt` file, which you can find in the code that gets downloaded to your Drupal install. You'll go learn more about this readme later in book. For now, I'll leave you to read the documentation on how to finish installing Views Slideshow on your own.

Summary

Ok, so that was about a half hour to an hour of playing around with some Drupal basics. This chapter covered some basics of Views, and you learned how to create different ways of viewing your content—all without needing any knowledge of HTML, JavaScript, or PHP. You learned about adding new content types and adding fields to content types to extend the type of data collected when creating your blogs, wikis, or whatever other content types you dream up. You can create fields to collect users' phone numbers, for example, or you can have users add pictures or videos, or sound files perhaps, all by adding fields to your nodes using the CCK, which comes with Drupal. You learned to add blocks to your site, using the out-of-the-box "most recent content" or "most recent comments" block, and add these blocks to the right sidebar, left sidebar, or any other region on the site. You also changed the theme of your site and learned how to download new themes, and you saw how quickly you can change the look and feel of your site by changing your site's theme. As well, this chapter went over how to download new modules to extend Drupal's functionality even further. There are hundreds of Drupal add-on modules to try out. This chapter has given you quite a lot to play around with and to explore.

CHAPTER 3

■ ■ ■

Getting Started with HTML

The most basic element of web programming is HTML, which stands for HyperText Markup Language, which is the core technology in creating web pages. In order to write HTML 5 code (the latest version of HTML is HTML version 5), you'll need to use a code editor. This chapter uses Komodo Edit in the examples. If you have not yet downloaded this free, open source program, you can do so at `http://komodoide.com/komodo-edit`. The free version of Komodo Edit is actually very good.

In this chapter you'll learn all about getting started with HTML so that you can use it later with Drupal. Specifically, you'll learn to create and display a simple web page created with HTML. You'll learn to add lists, tables, hyperlinks, and forms to your HTML page. By the end of the chapter, you'll have a pretty solid grasp of HTML.

■ **Note**   If you already know HTML, feel free to skip ahead to Chapter 4 to see how to fit HTML into Drupal modules, themes, and forms.

Creating Your First Web Page

As you learned in Chapter 1, all code editors work in basically the same way. A good editor will sense which language you're programming in and will format your code in a way that is easy for you—and others—to read. Komodo Edit is no exception.

Take a moment to review Figure 3-1, which shows a bit of HTML code written using Komodo Edit. (You'll see in the figure that I've chosen a dark base theme for Komodo; out of the box Komodo has a white background—changing the color scheme is not necessary.) Notice how the Komodo editor has color-coded the HTML tags (in gold in this case) so your eye can easily separate the tags from the English text of the document. Each editor has some preconfigured color schemes for color coding.

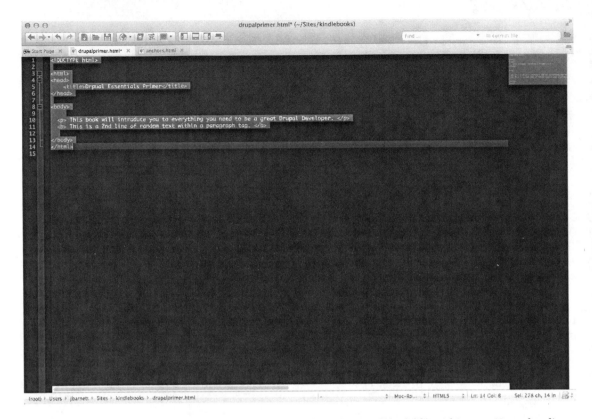

Figure 3-1. *Using Komodo Edit to write HTML. This is what HTML will look like within your Komodo editor*

■ **Note** I've created a video supplement to show you around how to use Komodo Edit. It's not too difficult, but there are a few tricks to know to use the tool. Check out `http://barnettech.com/content/drupal-web-programming-essentials-intro-and-code-editor-recommendation`.

Here is the code outside the context of the text editor as well for easier reading.

```
<!DOCTYPE html>

<html>
<head>
    <title>Drupal Essentials Primer</title>
</head>

<body>

  <p> This book will introduce you to everything you need to be a great
  Drupal Developer. </p>
  <b> This is a 2nd line of random text within a paragraph tag. </b>

</body>
</html>
```

Okay. So what are you looking at in Figure 3-1? It's helpful to break it down.

- The first line—`<!DOCTYPE HTML>`—declares the document to the web browser as being an HTML 5 document. HTML 5, as I mentioned, is the latest version of the HTML language, but it is still backward compatible with previous HTML versions.

- The second line, which contains simply `<html>`, is the opening tag that starts the HTML.

- The eighth line, `<body>`, is the opening tag that starts the body of the HTML document.

- The fourth line is a bit more complicated. It begins with the `<title>` tag and ends with `</title>`, and includes some text in between. This title element will define the text that shows in the browser's top tab area, it defines the title that shows up when the page is bookmarked, and defines the title that shows up in search engine results. In this case, the title is "Drupal Essentials Primer."

- Lines 5 and 6 wrap the text to be displayed in the browser in paragraph elements (`<p> some text </p>`). These paragraph elements define wrapped text as a single paragraph. The text included between these tags is what will be displayed on the web page when viewed in a browser.

- In line 7 `</body>` closes the body element, signifying to the browser that you are done declaring your body in your HTML document.

- Line 8 includes `</html>`, which closes the HTML element and signifies you are done with your entire HTML.

The preceding markup creates the very simplest of HTML documents, but honestly HTML is fairly simple. Don't sweat it—it doesn't get much more complicated than this.

The basic idea is that when you want to treat text a certain way, you "wrap" said text in a tag to declare how that text should be treated. For example,

- To treat text as a paragraph, wrap it in a `<p>` tag like so:

```
<p> I'm a new paragraph. </p>
```

- To treat text as bold, wrap it in bold tags:

```
<b> I'm bolded text. </b>
```

- To treat text with italics formatting, you would do this:

```
<i> I'm italicized. </i>
```

- To use header tags, use the `<h1>` tag. Your most important header tag is `<h1>`, and you can also use `<h2>`, `<h3>`, and so on through `<h6>`. As the number decreases, the importance (size of the text) decreases.

```
<h1> I'm an important header. </h1>
```

Notice that for each chunk of text, you have a beginning (or opening) tag, like `<b>`, and then you have the closing tag, which is the same tag but with a forward slash added to it, like `</b>`. This setup allows you to tell the browser when to start using said tag and when to stop; you include exactly the text want to display in the browser within said tag.

41

■ **Note**   Chapter 5 teaches you about basic Cascading Style Sheets (CSS) and explains how you can write CSS rules to govern exactly how these tags render in a browser. By using CSS you can make your particular text show as blue (or whatever color); you can set the font size; you can set indentation; etc.

So you've seen basic HTML in a file, now what? All you need to do is open your favorite web browser (mine is Chrome or Firefox depending on the task), and then in the upper left click File ➤ Open File and browse for your saved HTML document. You will see the HTML document you just created with your new knowledge of some HTML elements! Figure 3-2 shows an example of what HTML looks like when displayed in a web page.

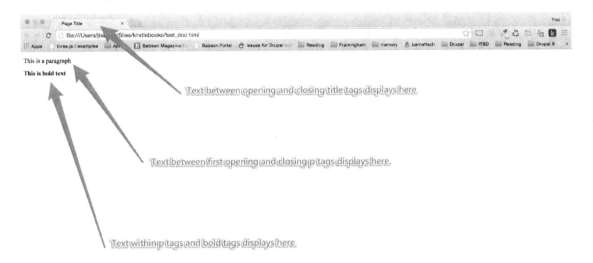

Figure 3-2. *Basic HTML displaying in a web page. The first line of text was placed within paragraph <p> </p> tags, and the second line was placed within paragraph tags and bold tags within the HTML document: <p><b> This is bold text </b></p>. Notice you can have "nested" tags (HTML tags within other HTML tags)*

Now that you've seen how some basic HTML works, it's time to give it a try. To begin, fire up Komodo Edit. Then complete the following steps.

1. From the Start Page, click File and then click New to display a list of different file types you can create. Choose the first item in the list to create a new HTML 5.html file type. Some default code will be generated for you; this is the basic essential code that makes up an HTML page.

2. In the editor that displays, type the following HTML code (see Figure 3-3) or feel free to use your own text:

```
<!DOCTYPE html>

<html>
<head>
    <title>HELLO WORLD</title>
</head>
```

```
<body>
  <h1> This is the header for the page. </h1>
  <p> This is a paragraph. </p>
  <b> This is bold text. </b>

</body>
</html>
```

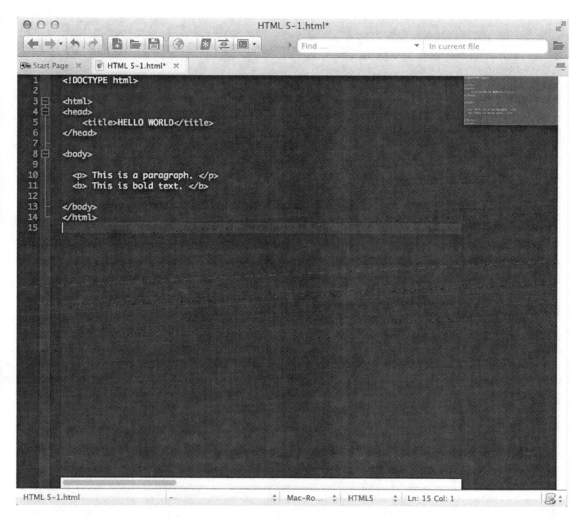

Figure 3-3. *Some basic HTML showing in the Komodo editor*

3. Click File ➤ Save As and then save the file in a place where you can easily find it with a filename of your choosing. Make sure your file has an `.htm` or `.html` extension.

4. Open your favorite web browser. In the upper left-hand corner, click File, click Open File, and then browse to choose the HTML file you saved in step 3. Your screen should resemble Figure 3-4.

This is the header for the page

This is a paragraph.

This is bold text.

Figure 3-4. *Basic HTML showing in a web browser*

Now that you've learned some of the basics of HTML, the rest of this chapter calls out some specific HTML tags that are a bit more complex.

■ **Note** Though you'll have a great grasp of HTML after reading this HTML Primer, I recommend the web site `www.w3schools.com/html/DEFAULT.asp` for further reading about HTML elements not covered in this chapter.

Adding Comments to Your HTML

You can put comments in your HTML code to document your code. These HTML comments do not get rendered by the web browser; they just serve to help document your code, making it more readable and more understandable to any other developer who reads your code. Comments in code are really important even for your own usage. If you write thousands of lines of code, which many developers do, it will serve you to annotate your code with comments so you can easily understand the code you vaguely remember you wrote at a later date. Comments are created as follows, included between the opening `<!--` tag and the closing comment tag, `-->`:

```
<!-- This is an HTML comment -->
```

Working with Images

To include an image on your web page, you use the following syntax, which includes the img element:

```
<img src="filename" alt="text to display if image cannot be shown">
```

The filename in the preceding line would just be something like `imagename.jpg`, and the image should be saved in the same location as your HTML file. `alt` is an attribute that allows you to display text that describes the image should the image not display in the web browser.

If you want to save your image(s) in a different location (i.e., not in the same folder as your HTML document), you can include a relative path to the image. For example, if I save an HTML document on my Mac in the /Users/barnettech/Sites/kindlebooks folder but I put the image in the /Users/barnettech/Sites/kindlebooks/images folder, I would write the preceding path as follows:

```
<img src="images/imagename.jpg" alt = "text to display if image
cannot be shown">
```

Because the path to the image is relative to where the HTML file lives, this is what is known as a "relative path." You will come across relative paths quite often when referencing files, so be sure to commit this new term to memory.

An absolute path gives the whole path to the file rather than a path relative to the current HTML document. The absolute (full) path to the image in the preceding case would be /Users/barnettech/Sites/kindlebooks/images/imagename.jpg.

Now, you'll practice adding code to your basic HTML document to add an image to the web page. I've moved an image (barnettech_logo.jpg) into the same folder as my HTML file. Then, after the line with the <b> and </b> tags, I've added the following line:

```
<img src="barnettech_logo.jpg" alt="text to display if image
cannot be shown">
```

Figure 3-5 shows the results of this action.

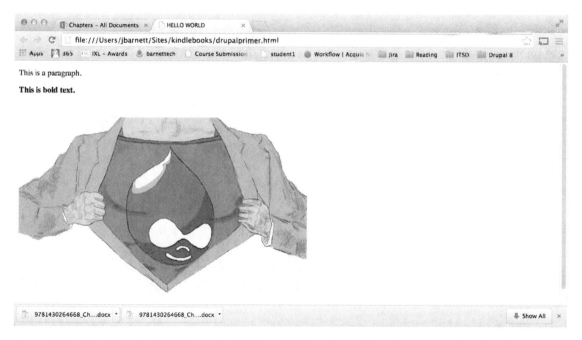

Figure 3-5. *This is how the HTML page looks after adding an image. (Thanks goes to my brother for creating this nice Drupal superhero image.)*

■ **Note**   It is always preferable to use relative paths so if your HTML page moves to another server with a different directory structure your code will still work. For instance, on my Mac the full path to a file always starts with `/Users/barnettech/Sites` and the full path might be `/Users/barnettech/Sites/your_html_file.html`, but on another system the beginning directory structure might be `/var/www` and the full path might be `/var/www/your_html_file.html`. So if you refer to an image file and hard code the full path which starts with `/var/www`, and then move that code to a different computer and try to load it into a browser, you will get an error that the web browser cannot locate the image. For the line `<img src="barnettech_logo.jpg" alt="text to display if image cannot be shown">`, the `barnettech_logo.jpg` file is located relative (a relative path is used) to where the HTML page is located. If you had an images folder in the same directory as your HTML file, the relative path would be `"images/barnettech_logo.jpg"`, and the full line would read `<img src="images/barnettech_logo.jpg" alt="text to display if image cannot be shown">`.

Creating Lists

With HTML you can create two types of lists: ordered lists and unordered lists. With an ordered list, each item in the list is numbered. With unordered lists, bullets appear prior to each item in the list. Here's the syntax.

Ordered list:

```
<ol>
  <li>Item 1</li>
  <li>Item 2</li>
</ol>
```

Unordered list:

```
<ul>
  <li>Item 1</li>
  <li>Item 2</li>
</ul>
```

Figure 3-6 illustrates what the two types of lists look like in a browser.

Figure 3-6. *Ordered lists and unordered lists in a web browser*

Notice that you first declare your opening tag for the ordered list, `<ol>`; then before you close out that tag with `</ol>` you have all your items within that list. Each item is declared with its own opening and closing tag. To start a list item, you open each one with `<li>`, add the item you want to display in the list, and then close out each item with `</li>`. After all the items are declared with their opening and closing tags, you tell the browser you're done with this ordered list by adding the closing tag for the ordered list: `</ol>`.

The unordered list works in exactly the same way, except you open the unordered list with `<ul>` and close it with `</ul>`.

■ **Note**   You will see this a lot, where you will "nest" tags within other tags. For example, `<li>` tags nest within `<ul>` tags. Within paragraph tags, `<p>`, you could have any number of tags, such as bolded text, or italicized, or an image could appear in your paragraph. These tags are "nested" within the paragraph tag. For example, consider this code: `<p> <b> hi there! </b> </p>`. The "hi there!" text is bolded, and occurs within, or is nested within, the paragraph tags. This is an important concept in HTML.

Creating Tables

Tables in HTML are much like ordered lists. First you declare the table opening tag `<table>` and then you declare a row with `<tr>`. Next you put in a nested column tag, `<td>`, then you put in your text, and you then close the column tag with `</td>`. You then repeat that code sequence for however many columns you would like in your table. When you are finished with your columns, you close the row with the `</tr>` closing tag. Then repeat for however many rows you would like, then close the table with the closing table tag `</table>`.

Figure 3-7 shows what a simple table might look like in your browser.

Figure 3-7. *A basic HTML table*

Here's the code that builds the table shown in Figure 3-7. Note that `border="1"` gives each cell in the table the visible borders of the cell; this is optional when creating a table.

```
<table border="1">
  <tr>
    <td>row 1, cell 1</td>
    <td>row 1, cell 2</td>
  </tr>
  <tr>
    <td>row 2, cell 1</td>
    <td>row 2, cell 2</td>
  </tr>
</table>
```

Figure 3-8 shows what the table would look like with column headings added.

Figure 3-8. *A basic HTML table with column headings*

Following is the code that creates the table shown in Figure 3-8:

```
<table border="1">
  <tr>
    <th>Header 1</th>
    <th>Header 2</th>
  </tr>
  <tr>
    <td>row 1, cell 1</td>
    <td>row 1, cell 2</td>
  </tr>
  <tr>
    <td>row 2, cell 1</td>
    <td>row 2, cell 2</td>
  </tr>
</table>
```

Note that to add the headers, the <th> tags are nested within the <tr> tags, which puts the headers on their own row, at the top.

Adding Anchors

An anchor in HTML makes it possible to set up your web page so that if a visitor clicks on a link, also known as a hyperlink, they will be taken to another section of the same web page. You often see this functionality in frequently asked question (FAQ) pages, where there is a list of the most common questions at the top of the page. Those questions are then linked to the answers, which appear lower down on the page.

To create this functionality, you need two pieces of HTML. First, you need to create a link that, when clicked, will take visitors to the other section that appears later on the page.

```
<a href="#section5">Visit Section 5</a>
```

Then lower on the page, where the content that you linked to appears, you would put an anchor on the page with an id as follows:

```
<a id="section5">Section 5</a>
```

In this case, if a visitor clicks on the text "Visit Section 5," that user will be taken to the text on the page "Section 5," which you wrapped with an id of "section5".

This is different from an "href" link, which will send visitors to another web page either within your web site or on another external site and the page will just be loaded normally. You can also use anchors to send visitors to another web page and have the focus of the web page be on the section you send the visitors to. For example, you might have something similar to the following:

```
<a href="http://www.barnettech.com/anchors.htm#section5">
Visit Section 5</a>
```

You can send the visitor to the www.barnettech.com web site, as an example, to the anchors.htm web page for viewing, and the visitor will be taken directly to the "Section 5" area. (This is a fictitious example as I have no anchor set up on my web site or an anchor.html page.)

What follows next is an example of some "real" code that illustrates how to use an anchor. The English text embedded in the code is just nonsense text I generated using a "lorem ipsum" generator—well, kind of, instead of generating random Latin text, it generates random vegetable names. Lorem ipsum generators are often used to make up some random text for use in the publishing industry or for web page mock-ups. The amount of random text has to be long enough so it scrolls off your screen in a web browser, so when you click to go to another portion of the screen using the anchor tag, the result will demonstrate the effect properly. For this example code to work, you might have to decrease the size of the window in your web browser to get this effect to work properly. For example, when you display the code in your web browser, you may need to decrease the window size from the bottom so that the window ends at the first line of text that reads "Take me back to the top!" as shown in Figure 3-8.

The code shows some <p> tags to create paragraphs on the page. Also notice the first anchor tag has no text, so it's a "hidden anchor" at the top of the page—later in the page, when the visitor clicks "Take me back to the top!" the visitor will be taken back to the top of the page to this hidden anchor tag.

```
<html>
  <body>
    <a id="top"></a>
    <h1>
      <p><a href="#section1">Visit Section 1</a></p>
      <p><a href="#section2">Visit Section 2</a></p>
</h1>

    <p><h2><a id="section1">Section 1</a></h2><p>
    <p>
      Veggies sunt bona vobis, proinde vos postulo esse magis
tigernut wakame jicama spring onion tatsoi zucchini yarrow.
Komatsuna amaranth catsear celery quandong zucchini chickweed chard
coriander spring onion winter purslane turnip greens
swiss chard radicchio bok choy mustard squash. Rock melon
carrot tomatillo cabbage rock melon leek courgette. Chickweed
beetroot tigernut epazote bitterleaf courgette dandelion bell
pepper earthnut pea salsify radicchio soko sea lettuce okra
pumpkin. Veggies sunt bona vobis, proinde vos postulo esse
magis tigernut wakame jícama spring onion tatsoi zucchini
yarrow.
    </p>
```

```
    <p>
        Komatsuna amaranth catsear celery quandong zucchini
chickweed chard coriander spring onion winter purslane turnip
greens swiss chard radicchio bok choy mustard squash. Rock
melon carrot tomatillo cabbage rock melon leek courgette.
Chickweed beetroot tigernut epazote bitterleaf courgette
dandelion bell pepper earthnut pea salsify radicchio soko sea
lettuce okra pumpkin.
    </p>
</p>
    <p><h2><a href="#top">Take me back to the top!</a></h2></p>
    <h2><a id="section2">Section 2</a></h2>
    <p>
        Peanut mustard chickweed lotus root yarrow summer purslane
desert raisin endive corn green bean rutabaga pumpkin lettuce.
Arugula zucchini courgette leek bunya nuts eggplant water spinach
tatsoi yarrow potato rock melon kohlrabi jícama bell pepper
shallot burdock. Pumpkin chicory caulie tigernut courgette
celery. Tigernut salad cress komatsuna earthnut pea cauliflower
bell pepper spring onion cucumber. Kale taro cress broccoli
beetroot corn salsify water spinach chickpea beet greens cucumber
dandelion arugula prairie turnip caulie cauliflower.
    </p>

    <p>
Peanut mustard chickweed lotus root yarrow summer purslane desert
raisin endive corn green bean rutabaga pumpkin lettuce. Arugula
zucchini courgette leek bunya nuts eggplant water spinach tatsoi
yarrow potato rock melon kohlrabi jícama bell pepper shallot
burdock. Pumpkin chicory caulie tigernut courgette celery.
Tigernut salad cress komatsuna earthnut pea cauliflower bell
pepper spring onion cucumber. Kale taro cress broccoli beetroot
corn salsify water spinach chickpea beet greens cucumber dandelion
arugula prairie turnip caulie cauliflower.
    </p>
    <p><h2><a href="#top">Take me back to the top!</a></h2></p>
</body>
</html>
```

Figure 3-9 shows how the page looks in a web browser. First, the page loads and we see the top of the page. If you click one of the anchors, say the one that says "Visit Section 2" at the top of the web page, then you'll be taken to the "Section 2" part on the web page, as shown in Figure 3-9.

Section 1

Veggies sunt bona vobis, proinde vos postulo esse magis tigernut wakame jÁcama spring onion tatsoi zucchini yarrow. Komatsuna amaranth catsear celery quandong zucchini chickweed chard coriander spring onion winter purslane turnip greens swiss chard radicchio bok choy mustard squash. Rock melon carrot tomatillo cabbage rock melon leek courgette. Chickweed beetroot tigernut epazote bitterleaf courgette dandelion bell pepper earthnut pea salsify radicchio soko sea lettuce okra pumpkin. Veggies sunt bona vobis, proinde vos postulo esse magis tigernut wakame jÁcama spring onion tatsoi zucchini yarrow. Komatsuna amaranth catsear celery quandong zucchini chickweed chard coriander spring onion winter purslane turnip greens swiss chard radicchio bok choy mustard squash. Rock melon carrot tomatillo cabbage rock melon leek courgette. Chickweed beetroot tigernut epazote bitterleaf courgette dandelion bell pepper earthnut pea salsify radicchio soko sea lettuce okra pumpkin. Veggies sunt bona vobis, proinde vos postulo esse magis tigernut wakame jÁcama spring onion tatsoi zucchini yarrow. Komatsuna amaranth catsear celery quandong zucchini chickweed chard coriander spring onion winter purslane turnip greens swiss chard radicchio bok choy mustard squash. Rock melon carrot tomatillo cabbage rock melon leek courgette. Chickweed beetroot tigernut epazote bitterleaf courgette dandelion bell pepper earthnut pea salsify radicchio soko sea lettuce okra pumpkin. Veggies sunt bona vobis, proinde vos postulo esse magis tigernut wakame jÁcama spring onion tatsoi zucchini yarrow. Komatsuna amaranth catsear celery quandong zucchini chickweed chard coriander spring onion winter purslane turnip greens swiss chard radicchio bok choy mustard squash. Rock melon carrot tomatillo cabbage rock melon leek courgette. Chickweed beetroot tigernut epazote bitterleaf courgette dandelion bell pepper earthnut pea salsify radicchio soko sea lettuce okra pumpkin.

Take me back to the top!

Section 2

Peanut mustard chickweed lotus root yarrow summer purslane desert raisin endive corn green bean rutabaga pumpkin lettuce. Arugula zucchini courgette leek bunya nuts eggplant water spinach tatsoi yarrow potato rock melon kohlrabi jÁcama bell pepper shallot burdock. Pumpkin chicory caulie tigernut courgette celery. Tigernut salad cress komatsuna earthnut pea cauliflower bell pepper spring onion cucumber. Kale taro cress broccoli beetroot corn salsify water spinach chickpea beet greens cucumber dandelion arugula prairie turnip caulie cauliflower. Peanut mustard chickweed lotus root yarrow summer purslane desert raisin endive corn green bean rutabaga pumpkin lettuce. Arugula zucchini courgette leek bunya nuts eggplant water spinach tatsoi yarrow potato rock melon kohlrabi jÁcama bell pepper shallot burdock. Pumpkin chicory caulie

Figure 3-9. *After clicking the "Section 2" link, you'll be taken to the anchor at the bottom of the page for Section 2*

Creating Forms

HTML can be used to create forms to pass data back to the server. You can add text fields, radio buttons, select lists, text areas, and other elements. To make a form, you use the `<form>` tag. You basically use the opening `<form>` tag and then nest the various input elements you want to use, such as radio buttons, within the opening and closing tags (`<form>` `</form>`), as follows:

```
<form>
  input elements
</form>
```

Now let's go over the input elements that you can choose to use (see Figure 3-10). These elements include text fields, password fields, radio buttons, drop-down menus, check box input fields, and text areas.

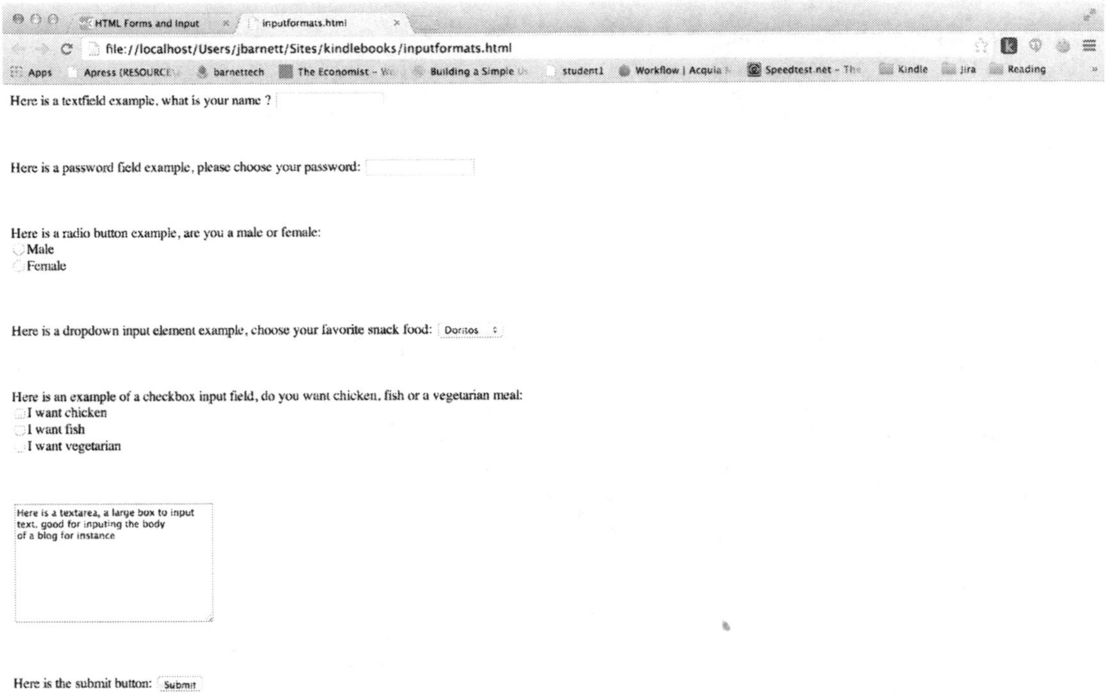

Figure 3-10. *Examples of input elements in an HTML form*

Text Fields

A text field is a basic text input box used to collect data from the person using your web site. A text field looks as follows:

```
<input type="text" name="yourname">
```

You can change "yourname" to be anything. When you learn some JavaScript or PHP in later chapters, you'll learn to process the data entered by referencing "yourname".

Password Fields

A password field is a bit different from a text field—as you type into the password field, each character you type is masked with a little circle so that no one standing behind you can see what you're typing. Here's how you create a password field.

```
<input type="password" name="password">
```

Radio Buttons

Here's how you form a radio button input element.

```
<input type="radio" name="sex" value="male">Male
<input type="radio" name="sex" value="female">Female
```

Again, you can change "sex", which is next to name= in the preceding code, to be anything you like. It will be used by the JavaScript or PHP or code you'll soon be learning to gather to act on the data entered into this input element.

Drop-downs

Here's an example of a dropdown input element.

```
<select name="snackfood">
<option value="chips">Chips</option>
<option value="popcorn">Popcorn</option>
<option value="nuts">Nuts</option>
<option value="raisins">Raisins</option>
</select>
```

As I mentioned earlier, what is next to name= (and in this case what is next to value=) can be changed and will be used to refer to the data to process the form. For example, you could change "snackfood" to be "junkfood" and value="chips" to be value="saltychip". The key is to keep your code readable by keeping your code clean and easy to follow with meaningful names.

Text Areas

Here's how to create a text area.

```
<textarea name="blogbody" rows="10" cols="30">Here is a
textarea, a large box to input text, good for inputting the
body of a blog, for instance.</textarea>
```

Again, name="blogbody" could be changed to anything that makes sense for your web site, like name="wikibody" or name="pagebody". It will be used to reference process, store, or act on the collected data in the text area by your JavaScript or PHP code. If you ever learn a different language like Java, .NET, or Ruby, these programming languages can also process forms, just like PHP can.

"Submit" Buttons

After you create your form, you need a way for users to submit their data. Enter the "Submit" button. You'll learn some JavaScript or PHP in later chapters to get the "Submit" button to function, but for now, here's how to display a "Submit" button.

```
<input type="submit" value="Submit">
```

All Together Now

Now that you've seen the input elements individually, let's put them all together. Here is all the code that created the form shown in Figure 3-10.

```
Here is a textfield example. What is your name? <input
type="text" name="yourname"> </br></br></br></br>
<!-- This is an HTML comment. It does not get rendered in your
web browser. It can be used to document your HTML code. I wanted
to mention that the </br> tags you see above just create some new
lines in your HTML. These tags create better spacing between
elements, to make them look a bit better in the web browser.
This is a crude way to create line breaks. Later you will learn how
to do this with CSS. -->

Here is a password field example. Please choose your password: <input type="password"
name="password"> </br></br></br></br>

Here is a radio button example. Are you male or female? </br>
<input type="radio" name="sex" value="male">Male </br>
<input type="radio" name="sex" value="female">Female </br></br></br></br>

Here is a drop-down input element example. Choose your favorite
snack food:
<select name="snackfood">
<option value="chips">Chips</option>
<option value="popcorn">Popcorn</option>
<option value="nuts">Nuts</option>
<option value="raisins">Raisins</option>
</select>
</br></br></br></br>

Here is an example of a check box input field. Do you want
chicken, fish, or a vegetarian meal? </br>
<input type="checkbox" name="mealtype" value="chicken">I want
chicken.</br>
<input type="checkbox" name="mealtype" value="fish">I want
fish.</br>
<input type="checkbox" name="mealtype" value="vegetarian">I
want vegetarian.</br></br></br></br>

<textarea rows="10" cols="30">Here is a textarea, a large box
to input text, good for inputting the body of a blog, for
instance.</textarea>
</br></br></br></br>

Here is the Submit button:
<input type="submit" value="Submit">
```

Using Layout Elements

Another HTML element type is a layout element. Layout elements are essential to help your web site to stay "looking good." The div element wraps whatever is nested within it inside of a "box." This is often called the "box model," and each area of a web page can be put into a box and then placed exactly the way you like it using CSS. You'll learn how to do this in Chapter 5.

There is another way to put your content in a box. You can put it into a <span> tag. The difference between a div and a span is that a div tag forces content that comes after it to the next line, whereas a span does not force a new line. So, for instance, you could wrap the earlier form code in a div element as follows:

```
<div>
  Here is a textfield example. What is your name? <input
  type="text" name="yourname"> </br></br></br></br>

Here is a password field example. Please choose your password:
<input type="password" name="password"> </br></br></br></br>

  Here is a radio button example. Are you male or female? </br>
  <input type="radio" name="sex" value="male">Male </br>
  <input type="radio" name="sex" value="female">Female
  </br></br></br></br>

  Here is a drop-down input element example. Choose your
  favorite snack food:
  <select name="snackfood">
  <option value="chips">Chips</option>
  <option value="popcorn">Popcorn</option>
  <option value="nuts">Nuts</option>
  <option value="raisins">Raisins</option>
  </select>
  </br></br></br></br>

  Here is an example of a check box input field. Do you want
  chicken, fish, or a vegetarian meal?</br>
  <input type="checkbox" name="mealtype" value="chicken">I want
  chicken.</br>
  <input type="checkbox" name="mealtype" value="fish">I want
  fish.</br>
  <input type="checkbox" name="mealtype" value="vegetarian">I
  want vegetarian.</br></br></br></br>

  <textarea rows="10" cols="30">Here is a textarea, a large box
  to input text, good for inputting the body of a blog, for
  instance.</textarea>
  </br></br></br></br>

  Here is the Submit button:
  <input type="submit" value="Submit">
</div>
```

Notice the opening div tag, `<div>`, and the closing div tag, `</div>`, after the form. Right now, when you put this in a web browser, you won't see a difference in how the page looks, but in later chapters, when you learn CSS, you'll be able to make use of these div and span tags to style a web page. To use the span tag in the preceding example, you would just replace the `<div>` `</div>` opening and closing tags with the opening and closing span tags, `<span>` `</span>`.

Summary

In this chapter you were introduced to HTML, the core ingredient of web page creation. To begin this chapter, you opened up Komodo Edit and added the HTML code necessary for creating a basic web page. You then learned how to use comments in your code. Next, you learned to enhance a web page by adding images and creating lists and tables. You also learned to use anchors, so that you could create links within a single web page or to other web pages. Finally, you gained experience working with forms, which are necessary when you want to gather input from visitors to your site. There are various types of input elements used with forms, including text fields, password fields, radio buttons, drop-downs, and text areas. At this point, you should be familiar with some of the basic elements used to code HTML pages.

CHAPTER 4

■ ■ ■

Creating a Basic Drupal Module with HTML Output

Now that you've gotten your feet wet with HTML, this chapter shows you how to use HTML to create your own custom web pages within the Drupal framework. In this chapter, I'm actually going to jump ahead a bit. Even though I'm going to assume you don't know any PHP (a server-side scripting language designed for web development), I'm going to give you just enough right now so you can play around with showing basic HTML in a programmatically created Drupal page—that is, via a Drupal module.

In order to create your module, you first need to locate your Drupal docroot directory, which is where your Drupal files are housed. You'll be placing your own files you create within the Drupal directory structure so that you can integrate your custom pages into your Drupal site.

Working with the Drupal Docroot Directory

So what is a docroot directory? Well, to begin, you need to know that there are two docroot directories: an Apache docroot and a Drupal docroot. Let's look at the Apache docroot directory first.

The Apache docroot is the location from which your local Apache web server will serve up web pages—any web pages, not just your Drupal installation. Often the name of the folder for the Apache docroot directory will be htdocs or the /var/www/ directory, which is the most commonplace on an Ubuntu server (the location of the docroot directory can also be configured to be in any other directory, but usually it is in the default location at /var/www).

Your Drupal docroot directory is the base, or "home," directory of your Drupal installation and it's where all your Drupal files and folders reside. You can really put the Drupal docroot anywhere within the Apache docroot directory. If you use Acquia Dev Desktop out of the box on a Mac, the Drupal docroot directory will just be within your Sites/devdesktop directory, which is within your user's home directory. On my Mac, mine is at, for example, /Users/jbarnett/Sites/devdesktop. On a Windows machine, the Drupal docroot directory is most often at C:/Users/your_username/Sites. Acquia Dev Desktop for Windows, puts the Drupal docroot within C:/Users/your_username/Sites/devdesktop. Within this devdesktop directory you'll find all the site folders for each Drupal installation you've created using Acquia Dev Desktop.

When you need to configure where your Drupal docroot is or you want to create another instance of Drupal on your local machine or on an Ubuntu server in the cloud (at Amazon, Rackspace, Linode, or any other server farm in the cloud), you will set up an Apache virtual host (something I won't get into now). Fortunately, Acquia Dev Desktop already sets this up for you, which allows you to proceed more quickly. An Apache virtual host is configured to "wire" it so your web server at a particular web URL serves up the correct files within your Apache docroot—whether they be Drupal files, HTML files, straight up PHP files, and so on.

Now that you know where your Drupal files are stored you can begin creating your first Drupal module.

Creating a Basic Drupal Module

In this section, we are going to create a basic Drupal module. Recall that a module is like a plug-in that extends Drupal's functionality. In this case, the module you create will be used to create a simple web page that looks like the one shown in Figure 4-1. Simply, this module will output the following HTML to the screen (as shown in Figure 4-1):

```
<p><b>Saying Hello World in Drupal 8 is cool!</b></p>
```

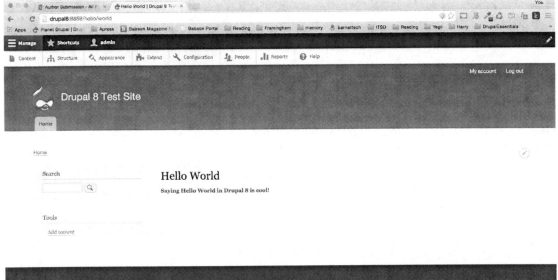

Figure 4-1. *A bare bones custom-created Drupal module showing some basic HTML*

■ **Note**   The code for this Drupal module is on Github: `https://github.com/barnettech/drupal8_book`.

Within a subfolder of your Drupal docroot directory (likely under /Users/your_username/Sites/devdesktop on a Mac or within C:/Users/your_username/Sites on a Windows machine), you'll see a file list that looks as follows:

```
README.txt          example.gitignore      robots.txt
composer.json       index.php              sites
composer.lock       modules                themes
core                profiles               web.config
```

You can navigate to your Drupal docroot folder within the file browser that comes with your Mac or with Windows, or you can use the command line if you're comfortable with that.

1. To begin, locate the modules folder. On my Mac it looks as follows: `/Users/jbarnett/Sites/devdesktop/drupal-8.0.0-beta6/drupal/modules`.

■ **Note** The Drupal 8 directory structure is different from previous versions of Drupal. In Drupal 7 and prior, the `modules` directory in Drupal's docroot directory contained core modules (modules that come with Drupal) only, and the contrib (community contributed) and custom modules used to live in the `sites/all/modules` directory. The Drupal community thought this was confusing and wanted something more intuitive. Now when a developer sees the Drupal docroot directory, and within it the `modules` directory, he or she can think, "Oh, that is where my modules I develop or download should go." Drupal core modules now live within the `core/modules` directory.

---

2. Within this `modules` directory, create two folders, if they don't exist already: a `contrib` folder and a `custom` folder. In the `contrib` directory, you'll be putting all the community-contributed modules that you download from `drupal.org` (or elsewhere), and in the `custom` directory you'll be putting any modules that you create from scratch. This is the standard convention used in the Drupal community for organizing your modules.

3. Within the `custom` folder that you just created, create a folder called `hello_world`, which will also serve as the name of your new custom module.

4. Create three files within this subdirectory (using your code editor or the Linux command line). First, create a file called `hello_world.info.yml` and then create a file called `hello_world.module`. Naming the files with the same name as the module name is essential. Finally, create a file named `hello_world.routing.yml`.

■ **Note** The code for this Drupal module is on Github: `https://github.com/barnettech/drupal8_book`. The code will be formatted better at Github compared to reading it on your Kindle device/e-reader because it includes syntax highlighting.

---

5. The first file we're going to create is the `hello_world.info.yml` file, and this file is a basic file that tells the Drupal system there is a new module and to look for the appropriate files and functions within it. Without this file, your module will not be recognized. Type the following into the `hello_world.info.yml` file:

```
name:  Hello World
type:  module
description:  'A basic Drupal 8 Hello World Module.'
package:  Custom Modules
version:  1.0
core:  8.x
```

The file hello_world.info.yml has a .yml extension and is a YAML file. YAML files are used to store metadata about all themes and modules, something that was done in .info files prior to Drupal 8.

■ **Note**   For users who've used Drupal 7 and previous versions, you may wonder why Drupal switched in Drupal 8 to using YAML rather than continuing to use just an .info file with standard text file format. I found this answer: "Why YAML, that's also by exclusion. First, we are looking for a file format that is both human editable and computer parsable. We did not want a Drupal-specific format (info files). We did not want XML because then the schema is the Drupalism (and XML has cooties). JSON (JavaScript Object Notation) doesn't allow comments and non-ASCII characters need escaping, that's not nice for humans. So, YAML." (Excerpt by NK at www.drupal4hu.com/node/377.)

---

6. The next bit of code wires the Drupal system to register the new hello/world URL and connects (routes) that URL to the code located in the HelloWorldController and specifically to the code in the method (a grouping of code) myCallbackMethod. This code also sets the permissions to be only for those with the right to "access content." Type the following code into the hello_world.routing.yml file:

```
hello_world_settings:
  path:  '/hello/world'
  defaults:
    _controller:  '\Drupal\hello_world\Controller\HelloWorldController::
myCallbackMethod'
    _title: 'Hello World'
  requirements:
    _permission: 'access content'
```

7. Now we need to make a few more directories and one more file, and we'll be done. Make sure you're within the hello_world module directory and then create a directory called src. Within the src directory, create a folder called Controller. The directory structure should look like this: hello_world/src/Controller.

■ **Note**   This directory structure is very different from Drupal 7 and prior versions; we never needed to create this kind of directory structure previously, but with the new object-oriented way of doing things, it is now necessary. If the directory structure is at all confusing, look at the code in Github—you'll be able to see the directory structure. You can also download ("clone") the project from Github, which will bring the files and directory structure down to your own computer.

---

8. The next file, as stated earlier, houses the myCallbackMethod, which gets invoked in the hello_world.routing.yml you just set up. That method will house the HTML code that will display within the new web page you're creating at the hello/world URL.

▪ **Note**   A method in object-oriented coding is very similar to a function in the procedural (non-object-oriented) code you may be more familiar with. It is a block of code that is grouped together for easier invocation. The hello_world.routing.yml file (specifically, the line following _controller: invokes this myCallbackMethod) you created earlier is the file that invokes this myCallbackMethod so its code will get executed.

---

9.   Within this new hello_world/src/Controller directory, create the file HelloWorldController.php and type the following code in this file:

```php
<?php
/**
 * @file
 * Contains \Drupal\hello_world\HelloWorldController.
 */

namespace Drupal\hello_world\Controller;
/**
 * Provides route responses for the hello world page example.
 */
class HelloWorldController {
  /**
   * Returns a simple hello world page.
   *
   * @return array
   *   A very simple renderable array is returned.
   */
  public function myCallbackMethod() {
    $element = array(
      '#markup' => '<p><b>Saying Hello World in Drupal 8 is
cool!</b></p>',
    );
    return $element;
  }
}
```

10.   Notice the following line which is the specific line that houses all the HTML code that will display to the user on the new web page:

```php
$content = '<p><b>Saying Hello World in Drupal 8 is
cool!</b></p>';
```

■ **Note** The code you've seen so far is the amount of coding it takes to put some basic HTML on a page in Drupal 8. The boilerplate code is a bit more complex than in previous versions of Drupal, as Drupal 8 incorporates the Symphony routing system. Drupal 8 has taken on new, more "modern" architecture from the Symphony PHP framework (`http://symfony.com/`), and Drupal 8 leaps to try to adopt more modern architectural paradigms, which Symphony already handles well. This leap for the Drupal community brings Drupal more up to date with other object-oriented frameworks. Don't worry for now if you don't understand every line of PHP code presented.

---

11. Locate the admin toolbar, click the Manage tab, and then click Extend (or in your browser, go to the `...admin/modules` URL). Enable your new module by clicking the check box next to "Hello World" and then click the "Save configuration" button. See Figure 4-2 as an example of what your new module should look like on the module management page.

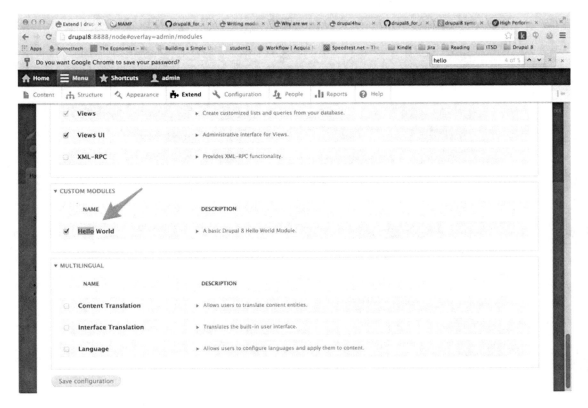

Figure 4-2. *Enabling your new custom module, which outputs some HTML to the screen*

12. In your browser open your Drupal site to: `http://localhost/hello/world`. Be sure to replace `localhost` with whatever the URL is for your Drupal site. (On my computer, it's `http://drupal8:8888/hello/world`.)

You'll now see your simple Drupal page in all its glory, showing some basic HTML on the page (see Figure 4-3). Your screen may look different if you've installed a different Drupal theme.

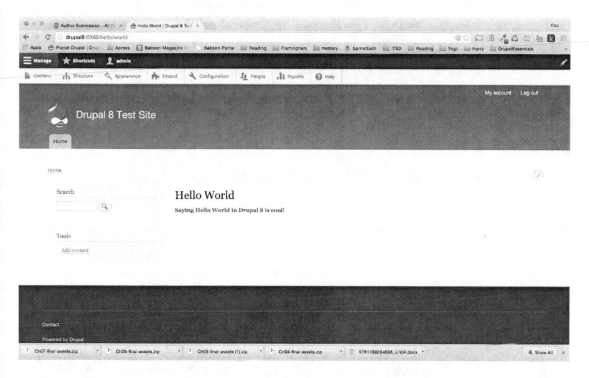

Figure 4-3. *The module outputted the basic HTML into the center of the Drupal page*

Now when I introduce you to CSS, PHP, JavaScript, and so on later in the book, I can show you the featured technology as used outside Drupal, and also within a Drupal module, within the Drupal framework. We'll be adding to this Drupal module to showcase each new technology. The example code you just looked at is pretty simple, only displaying some HTML on the screen, but this code is the framework you'll add to in order to create more complex web pages.

If any of the code presented just now is confusing, don't worry too much. For now just imagine this code as a bunch of magic and put your HTML within the quotes within the line `$content = '<p><b>Saying Hello World in Drupal 8 is cool!</b></p>'`, and that HTML will be the output on the web page.

Looking at the Model, View, Controller Design Pattern

To get into the wisdom behind the architecture you're seeing in Drupal 8, it's necessary to talk about the controller you just saw in the Hello World module (the `HelloWorldController.php` file you just created). The controller is the "C" in the Model, View, Controller (MVC) architecture, which is popular in almost all coding languages, and it separates "concerns," separating the view code, logic, and data. By separating these different pieces of architecture, the code is more organized, and it helps in keeping "themers" in the "view" and developers on the back end, which means themers and developers should experience less collision when working together.

■ **Note** You can read more about controllers at `https://drupal.org/project/controller`.

The system separates the view (the theming/presentation layer) from the back-end data (the model), and the logic/strategy (in the controller) of responding to the user's actions they initiate in the view. For example, the view—the look and feel of the site—can be replaced or heavily modified, and the core data and logic behind the view can be unaffected by the change. This system also allows you to have multiple views of the back-end data (the model) and allows a change to the model to affect all views of the data—the key idea of the "observer pattern" in software architecture. You can read more about MVC in the book *Design Patterns* by Richard Helm, Ralph Johnson, John M. Vlissides, and Craig Larman (often referred to as "The Gang of Four") (Addison-Wesley, 1994).

Showcasing Different HTML Elements Within the Drupal Module

Most HTML elements you saw in Chapter 3, like tables and lists, can be easily put into your new Drupal module's output. The exception is forms, which are more complicated and will be covered in Chapter 14.

■ **Note** When you put HTML into your Drupal module you omit the `<html>`, `<head>`, and `<body>` tags. Drupal puts these tags in for you.

Take, for example, the code to create anchors (see Chapter 3). You can easily put this code into the new Drupal module in the `HelloWorldController.php` controller file. The new file will now look as follows:

```php
<?php
    /**
     * @file
     * Contains \Drupal\hello_world\HelloWorldController.
     */

    namespace Drupal\hello_world\Controller;

    /**
    * Provides route responses for the hello world page example.
     */
    class HelloWorldController {
      /**
       * Returns a simple hello world page.
       *
       * @return array
       *    A very simple renderable array is returned.
       */
```

```
      public function myCallbackMethod() {
        $content = '
<a id="top"></a>
   <h2>
     <p><a href="#section1">Visit Section 1</a></p>
     <p><a href="#section2">Visit Section 2</a></p>
     <p><a href="#section3">Visit Section 3</a></p>
     <p><a href="#section4">Visit Section 4</a></p>
     <p><a href="#section5">Visit Section 5</a></p>
   </h2>

   <p><h2><a id="section1">Section 1</a></h2><p>
   <p>
        Veggies sunt bona vobis, proinde vos postulo esse magis
tigernut wakame jícama spring onion tatsoi zucchini yarrow.
        Komatsuna amaranth catsear celery quandong zucchini chickweed
chard coriander spring onion winter purslane turnip greens swiss chard
radicchio bok choy mustard squash. Rock melon carrot tomatillo cabbage
rock melon leek courgette. Chickweed beetroot tigernut epazote bitterleaf
courgette dandelion bell pepper earthnut pea salsify radicchio soko sea
lettuce okra pumpkin. Veggies sunt bona vobis, proinde vos postulo esse
magis tigernut wakame jícama spring onion tatsoi zucchini yarrow.
```

... *text ommitted here to save space* ...

```
   </p>

   <p><h2><a href="#top">Take me back to the top!</a></h2></p>

     <h2><a id="section2">Section 2</a></h2>
     <p>

        Peanut mustard chickweed lotus root yarrow summer purslane desert
raisin endive corn green bean rutabaga pumpkin lettuce. Arugula zucchini
courgette leek bunya nuts eggplant water spinach tatsoi yarrow potato rock
melon kohlrabi jícama bell pepper shallot burdock. Pumpkin chicory caulie
tigernut courgette celery. Tigernut salad cress komatsuna earthnut pea
cauliflower bell pepper spring onion cucumber. Kale taro cress broccoli
beetroot corn salsify water spinach chickpea beet greens cucumber dandelion
arugula prairie turnip caulie cauliflower.  Peanut mustard chickweed lotus
root yarrow summer purslane desert raisin endive corn green bean rutabaga
pumpkin lettuce. Arugula zucchini courgette leek bunya nuts eggplant
water spinach tatsoi yarrow potato rock melon kohlrabi jícama bell pepper
shallot burdock. Pumpkin chicory caulie tigernut courgette celery. Tigernut
salad cress komatsuna earthnut pea cauliflower bell pepper spring onion
cucumber. Kale taro cress broccoli beetroot corn salsify water spinach
chickpea beet greens cucumber dandelion arugula prairie turnip caulie
cauliflower.
```

... *text ommitted here to save space* ...

```
     </p>
   <p><h2><a href="#top">Take me back to the top!</a></h2></p>
```

```
    <h2><a id="section4">Section 4</a></h2>
    <p>
        Artichoke arugula collard greens kale tomato scallion catsear
celery turnip bunya nuts endive seakale wattle seed nori daikon fava bean
parsnip. Burdock zucchini caulie garlic rock melon pumpkin. Eggplant
endive kombu asparagus tomatillo artichoke. Artichoke arugula collard
greens kale tomato scallion catsear celery turnip bunya nuts endive
seakale wattle seed nori daikon fava bean parsnip. Burdock zucchini caulie
garlic rock melon pumpkin. Eggplant endive kombu asparagus tomatillo
artichoke.
```

... text ommitted here to save space ...

```
    <h2><a id="section5">Section 5</a></h2>
    <p>
        Artichoke parsley ricebean desert raisin caulie grape kakadu plum
collard greens leek courgette seakale mustard nori sorrel amaranth
courgette peanut beetroot. Maize corn beet greens lettuce broccoli parsnip
garlic chickweed groundnut garbanzo brussels sprout kombu rock melon bamboo
shoot seakale endive cauliflower. Celery cucumber coriander cress desert
raisin silver beet pumpkin quandong cauliflower kombu garlic squash.
Artichoke parsley ricebean desert raisin caulie grape kakadu plum collard
greens leek courgette seakale mustard nori sorrel amaranth courgette peanut
beetroot. Maize corn beet greens lettuce broccoli parsnip garlic chickweed
groundnut garbanzo brussels sprout kombu rock melon bamboo shoot seakale
endive cauliflower. Celery cucumber coriander cress desert raisin silver
beet pumpkin quandong cauliflower kombu garlic squash.
```

... text ommitted here to save space ...

```
    </p>
    <p><h2><a href="#top">Take me back to the top!</a></h2></p>
    ';
    $element = array(
      '#markup' => $content,
    );
    return $element;
  }
```

Notice the code ported over from the HTML from Chapter 3; we only needed to omit the <html>,
<head>, and <body> tags. Figure 4-4 shows what the anchor code from Chapter 3 looks like in the Drupal
module.

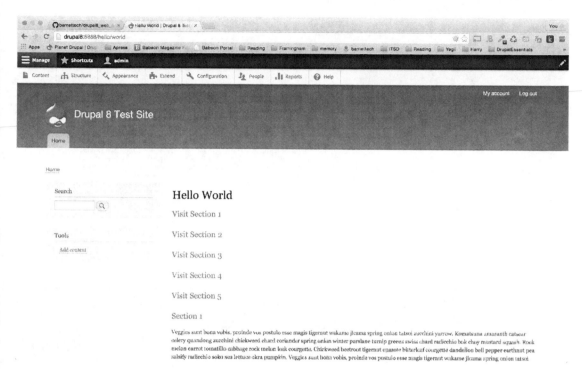

Figure 4-4. *HTML anchors in a simple Drupal module*

Now, for example, if you click "Visit Section 5" at the top of the screen, you are sent to Section 5, which is much farther down the page (see Figure 4-5). The anchor HTML code works just as expected within the HelloWorldController.php file.

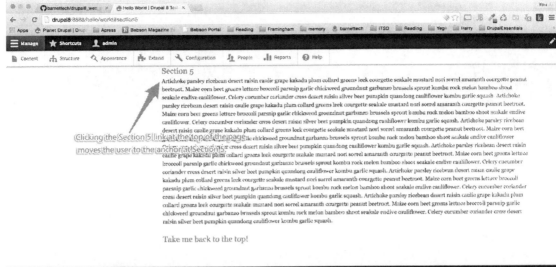

Figure 4-5. *The anchor at Section 5*

■ **Note** In Chapter 12, you'll learn a better way to handle HTML output—by creating theme functions—to further separate the view of the web page from the controller logic.

If you want to put a basic HTML table into the `HelloWorldController.php` file, it would look as follows:

```php
<?php
/**
 * @file
 * Contains \Drupal\hello_world\HelloWorldController.
 */

namespace Drupal\hello_world\Controller;

/**
 * Provides route responses for the hello world page example.
 */
class HelloWorldController {
  /**
   * Returns a simple hello world page.
   *
   * @return array
   *   A very simple renderable array is returned.
   */
```

```php
public function myCallbackMethod() {
    $content = '
<table border="1">
  <tr>
    <th>Header 1</th>
    <th>Header 2</th>
  </tr>
  <tr>
    <td>row 1, cell 1</td>
    <td>row 1, cell 2</td>
  </tr>
  <tr>
    <td>row 2, cell 1</td>
    <td>row 2, cell 2</td>
  </tr>
</table>
    ';
    $element = array(
      '#markup' => $content,
    );
    return $element;
}
```

Again, you omit the `<body>`, `<html>`, and `<head>` tags. Figure 4-6 shows what the Drupal page looks like at the ...hello/world URL.

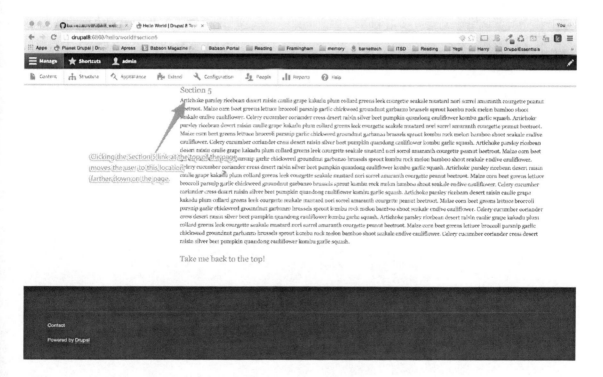

Figure 4-6. *The Basic Drupal module with HTML in it to create a table*

And finally, here is our `HelloWorldController.php` file with HTML code to create both unordered lists and ordered lists.

```php
<?php
    /**
     @file
     * Contains \Drupal\hello_world\HelloWorldController.
     */
    namespace Drupal\hello_world\Controller;
    /**
    Provides route responses for the hello world page example.
     */
    class HelloWorldController {
      /**
       * Returns a simple hello world page.
       *
       * @return array
       *   A very simple renderable array is returned.
       */
      public function myCallbackMethod() {
        $content = '
ORDERED LIST:
<ol>
    <li>Item 1</li>
    <li>Item 2</li>
</ol>
UNORDERED LIST:
<ul>
    <li>Item 1</li>
    <li>Item 2</li>
</ul>
        ';
        $element = array(
          '#markup' => $content,
        );
        return $element;
```

See Figure 4-7 for an example of what the Drupal page looks like with the HTML creating both ordered and unordered lists.

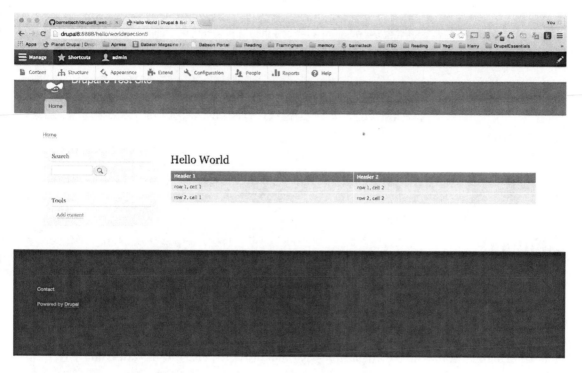

Figure 4-7. *Our simple Drupal module with HTML output creating first an ordered list and then an unordered list*

Renaming a Module—and How to Create a Module Not Named "hello_world"

If you would like to change the name of your module, you must change all the filenames and function names in the module. You also must change the folder name that houses the module's files. So In the case of the example module, the folder name was hello_world. So if you wanted to change the module name to my_module, you would need to change the folder name to my_module. Then, within the my_module folder, you would need to change the hello_world.info.yml file to my_module.info.yml instead. Also the hello_world.module file would be renamed to be my_module.module. Then within the my_module.info.yml file, you would change the name of the module if you wish to. Then within the my_module.module file, you would change *all* the function names to begin with my_module rather than hello_world. So if you have functions called hello_world_cron (to have Drupal run new cron tasks; cron tasks refer to tasks to be run on a schedule) and hello_world_permission (to create new Drupal permissions) which implement the hook_cron and hook_permission Drupal hooks respectively, you would change these function names to my_module_cron and my_module_permission.

■ **Note** Hooks are bits of code that allow you to alter or add to Drupal functionality. It's important to preface all your hooks with your module's name; otherwise, they will not run.

Drupal looks for any hook declarations that are in your Drupal installation, and runs the code at the appropriate time based on what type of hook it is. `hook_cron` is a hook in the Drupal system that has Drupal run the code within the `hook_cron` function on a schedule. `hook_permission` is a Drupal hook which allows you to define new Drupal permissions.

If you create a new module from scratch, the same conventions apply: The folder name must match the prefix of your function names, and the filenames must contain the name of your module.

Summary

In this chapter you took the HTML skills you acquired in Chapter 3 and learned to output HTML in a Drupal module. You learned the basic structure of a Drupal module and about the different pieces needed to create a module that included a controller and some YAML configuration files. We learned that the directory structure and how we name our files matter to wire up a Drupal module to work. Finally, you took a first look at how hooks work in Drupal to alter and add to Drupal.

As you learn about PHP later in the book, the boilerplate code used to create a module will make more sense to you. For a beginning Drupaler, copying and pasting boilerplate code and editing the code to do what you need it to do can take you a long way toward being a successful Drupal programmer. To fully understand the new code needed to create a Drupal hello world module, you would need to study object-oriented PHP programming. My favorite book on the subject is *PHP 5 Objects, Patterns, and Practice* by Matt Zandstra (Apress, 2005) (see www.apress.com/9781590593806). This chapter fearlessly showed you how to create a Drupal module without assuming you had read a book on object-oriented programming. Know that a primary paradigm in object- oriented programming is to create a bit of code (a class) that can be extended easily by other programmers to accomplish a task. In fact, the whole point is to abstract the coding behind the scenes, so other programmers can build upon what has already been done, not needing to concern themselves necessarily with what has already been built.

Abstraction is key to all engineering. We can program in a programming language because other engineers have already created a computer for us. All we need to do is write Drupal code. I don't concern myself (often) with how the computer I'm using was made. This is abstraction, and in my mind is the basic idea behind the quote, "We stand on the backs of giants." So don't be overly concerned if the boilerplate code in creating a Drupal module is a bit of a black box. You now have learned the basic skills of creating a Drupal module, which is a highly valuable skill by itself.

■ ■ ■

## CHAPTER 5

A CSS Primer for Drupal

So now you have wet your chops and know some HTML. Recall that HTML stands for HyperText Markup Text. And it's exactly that: a way to *mark up* the structure of your web pages. Well now you'll want to *style* those web pages with some CSS magic. Cascading Style Sheets (CSS) is a simple design language intended to simplify the process of making web pages presentable. CSS handles the "look and feel" part of a web page. Using CSS, you can control the color of text, the style of fonts, the spacing between paragraphs, how columns are sized and laid out, and what background images or colors are used, as well as a wide variety of other effects.

In this chapter you will learn to add CSS to HTML outside the Drupal framework to gain a basic understanding of what CSS can do. Then in Chapter 6, you'll learn to add CSS into the Drupal framework to style the HTML in your custom Drupal module.

A Quick Look Back at the Limits of HTML

Before diving into CSS, let's take a moment to look at the limitations of some basic HTML. Consider again the following code from Chapter 3:

```
<html>
  <head>
    <title> HELLO WORLD </title>
  </head>
<body>
  <h1>HELLO WORLD!</h1>
  <p>  This is a paragraph. </p>
  <p><b> This is bold text. </b></p>
  <p><i> This is italicized text. </i></p>
</body>
</html>
```

Figure 5-1 shows how this code will display in a browser—absolutely boring and without much style (CSS).

HELLO WORLD!

This is a paragraph.

This is bold text.

This is italicized text.

Figure 5-1. *Some boring basic HTML, with no CSS*

So what can you do to add some color and pizazz? Read on.

Styling Your Text with an External Style Sheet

CSS provides you with many ways to style your text. This section starts with a simple example. You'll use some CSS styles to turn some of the black text blue, in order to call more attention to it. To do this, you'll create an "external style sheet." An external style sheet is a separate file used to store CSS—with an external style sheet, your CSS styles are not stored within the same file as your HTML.

External style sheets encourage a uniform look and feel for a site, and they encourage only needing to define a style once in your CSS code, to be used throughout your site. A good coding practice is always to avoid redundant code! It will be easier to manage and keep track of all your site's styles, and it will be easier to rework styles when you're ready for your site's big redesign someday as well. Preference in the development community is most definitely to use external style sheets, which provides better code organization.

Let's practice creating an external style sheet and adding a reference to it in your HTML file.

1. Open Komodo Edit or your favorite code editor and, in the same directory in which you saved your HTML file, create a new file named something like `some_style.css`. (You can actually name this file anything you want, but it does need the `.css` extension.)

2. In the HTML file you created previously, after the opening `<html>` tag, start a new line and type the following:

    ```
    <head>
    <link rel="stylesheet" type="text/css" href="some_style.css">
    </head>
    ```

Your HTML should now look as follows in your editor:

```
<html>
  <head>
    <title> HELLO WORLD </title>
    <link rel="stylesheet" type="text/css" href="some_style.css">
  </head>
```

```
<body>
  <h1>HELLO WORLD!</h1>
  <p>  This is a paragraph. </p>
  <p><b> This is bold text. </b></p>
  <p><i> This is italicized text. </i></p>
</body>
</html>
```

So these magic lines you just added tell your browser that when it loads up this HTML page, it also needs to load up a style sheet called `some_style.css`.

3.   In `some_style.css`, put in these lines (these CSS styles):

```
h1 {
  color: blue;
}
```

This code, known as a "CSS rule," will make any text in your HTML page that is wrapped in an `<h1>` tag blue. In this case, the only text marked up by the `<h1>` tag is "HELLO WORLD!" Each CSS style rule has three parts: the selector (in this case the `h1` element), the property (in this case `color`), and the value (in this case `blue`).

4.   Save this CSS file and then reload your HTML file. Your web page should resemble Figure 5-2.

Figure 5-2. *Some HTML with very basic CSS styling*

Wow, that's some style—the text within the `<h1>` tag is now blue! Joking aside, I provide the simplest example just to show how easy CSS can be. Throughout the rest of this chapter, we'll take it up a notch.

Using <div> and <span> Tags

The preceding example used the simple `color` CSS style, which sets the color of text. Rest assured, there are plenty of other ways to decorate your web page. This section looks at how `<div>` and `<span>` HTML tags are used to box up sections of your HTML for styling with CSS.

Take this slightly modified HTML—try this now on your own as well in your code editor.

```
<html>
  <head>
    <link rel="stylesheet" type="text/css" href="some_style.css">
  </head>
```

```
<body>
  <span id="the-title"><title> HELLO WORLD </title></span>
  <h1>HELLO WORLD!</h1>
  <p>  This is a paragraph. </p>
  <div class="to-the-right"><b> This is bold text. </b></div>
  <i> This is italicized text. </i>
</body>
</html>
```

Notice the <div> and <span> tags. These tags simply "wrap" some HTML, often for the sole purpose of having CSS act on that wrapped HTML, which is the HTML that appears between the opening and closing <div> or <span> tags. Without CSS rules decorating them, the <div> and <span> tags will not change how your HTML document looks by themselves, except that a <div> will put your code in a "box." Then, anything after the <div>, will be put on a new line. The <span> tag also puts any HTML code within it in a "box," but it doesn't force there to be another line for any content after the closing </span> tag. Even these default behaviors can be overridden with CSS rules.

Also notice the <span> in the preceding code has an id of "the-title", and the <div> has a class of "to-the-right". You will use these id and class tags later in this chapter to identify in the CSS what to decorate in your HTML.

Commenting Your CSS

Like HTML, CSS has a way for you to leave comments within your code. Again, the browser will ignore these comments, but they will serve as good documentation for your code. All good coders (who work well as team players) document their code well; it also helps you to remember what you've done, not a trivial thing as a professional programmer when you're writing thousands of lines of code!

In CSS you put your comments between /* and */, as follows:

```
/* This is a comment, which will be ignored by the browser. */
```

Creating Additional Styles

Blue text isn't all that exciting. In this section, you'll take your CSS a bit further, by adding a background image and some other pizazz. Take a look at the following CSS, with comments, to clue you in on what each line does—and the resulting change in your HTML:

```
/* The CSS style below takes everything that is wrapped in
the body tag and slaps a background image called ocean.jpg
behind it. */
body {
  background-image:url('ocean.jpg');
}

/* The CSS style below colors all text wrapped in an h1 tag
blue. */
h1 {
  color: blue;
}
```

```
/* The CSS style below takes all text wrapped with the div
with an id of "the-title" and centers it. Notice that to
reference an id in your HTML you just put a # sign in front
of the id name in order to use it within the CSS file. */
#the-title {
  text-align: center;
}
```

```
/* The CSS style below takes all text wrapped with a div
with class "to-the-right" and gives it a margin of 200px.
"px" stands for pixels and is one commonly found standard
of measurement in the world of CSS. Notice that to reference
a class in your HTML you just put a dot "." in front of the
class name (in this case "to-the-right" is the class name).
*/
.to-the-right {
  margin-left: 200px;
}
```

1. Take the preceding CSS and put it into the CSS file you created earlier in this chapter—just replace the CSS that was in there previously.

2. Save any image you like to replace ocean.jpg in the CSS. Make sure the image is a .jpg, .gif, or .png file. (I'm referring to the file's extension here ... what comes after the period in the filename.) Replace the filename ocean.jpg in the CSS with the filename of the image you want to use.

USING A FOLDER FOR YOUR IMAGES

If you put your image file in the same directory as your HTML file, you won't need to change the code shown. But if you want to put the image in an images folder (and the images folder is in the same directory as your HTML file), the new CSS would look like what's shown here (the URL, or uniform resource locator) to the image is relative to where your HTML file lives in the file system).

Here's how it looks if you move the ocean.jpg image into an images folder:

```
body {
  background-image:url('images/ocean.jpg');

}
```

3. Save your CSS file and then refresh your browser with the HTML you've written with its new CSS. It should look something like Figure 5-3. Much more stylish than before!

Figure 5-3. Some HTML jazzed up using the CSS background-image property

You can see that some basic CSS styling can jazz up the page, rather than just presenting plain text to web site visitors.

Choosing Between Classes and IDs

When creating CSS rules, you usually will pick between using a class or using an id. Use classes when that CSS style will be used in more than one place on your site. This is convenient when you have, say, a header that occurs often in your site and you will frequently be reusing this same header elsewhere in your site. By using a class, you won't have to put in another CSS rule. Instead, you'll be able in your HTML to just use the same class name to wrap some HTML. That same look and feel you defined for that CSS rule will then show up wherever in your HTML you wrap HTML in that same class name! Very convenient—and a core idea of CSS. CSS allows for easily maintaining a consistent look and feel on web sites. You can make sure that you're using the same font, for instance, across all the pages of your site.

Conversely, use a CSS id tag when referring to something that will occur only once on any given HTML page. For example, the top blog post on your home page might have unique styling because it's a featured post, and so you would use an id rather than a class. You cannot have the same id name show up multiple times on a single HTML page. Although the page will display, you'll quite possibly be scratching your head later trying to figure out why you're seeing strangeness in the rendering of your HTML document or misbehavior of your JavaScript.

Working with Conflicting Styles

So what if there are conflicting styles? The more specific that style, the higher the precedence it takes. For example, if you have a CSS style on the body element of your web page and on a class within the body element, those are conflicting styles.

For example, consider the following HTML:

```
<html>
<head>
<link rel="stylesheet" type="text/css" href="some_style.css">
</head>
<body>
  <span id="the-title"><title> HELLO WORLD </title></span>
  <h1 class="specific-class">HELLO WORLD!</h1>
  <p>  This is a paragraph. </p>
  <div class="to-the-right"><b> This is bold text. </b></div>
  <i> This is italicized text. </i>
</body>
</html>
```

And this CSS:

```
h1 {
  color: blue;
}

/* The style above would not take precedence over
   the one below, which is more specific, so the
   text color would become red and not blue. */

h1.specific-class {
   color: red;
}
```

You can see you can "chain" elements, classes, and ids together to tell CSS what elements you want to target with your CSS styles.

For example, consider the following HTML:

```
<html>
<head>
<link rel="stylesheet" type="text/css" href="some_style.css">
</head>
```

```
<body>
  <title> HELLO WORLD </title>
  <div id="my-id-name"><h1>HELLO WORLD!</h1></div>
  <p>  This is a paragraph. </p>
  <div class="to-the-right"><b> This is bold text. </b></div>
  <i> This is italicized text. </i>
</body>
</html>
```

To be specific about the preceding bold line, you could write the following two rules. The second rule, being much more specific, would win out, and in a browser the line would show as red (not blue):

```
h1 {
  color: blue;
}

/*  The line below wins, not the one above, so the text is red, not blue. */
body #my-id-name h1{
  color: red;
}
```

Knowing how to be more specific to override a specific piece of CSS, as was just discussed , is a great thing to understand. Next, we'll talk about using internal style sheets.

Using Internal Style Sheets

So far we've introduced you to declaring an external style sheet in the <head> of your HTML document referencing your external CSS file. It is preferable to use an external style sheet (or sheets) to manage all your CSS for all your web pages in one central place You can also put your styles directly within the <head> portion of the HTML file, as follows (this is known as using an internal style sheet):

```
<html>
<head>
<style>
body {
  background-image:url('ocean.jpg');
}

h1 {
  color: blue;
}

body #my-id-name h1{
  color: purple;
}

#the-title {
  text-align: center;
}
```

```
.to-the-right {
  margin-left: 200px;
}
</style>
</head>
<body>
  <title> HELLO WORLD </title>
  <div id="my-id-name"><h1>HELLO WORLD!</h1></div>
  <p>  This is a paragraph. </p>
  <div class="to-the-right"><b> This is bold text. </b></div>
  <i> This is italicized text. </i>
</body>
</html>
```

Again, the code we're interested in is shown in bold. Notice, to put the styles directly in your HTML document you need to put your CSS styles within <style> tags, and the style tags need to live nested within the opening and closing <head> tags. If you're just making a single, quick page of HTML, you might use an internal style sheet. If you're going to create multiple pages or an entire web site, you're better off to use an external file (known as an external style sheet) to hold all your CSS. The external style sheet, as mentioned previously, can define styles across web pages—you won't need to rewrite the same CSS rules multiple times. Using this approach keeps your styles consistent among your different web pages.

Using Inline Styles

You can also include "inline styles," which take precedence over any internal or external styles. Following is an example of an inline style:

```
<p style="color:purple;margin-left:200px">This is a paragraph
with inline styles being applied to it.</p>
```

I do not recommend the use of inline styles because to override these styles you'll have to locate all the inline styles in your code to change them. I mention inline styles here so you know they exist, but again, I don't see them used often, because it's a better practice to use external style sheets. For example, if you set it up it so that a class name turns all your text blue and one day you decide you want your text red, you have to first change the CSS in your external style sheet to make it red. Easy enough, right? But what if you forgot you had some inline styles in your code that make the text blue? Then you would have to go and hunt down all the inline styles and manually change them all. Either that or you would have to remove them all so that your external style sheet can control things again.

Understanding the Cascade Order

Cascading Style Sheets get their names because, when multiple methods of styling are applied to an element, the styles "cascade" in order of precedence. Following is the cascade order, or the order of precedence, that your styles will be displayed in, when the same element is styled in multiple conflicting ways:

1. First the browser's default styles will be used for the element, each browser by default will show elements a certain way.

2. Next, external style sheets will be considered.

3. Next, internal style sheets will be looked at and will override any styles defined in steps 1 or 2.

4. Next, inline styles will be used and will take precedence over any styles defined in steps 1–3.

Working with Commonly Used CSS Styles

Although it would take an entire book to cover all of the available CSS styles, this section describes some commonly used CSS styles: text styles, fonts, links, tables, backgrounds, and positioning. In the following sections, you'll learn to apply each of these styles.

Text Styles

You can change the color of your font with the `color` property, which you used earlier in this chapter. Following is an example that would color all your text within the `<body>` tags of your document red:

```
body {color:red;}
```

If you want more control over your colors—that is, you want a wider variety of colors to choose from—you can use color codes. For example, the following code, using color code #006400, would apply a nice green color to your text:

```
body {color: #006400;}
```

■ **Note** For a list of all the available HTML color codes, check out `www.w3schools.com/html/html_colornames.asp` and `http://html-color-codes.info/`.

You can also align text right, left, or center. Consider the following two examples:

```
/* The next line centers the h1 text on the page. */
h1 {text-align:center;}

/* The next line puts text in the paragraph with the class of
"heading-top" aligned to the right of the page. */
p.heading-top {text-align:right;}
```

You can indent text as seen in the code that follows:

```
/* The CSS below indents all paragraph text 25 pixels. */
p {text-indent: 25px;}
```

You can also decorate text by underlining it or by adding a strikethrough (a line through the letters of text). Following are examples:

```
/* The following CSS puts a line through all text in paragraph
tags that have the class "line-through". */
p.line-through {text-decoration:line-through;}

/* The following CSS below underlines text within a paragraph
tag that has the class "underlined-text". */
p.underlined-text {text-decoration:underline;}
```

Fonts and Font Sizes

You can set a "font family," where you name several fonts you want to use in order of preference. If the user's browser supports the first font in the list, that font is used; if not, the browser uses the next font in the list, if available, and so on. You can list as many fonts as you like. If the font name has multiple words in its name, it must appear in quotes. Here's an example:

```
p{font-family:"Times New Roman", Arial, "Comic Sans MS";}
```

You can set the font style:

```
/* The CSS style below sets all text in a paragraph tag that
has a class of "normal" to have a normal default style. */
p.normal {font-style:normal;}

/* The CSS style below sets all text in a paragraph tag that
has a class of "italic" to be in italics. */
p.italic {font-style:italic;}
```

You can also set the font size:

```
/* The CSS style below sets all h1 text to have a size of
40 pixels. */
h1 {font-size:40px;}

/* The CSS style below sets all h3 text to have a size of
20 pixels */
h3 {font-size:20px;}

/* The CSS style below sets all text within paragraph tags
to have a size of 12 pixels. */
p {font-size:12px;}

/*You could also combine a bunch of these styles into one
CSS rule like this:*/
p {
    font-family:"Times New Roman", Arial, "Comic Sans MS";
    font-size:20px;
    font-style:italic;
  }
```

Links

You can style the different states of links on your HTML page, having one style to show an unvisited link, another for a link a user has already clicked (a visited link), a style for when you mouse over a link, and a style for a selected link. Here's the code.

```
a:link {color:#254117;}      /* An unvisited link will show
as forest green, which is color code #254117 */

a:visited {color:#6CC417;}    /* A visited link will be alien
green, which is color code :#6CC417; */

a:hover {color:#99C68E;}      /* A mouse-over link will show as
frog green, which is color code :#99C68E; */

a:active {color:#0000FF;}     /* A selected link will show as
the color snake green, which is color code #6CBB3C; */
```

Tables

You can also style tables with CSS. If you want your HTML table to have a border, you could use the following code for example, which gives the table a solid black border 1 pixel wide:

```
table {
  border: 1px solid black;
}
```

Here's a full example with an internal style sheet showing a table with a border created via CSS. You'll notice that the td and th elements are assigned the CSS style as well giving the elements a border.

```
<!DOCTYPE html>
<html>
<head>
<style>
table, td, th
{
border:1px solid black;
}

</style>
</head>

<body>
<table>
<tr>
<th>Firstname</th>
<th>Lastname</th>
<th>Attending?</th>
</tr>
```

```
<tr>
<td>Peter</td>
<td>Pumpkineater</td>
<td>yes</td>
</tr>
<tr>
<td>Green</td>
<td>Lampost</td>
<td>yes</td>
</tr>
</table>
</body>
</html>
```

Figure 5-4 shows how it looks.

Figure 5-4. *A basic table created using HTML*

You can also set the table to have padding, which is the amount of white space surrounding the content in a table cell:

```
td {
  padding:25px;
}
```

The preceding CSS rule would make the earlier table cells look like Figure 5-5, with 25 pixels (px) of whitespace:

Figure 5-5. *A basic HTML table with some CSS padding (25 px)*

Here is a rule giving the table double the padding as it had previously:

```
td {
  padding: 50px;
}
```

85

The table with double the whitespace (double the padding) in each cell looks like the one shown in Figure 5-6.

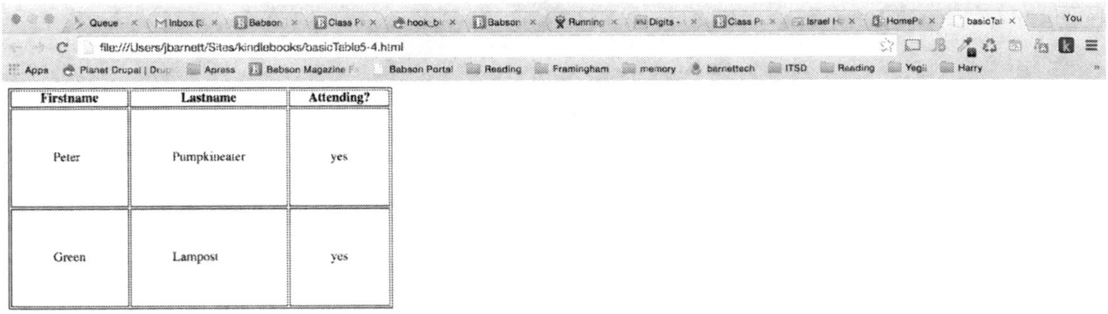

Figure 5-6. *A basic HTML table with even more padding (50 px)*

You can set the table width and height using CSS either in pixels or with a percentage:

```
table
{
  height: 200px;
  width:  250px;
}
```

You can align text in cells left, right, or center.

```
td {
  text-align: left;
}
```

You can set a background color for the table itself or its header.

```
th, table{
background-color:green;
color:white;
}
```

Backgrounds

You can set the background color for an element. In the CSS rule that follows, the background of the entire HTML document would be green. The text is set to white so that it will show up well on the green background.

```
body
{
background-color:green;
color: white;
}
```

In the following CSS style, a background image is set to be included behind the entire body element:

```
body {
  backgound-image: url('my_sample_image.jpg');
}
```

Positioning

You can position elements on the page in a fixed manner, or with relative or absolute positioning with CSS. With fixed positioning, the position remains fixed on the screen, even if the user scrolls the window. With fixed positioning, you specify exactly where the content should display on the page. Following is an example rule using fixed positioning:

```
/*  In this CSS rule the element is placed 35 pixels from
the top and 55 pixels to the right on the page. */
.positioned-element{
  position:fixed;
  top:35px;
  right:55px;
}
```

An element can also be placed on the screen using relative positioning. This means the element will move relative to where it would have normally have displayed on the page if not acted upon by CSS positioning rules.

```
/* With the CSS rule below, whatever text or HTML is wrapped
in the class "positioned-element" is brought up on the page
from wherever it would have normally been by 50 pixels (even
if it means it will overlap with other text or HTML). */
.positioned-element{
  position:relative;
  top:-50px;
}
```

Absolute positioning is another way to position an element in a spot that you specify, but it is placed relative to the first parent element that is not a fixed element.

```
.positioned-element{
  position:absolute;
  left:100px;
  top:150px;
}
```

The CSS snippets from the preceding section are some of the most commonly found CSS rules you'll come across. In the next section, I introduce you to a piece that is important to understanding CSS and page layouts: the CSS box model.

Working with the CSS Box Model

Consider the following HTML, named boxmodel.html. You'll see that there is also an included style sheet, boxmodel.css (a discussion of which follows the HTML discussion), which is invoked in the <head> of the HTML document.

```
<!DOCTYPE html>
<html>
  <head>
    <link rel="stylesheet" type="text/css" href="boxmodel.css">
  </head>
  <body>
        <title> Drupal Web Essentials Primer </title>
        <div class="one box"> Here is a box with a class of one.
</div>
    <div class="two box"> Here is a box with a class of two. </div>
    <div class="one box"> Here is another box with a class of one. </div>
    <div class="two box"> Here is another box with a class of two.
</div>
    <div class="three box"> Here is a box with a class of three,
    absolutely postioned on the page using pixel coordinates. </div>
    <div class="four box"> Here is a box with a class of four,
    positioned using pixels relatively to where the element would
    normally have been displayed on the page based on the HTML. </div>
    </body>
</html>
```

The preceding HTML creates a bunch of boxes, and without the style sheet boxmodel.css, it looks Figure 5-7. Notice that you don't really see any boxes at all; you just see that where there are <div> elements surrounding text, the <div>s force the text to a new line. In reality, <div>s don't just force text to a new line; they create a "box" around the HTML and text that is nested within them. The CSS file, when we allow it to load, showcases this CSS "box" model behavior.

Figure 5-7. *The box model with no CSS applied, so the boxes created aren't apparent*

Figure 5-8 shows what the page looks like when you add the style sheet boxmodel.css.

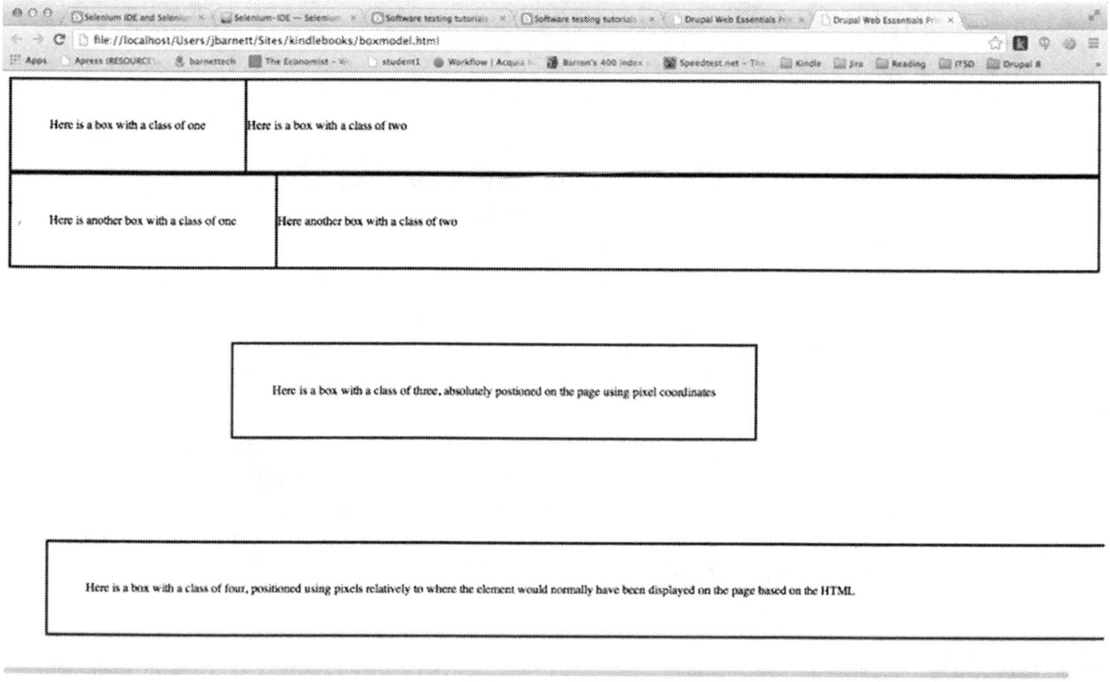

Figure 5-8. *Some HTML showing the CSS box model with some CSS to showcase the boxes created*

So let's look at the CSS in the boxmodel.css file.

```
/* This line tells the browser to keep the boxes with a class
of "one" to the left and let other elements "float" around it.
This will allow the boxes with a class of "two" to 'float'
immediately to the right of it. */
.one {
  float: left;
}


/* This CSS rule applies to all the boxes, apply some padding
to it (to make the box bigger) and put a solid border around
each box so we can really see each box created clearly. */
.box {
  padding: 50px;
  border: solid;
}


/* This CSS rule will put the box with a class of "three" at
the position specified using absolute positioning, so the box
as you see in Figure 5.5 is a bit farther down the screen and
to the right. */
```

```
.three {
  position:absolute;
  left:300px;
  top:350px;
}

/* This rule positions the box with a class of "four" using
relative positioning, and it positions it relative to where
the box would normally fall on the page. */
.four {
  position:relative;
  left:50px;
  top:350px;
}
```

The CSS you just added to the boxmodel.html file serves to illustrate that the <div>s and classes within those <div>s carve up our HTML into boxes so you can better position them and create a layout for your HTML to achieve your theming goals. Remember that <div>s create boxes and force elements that come after it to another line; <span>s create boxes and don't force a new line. (CSS can override these behaviors as well.) Then your CSS can "manage" these boxes. What you've just learned is called the CSS box model.

Summary

This chapter looked at CSS. Each CSS rule has a selector, a property, and a value. When working with CSS, it's best practice to use an external style sheet, placing all your CSS rules into an external file. You can also use internal style sheets, placing all your CSS rules into the head section of your HTML file. Or you can use inline styles, which allow you to place CSS rules directly into the flow of your HTML (although it's not best practice to do so). This chapter showed that when there are two conflicting CSS rules, the more specific rule always wins out. Finally, you looked at the cascade rules that CSS follows, showing the order in which the CSS rules are carried out and how this affects any conflicting styles.

In the next chapter, you'll look at how to use the CSS you just learned about within the custom Drupal module you began working on earlier.

## CHAPTER 6

Adding CSS to Your Drupal Module

By using CSS (Cascading Style Sheets), you have the ability to give your Drupal web pages their own custom look. In this chapter, you will add CSS, which will add color and styling to your Hello World module.

Note The code for this Drupal module is on Github: `https://github.com/barnettech/drupal8_book/tree/with_css`.

Using CSS Within Your

We're going to add to the hello_world basic module you created earlier by adding some color and styling to the page with CSS. We'll be adding some CSS to add a background image to our HTML, and we'll change the font color and size of some other HTML elements within our page.

Following are the updated files needed in our `hello_world` module with the newly added CSS.

The `hello_world.info.yml` will still contain the following:

```
name:  Hello World
type:  module
description:  'A basic Drupal 8 Hello World Module.'
package:  Custom Modules
version:  1.0
core:  8.x
```

You will need to create a `hello_world.permissions.yml` file. This version of the Hello World page will be gated with a new permission, which you'll create in this `hello_world.permissions.yml` file. This file defines a new permission: view hello world. To view this web page in this version, you'll need to give users permissions on the Drupal permissions page (see Chapter 2, where we covered granting user permissions; look on the permissons page for the new permission "view hello world").

The `hello_world.permissions.yml` file looks as follows:

```
view hello world:
  title: 'View hello world'
  description: 'Allow access to view the hello world page.'
  restrict access: TRUE
```

The hello_world.routing.yml file remains the same and looks like this. Again, this file maps URLs (uniform resource locators) to what code to run and display on the page.

```
hello_world_settings:
  path: '/hello/world'
  defaults:
    _controller: '\Drupal\hello_world\Controller\HelloWorldController::
myCallbackMethod'
    _title: 'Hello World'
  requirements:
    _permission: 'view hello world'
```

1. Add a folder called css within the hello_world directory, and then add a folder called images within the css folder.

2. Within the css folder you just created, add the CSS file called hello_world.css with the following code:

   ```
   .myDiv {
       position: relative;
       z-index: 1;
   }

   .myDiv .bg {
     position: absolute;
       z-index: -1;
       top: 0;
       bottom: 0;
       left: 0;
       right: 0;
       background: url(images/scribble.jpeg) center center;
       opacity: .2;
       width: 100%;
       height: 100%;
   }

   .block-title {
     font-size: large;
     color: red;
   }
   ```

3. Add a new file hello_world.libraries.yml or your_module_name.libraries.yml, which contains the following code:

   ```
   hello-world:
   version: 1.x
   css:
     theme:
       css/hello_world.css: {}
   ```

This file and the code within define any CSS and JavaScript libraries you'll use in your module. In this chapter you'll focus on adding CSS; Chapter 8 covers adding JavaScript to Drupal.

Next, in the `HelloWorldController.php` file you'll call this library in your render array. This will add the CSS your HTML will use.

Your `HelloWorldController.php` file should now look this. Note that some extra HTML has been added, which is not highlighted. The line where you add your CSS file is highlighted. Also notice the added divs and classes to the HTML; the new class names have been highlighted as well.

```php
<?php
    /**
     * @file
     * Contains \Drupal\hello_world\HelloWorldController.
     *

    namespace Drupal\hello_world\Controller;

    /**
     * Provides route responses for the hello world page example.
     */
    class HelloWorldController {
      /**
       * Returns a simple hello world page.
       *
       * @return array
       *   A very simple renderable array is returned.
       */
      public function myCallbackMethod() {
        $content = '
        <div class="myDiv">
          <div class="bg"></div>
          <div class="block-title">A basic Drupal page
          created programmatically, Hello World</div>

          Some random text to show off this transparent
        background ....
          Lorem ipsum dolor sit amet, consectetur adipiscing
        elit. Morbi nisi purus, gravida sit amet molestie
        et, facilisis vel nulla. Mauris faucibus augue eu
        quam feugiat at lacinia velit malesuada. Sed
        bibendum faucibus mattis. Maecenas quis ligula
        nibh, sit amet iaculis metus. Aenean lobortis
        massa ut nulla tristique eu vestibulum leo
        eleifend. Maecenas arcu lectus, facilisis in
        mattis sed, pretium et metus. Phasellus elementum,
        elit fringilla mollis sollicitudin, ipsum odio
        vestibulum quam, vitae tristique odio tortor eu
        augue. Pellentesque volutpat placerat neque, sit
        amet vehicula lectus commodo vitae. Aliquam nec
        ultricies eget libero. Donec mollis malesuada est
        a varius. Vestibulum dignissim venenatis nisl, nec
        semper massa tincidunt egestas. Maecenas a erat sem.

          Vestibulum semper eleifend eros at semper. Phasellus
        neque augue, eleifend ut congue pharetra, sagittis
        in neque. Duis sit amet es et risus sodales vulputate
```

sed ut sapien. Vestibulum consequat est lobortis ligula aliquam ac sodales ante sodales. Fusce dict um tortor ut est vehicula sit amet imperdiet dolor consequat. Maecenas nec risus sed quam accumsan vestibulum id ac urna. Suspendisse suscipit dictum dolor condimentum rutrum. Duis augue sem, mattis vel tincidunt ut, interdum in mauris. In quis feugiat ipsum. Donec euismod massa et tortor rhoncus lacinia. Nunc felis ligula, tincidunt eu viverra at, auctor quis magna.

Nullam sapien augue, venenatis sit amet ornare et, blandit nec velit. Morbi eu ligula a lacus commodo lacinia vel et neque. Sed at nisi at sapien adipiscing accumsan in fringilla ligula. Nunc fringilla, est vel ullamcorper tincidunt, tellus ligula lobortis turpis, vel gravida purus lacus a dui. Quisque et massa vestibulum nisi dictum lacinia vehicula ac nisi. Nulla facilisi. Cum sociis natoque penatibus et magnis dis parturient montes, nascetur ridiculus mus. Phasellus sed neque ante, venenatis sagittis dui. Cras lorem ipsum, scelerisque tempor aliquet quis, imperdiet in augue. Curabitur tellus est, ultrices eu sagittis et, pellentesque id enim. Nunc lobortis mattis viverra. Sed non purus ipsum. Aenean ac justo sed urna eleifend consequat.

```
    </div>';
    $element = array(
      '#markup' => '<p><b>Saying Hello World in Drupal 8
      is cool!</b></p>' . $content,
      '#attached' => array(
        'library' => array(
          'hello_world/hello-world',
        ),
      ),
    );
    return $element;
  }
}
```

Within the bold code you just added to the $element array, add the following lines:

```
$element = array(
    '#markup' => '<p><b>Saying Hello World in Drupal 8
    is cool!</b></p>' . $content,
    '#attached' => array(
      'library' => array(
        'hello_world/hello-world',
      ),
    ),
  );
```

These lines attach the CSS file `hello_world.css`, which lives in the library you created in your `hello_world.libraries.yml` page, to this HTML page. Notice you added the library by adding `'hello_world/hello-world'`—this being the module name, then a slash, and then the library name.

Find your own background image and download it into the `images` folder you created. You can call the file anything you like; I called mine `scribble.jpeg`—just make sure to replace the name `scribble.jpeg` with your file's name. Figure 6-1 shows my work to this point. You can see that I've successfully added some CSS to make the Drupal module a bit more stylish.

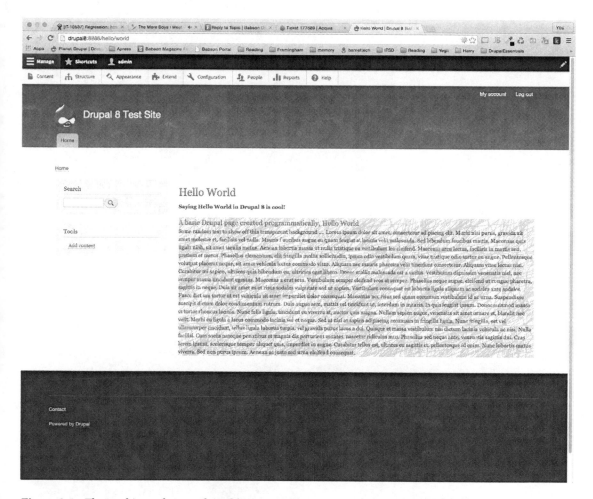

Figure 6-1. *The resulting web page after adding some CSS to the Hello World Drupal module*

Summary

In this chapter you've seen just how to use CSS to decorate your Drupal web pages. You also learned how to add CSS to a custom-created Drupal module.

■ ■ ■

## CHAPTER 7

A JavaScript Primer for Drupal

So now you know what HTML (HyperText Markup Language) and CSS (Cascading Style Sheets) are, and you've come to know all the different CSS selectors and HTML elements available to you to create very rich web pages. So now let's add some JavaScript to make your pages dynamic and very "Web 2.0." JavaScript lets you program your web page to respond to users moving their mouse, or clicking a particular HTML element, or maybe you want some time-based events to occur. JavaScript is very exciting and can add lots of cool features to your site. In this chapter you'll learn to add JavaScript to web pages; then in Chapter 8 you'll learn to add JavaScript to custom-created Drupal pages. Remember that HTML, CSS, and JavaScript can all run independently of Drupal, but the Drupal system does use these same building blocks to create pages.

Getting Started with JavaScript

JavaScript can bring your page alive, allowing you to respond to user clicks and other events on the page, without the need to reload the page. I believe that JavaScript and jQuery can really make for a great user experience, minimizing the need to reload the page to get your users the information they need. JavaScript also allows you to create some really great features where your users can drag items, click items, and create entire intricate interactive games. Google's e-mail interface at http://www.gmail.com has hundreds of thousands of lines of JavaScript and is one of the world's most intricate examples of how much you can do with JavaScript.

For now, though, let's start with a simple Hello World script (a ubiquitous way programmers teach how to get a programming language to speak its first words to your screen—which inevitably are "Hello World"). Get ready to start the JavaScript "Hello World" exercise.

1. Put the following line of code into the HTML page you've been working on, within the <head> tags and before the <style> tag:

```
<script>
alert("Hello World!");
</script>
```

Here's what the basic JavaScript code (highlighted in bold) looks like in the larger HTML page:

```
<html>
<head>

<script>
// Below line will show a popup stating "Hello World!"
// The alert command in JavaScript creates a popup box showing
```

```
// whatever is in the quotation marks and parentheses that
// directly follows the alert command.
alert("Hello World!");
</script>

<style>
body {
  background-image:url('ocean.jpg');
}

h1 {
  color: blue;
}

body #my-id-name h1{
  color: purple;
}

#the-title {
  text-align: center;
}

.to-the-right {
  margin-left: 200px;
}
</style>

</head>
<body>
  <title> HELLO WORLD </title>
  <div id="my-id-name"><h1>HELLO WORLD!</h1></div>
  <p>  This is a paragraph. </p>
  <div class="to-the-right"><b> This is bold text. </b></div>
  <i> This is italicized text. </i>
</body>
</html>
```

Notice the lines that begin with //. Comments in JavaScript are denoted by starting a line with a double forward slash: //. Or for multiline comments, you would write the comment as follows, wrapping your comment text in a forward slash and an asterisk, and closing the comment with an asterisk and a forward slash:

```
/* Here is my sample comment. */
```

Notice each line of JavaScript must end with a semicolon (well you can omit them but it is not recommended).

When you display your HTML page in your web browser, you should get an annoying pop-up that says "Hello World!" It should look like the one shown in Figure 7-1. This is one easy way of including just a bit of JavaScript in your HTML page. When you click OK, the alert will close, and you'll return to your web page.

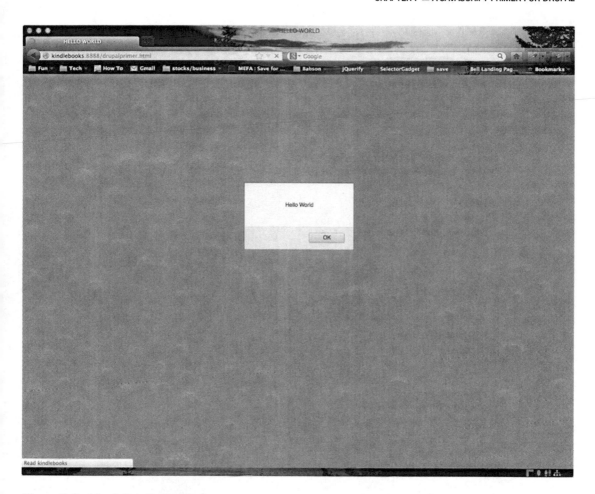

Figure 7-1. *A basic JavaScript alert*

While it is possible to include JavaScript within your HTML file, just like you might include CSS directly within the file, it's also possible to include a reference to the JavaScript file. We'll do that next.

Adding Basic JavaScript to a Web Page

An even better way to include JavaScript in your pages, just as in CSS, is to put all your JavaScript code in an included JavaScript file rather than directly in your HTML file. Again, this will provide you with better code organization, which becomes essential when your code base gets to be over 10,000 lines of code in a big collaborative project with many other developers! In this section, you'll create a basic JavaScript file and call it from within the HTML file.

1. Create a file with a .js extension. I'm going to call mine basic_javascript.js. (You can use your code editor to create the file.)

2. Add the following code to your HTML file. You can discard the previous JavaScript code you entered.

```
<html>
<head>

    <script type="text/JavaScript" src=
    "basic_javascript.js"></script>

    <style>
      body {
        background-image:url('ocean.jpg');
      }

      h1 {
        color: blue;
      }

      body #my-id-name h1{
        color: purple;
      }

      #the-title {
        text-align: center;
      }

      .to-the-right {
         margin-left: 200px;
      }
    </style>

</head>
<body>
  <title> HELLO WORLD </title>
  <div id="my-id-name"><h1>HELLO WORLD!</h1></div>
  <p>  This is a paragraph. </p>
  <div class="to-the-right"><b> This is bold text. </b></div>
  <i> This is italicized text. </i>
</body>
</html>
```

Notice the preceding highlighted code. The purpose of this code is to include the file basic_javascript.js for use by your web page. It pulls in the JavaScript, which you type into this file next.

3. In the file called basic_javascript.js (or whatever you decided to call it), put in the following line:

```
alert("Hello World!");
```

4. Save your file.

Normally, at this point, I'd have you load your web page in a browser. Instead, I'm going to take a moment to introduce you to Firebug, which is a Firefox add-on that many developers use on a daily basis to makes their coding lives easier.

■ **Note** Chrome also has a very good equivalent to Firebug, which is built into the chrome web browser, if you right-click and choose Inspect Element, you'll be able to use that one instead of Firebug if you prefer Google Chrome.

Installing Firebug

Firebug is an add-on that enables you to debug your web pages within the web browser itself. Before you can use Firebug (which works on a Mac or in Windows), you need to download the latest version of Firefox (if you don't have it on your computer already) and install Firebug.

- On a Mac, open Firefox. In the upper menu, click Tools, then click Add-ons, then click Get Add-ons. Search for the Firebug add-on and follow the directions to install it. Restart Firefox.

- In Windows, open Firefox. Click the little white arrow at the top of the browser within the little orange box that says "Firefox," then click Add-ons, then click Get Add-ons and search for the Firebug add-on. Follow the directions to install Firebug. Restart Firefox.

Now, when you use Firefox, you will see a little bug icon in the top right corner. You'll also see the Firebug tools, which display at the bottom of the Firefox window. (See Figure 7-2.)

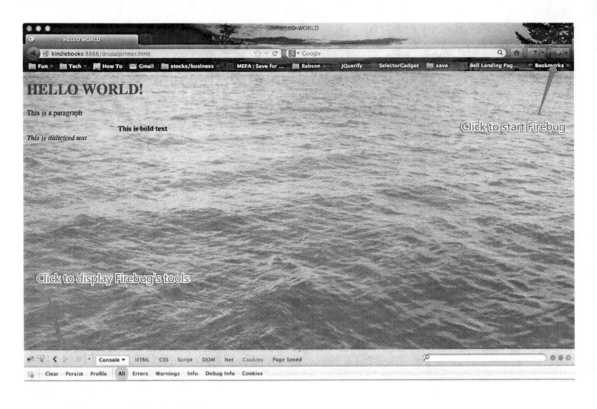

Figure 7-2. *The Firefox browser with Firebug installed*

Using Firebug

To practice using Firebug, redisplay your web page (your HTML file) in Firefox. Then complete the following steps:

1. Click the Net tab. You can use this tab to make sure all your files are loading, such as your JavaScript file or your CSS external file, as shown in Figure 7-3. Note that it shows that your drupalprimer.html, basic_javascript.js, and ocean.jpg files all load successfully. If they didn't, the missing file(s) would show up in red, and under the Status column, you would see an error code.

Figure 7-3. *The Firebug Net tab*

The Net tab is also great for looking at the timeline, to see what assets are taking a long time to load. The onload time for this page was 1.45 seconds. Onload refers to how long it took for Firefox to load your CSS, JavaScript, and images.

2. Locate the Firebug tools and then click the icon that displays a small rectangular box with an arrow in it. Now, when you click any piece of HTML, this tool will show you all the CSS styles associated with that HTML in a pane on the right-hand side of the window. (See Figure 7-4.)

Figure 7-4. *Using Firebug to help with your CSS*

You can see Firebug is extremely useful for quickly seeing what CSS is within a web page. But you can do more than just look at the styles. Within the pane that displays on the right-hand side, you can actually modify the CSS to alter the web page in real time. If a web page does not look exactly like you want it to, this pane provides the perfect way to modify the CSS—you can edit the CSS and try out different styles to get things looking the way you want them to. After experimenting to your liking in Firebug, you can go back and edit your CSS file to make the changes permanent. Firebug is a fabulous debug tool for CSS and really helps you tweak your CSS to be the perfection you're aiming for. And as you'll see, it's just as fabulous for debugging JavaScript.

Modifying JavaScript Code

In this section you modify your JavaScript from the earlier exercise so that instead of showing `alert('Hello World');` it shows `console.log('Hello World');`. This change allows you to see how to use Firebug's Console tab.

1. Load your HTML page and modify the JavaScript from `alert('Hello World');` to `console.log('Hello World!');`. Save your file.

2. If your Firebug debugger is not already open, open it. In Firebug click the Console tab.

3. Load the revised web page (see Figure 7-5). This time you won't see that annoying pop-up that says "Hello World." Instead, you'll see "Hello World" show up as a message within the Console tab.

Figure 7-5. *Using Firebug's console to output debug log messages from your JavaScript code*

The area below the Console tab will show you if you have any JavaScript errors. This is going to help you quite a bit! As well, you can put in console messages to print out values of variables to make sure they are the values you're expecting. (You explore variables and some basic JavaScript programming structures later in this chapter. For now, just keep this tool in mind because it's one you're going to need.)

■ **Note**   Do not leave in those console.log messages when you move your code into a production (live) environment. Internet Explorer browsers have problems with it and will show JavaScript errors unless the user presses F12 and opens his or her browser's developer tools (not something an average user would do, of course).

Working with JavaScript Programming Constructs

So now I'm going to start introducing basic programming constructs (essential elements of programming languages). I'll be teaching you basic JavaScript, but the basic concepts apply to any programming language (PHP, JAVA, Ruby, etc.).

Variables

Let's start with what variables are. Remember basic algebra, where you learned $1 + x = 3$ and solved for x? Well, x is a variable. In programming languages, variables can store information, and they are often modified and retrieved for use within the flow of a page (or pages) of programming.

Now let's use JavaScript with variables to look at similar basic math.

```
y=5;
z=2;
x=y+z;
console.log('the value of y + z is ' + x);
```

If you plug the preceding code into your JavaScript file (you can just put the code in after the code already in there), the output in your Firebug console will be: the value of y + z is 7.

■ **Note**   If you are copying and pasting into your code editor, you may have to delete the quotation marks and then replace them. The fonts used in Microsoft Word or other nonprogramming utilities use quotation mark characters that are commonly incompatible with programming.

ADDITION VERSUS CONCATENATION

Notice in the `console.log` line in the previous section that I used the + sign not for addition but to concatenate (join together) the words "the value of y + z is" and the value of x. When a variable consists of text, or a series of characters (any mix of letters, numbers, and symbols), it is called a *string*. You define a string within quotes, either single or double quotes

When a variable consists of numbers, it is considered an integer—but only if you do not put quotes around the number. For example, I may want to just talk about the number "1234" and not treat it as an integer. In fact, you can "cast" (make) "1234" as a string or an integer in programming languages. Sometimes the computer just figures out if you intend it to be an integer or string based on context and

---

what you're trying to do, and sometimes you have to actually tell the computer (known as "casting" the variable) how you want to treat your variable (as a string or integer). Just to clarify, if you put quotes around a number, it will be treated as a string; if you don't, it will be treated as a number and you'll be able to do arithmetic with numeric (non-string) variables.

In the preceding case, the computer knew in JavaScript when you coded x=y+z that you wanted to compute the value of 5+2, (the values of y and z, respectively). When you wrote + x next to the string 'the value of y + z is' the computer knew you just wanted to concatenate the first string with the value of x. String concatenation is used quite often in programming.

Variables as Integers/Numbers

Following are two examples of using variables as basic integers/numbers:

```
x = 7;
y = 236;
```

Variables as Strings

Here are some examples of variables that store strings.

```
x = 'Here is my string, which can be any sequence of characters,
which can be letters, numbers, or symbols'

myString = "I am a string also, notice you can call your string
anything you like, this time the variable's name is myString";
```

Note that if you enclose the string with double quotes, you cannot write something like the following within the string:

```
myString = "Hello I cannot use "quotes" within my string without
escaping (putting a forward slash in front of them) them";
```

You cannot use the double quotes within the string again because the browser will get confused and not know where your string begins and ends, the opening and closing quotes tell the web browser where your string begins and ends.

The same holds true if you wrap your string with single quotes—you cannot use single quotes again in the string. Here's how you get around this.

```
myString = "I can use a single quote in this string because I'm
wrapping my string in double quotes";
```

So you can do it that way or you can "escape" your quotes like this and it tells the browser not to apply any special meaning to your use of this quote character—the quote is simply a quote. Escaping the quote characters in a string would look like the following:

```
myString = "I can use my single quote again in this string I\'m
very happy!";
```

Notice the forward slash "escaped" the single quote, making it usable again within the string. Usually if I've created my string by putting double quotes around it, then I use single quotes within the string for apostrophes. Also the reverse is true—if you enclose your string in single quotes, then double quotes can be used within the string.

Strings and numbers are two different data types that are pretty straightforward. In the next section I introduce you to arrays, objects, and Booleans, which I indent to make just as straightforward.

Arrays

Think of arrays as a compartmentalized container with slots for each item so you can easily reference and find each item, kind of like a file cabinet with as many drawers (rows in the array) as you need. So . . . an array is a single variable that can store more than one piece of information.

Consider the following `car` variable, which is declared as an array:

```
car = new Array();
car[0] = "Nissan";
car[1] = "Ford";
car[2] = "Volvo";
```

You can also write the preceding array as follows:

```
cars = new Array("Nissan", "Ford", "Volvo");
```

All three car types are data elements of the `car` array variable.

Arrays are zero based, so even when you declare it the way I did, `cars[0]` is equal to the string `"Nissan"`. You'll find in computer languages, you usually will start counting from zero, and not one.

To reference an item from the `car` array, you would do this:

```
console.log('I think I am going to buy a  ' + car[0] + ' when
I need a new car');
```

The preceding line will print out this text in your Firebug console: I think I am going to buy a Nissan when I need a new car.

Arrays are a nice way to pass along lots of data in a single variable. Another way to do the very same thing is with objects.

Objects

Objects are another way to store data. Just like an array, one object can contain many "properties." Take a look at the following:

```
user = new Object();
user.firstname = "Jimmy";
user.lastname = "Greyson";
/* Note below there are no quotes around 45 so it's treated as
an integer and not a string. */
user.age = 45;
```

All the preceding data elements—"Jimmy", "Greyson", and the age of 45—belong to the single object stored in the `user` variable.

Now, in your JavaScript file—after declaring the preceding object—you can type the following:

```
console.log("Hello fictitious person " + user.firstname + " " +
user.lastname);
```

Sure enough, if you load these lines in your Firefox browser, you'll see in the Firebug console that it reads: Hello fictitious person Jimmy Greyson.

Booleans

Booleans, like those shown here, simply define a variable as true or false:

```
myVar = TRUE;
myVar = FALSE;
```

The preceding variables are Booleans. Boolean variables are often used in conditional statements and can be used as a flag to check if a condition was true or false. For example, the following bit of code will evaluate the variable `flag` as `true` and will run the code within the `if` statement. As a result, an alert box will appear with the message "Good day to you!"

```
var flag = true;
if (flag) {
    alert("Good day to you!");
}
```

Now that you are equipped with some of the basics, I can show you why JavaScript is very, very cool.

Creating JavaScript Events

JavaScript can respond to what the user is doing in the browser, responding to "events." Here is a list of some of the more frequently used events.

- The user clicks a particular HTML element—a button, for example—in the browser. You might use this event so that if the user clicks a button, some other text or another section of the page becomes visible. By hiding elements until a click event occurs, you can minimize clutter on the screen, showing certain elements only on demand.

- The user's web page has finished loading. With this event you run some additional code after the user's web page fully loads. This event gives users a good experience— fast-loading pages. Because the additional code runs only after the page load, it doesn't interfere with the user being able to see the full page in his or her browser as fast as possible.

- The mouse moves over (hovers over) an HTML element. This event can be useful, for example, when you want to display additional help text about an element when a user hovers over that element.

- A user presses a key (could be any key or a particular key on the keyboard). One common use case might be showing users, as they are typing within a text area, how many characters they have to left to type (if you are limiting the length of the text they are allowed to type).

Now that you know more about using events in JavaScript, it's time to put that knowledge to work. In a new HTML file, type the following code. Save it as event_lab.html.

```
<!DOCTYPE html>
<html>
  <head>
  </head>
  <body>

    <p>Click the button to say hello. </p>

    <!-- the next line will create a button on the web page --!>
    <button id="myButton">Click Me</button>

    <!-- in area below within the paragraph tags that have the
    id of targetId we'll upon button click insert the word
    "Hello!!!!!" -->
    <p id="targetId"></p>

<script>
// The line below says: When the user clicks on the element
// with the id of "myButton", run the function sayHello. A
// function is a block of code you can invoke. Notice the
// sayHello function's block of code is within the
// brackets "{}" and that code says make the HTML of the
// element with an id of "targetId" be "Hello!!!!!"
document.getElementById("myButton").onclick=function()
{sayHello()};
function sayHello() {
  document.getElementById("targetId").innerHTML="Hello!!!!!";
}
</script>
  </body>
</html>
```

Figure 7-6 shows how the page would display in a browser prior to clicking the Click Me button.

Figure 7-6. *Clicking the Click Me button causes an event in the browser*

Figure 7-7 shows what the page would look like after clicking the Click Me button.

Figure 7-7. *The browser says hello after responding to a JavaScript click event*

The key line in the preceding code is shown again here.

```
document.getElementById("targetId").innerHTML="Hello!!!!!";
```

This line of code says to look in the document for the id of targetId, and then replace the HTML (innerHTML just refers to the HTML for this id area) with "Hello!!!!!". The string "Hello!!!!!" could have contained HTML like <p>Hello!!!!</p> with paragraph tags or other HTML tags, but I chose to just put text in this area, which works also. Replacing the innerHTML of the area with this id also means you can put whatever text you like in that area—I just put in "Hello!!!!!"

You now understand the basic idea behind enabling user interaction in web pages.

Using the jQuery Library

In the preceding section, you saw an example with getElementById. You can also reference a class with getElementByClassName, and you can reference regular HTML elements like paragraph <p> tags or table elements with the getElementByName function. In this section, I introduce an even easier way to do this using a JavaScript Library called *jQuery*. There are other libraries, but this is by far the most popular, and it allows you to do some really cool stuff with very little coding.

■ **Note** For more examples of reacting to browser events, be sure to check out my favorite WC3 tutorial: http://www.w3schools.com/js/js_htmldom_events.asp.

A JavaScript *library* is essentially a bunch of JavaScript that another programmer has made time to abstract for you to hide its complexity, and instead offers himself and others the luxury of just using his or her hard work in a very simple manner. You'll see this idea in programming over and over again—reusable code, and abstraction to simplify the use of code.

By including the jQuery library (http://jquery.com/), you can quickly do some really cool things. For example, you can use the accordion effect on your HTML. To see this effect in action, refer to the jQuery documentation, which includes a live demo: http://jqueryui.com/accordion/.

To include the accordion effect in your web page, put the following code into your HTML file and save it:

```
<html lang="en">
<head>
<title>jQuery UI Accordion</title>
  <link rel="stylesheet"
  href="http://code.jquery.com/ui/1.10.2/themes/smoothness/
  jquery-ui.css" />
  <script src="http://code.jquery.com/jquery-1.9.1.js"></script>
  <script src="http://code.jquery.com/ui/1.10.2/jquery-ui.js">
  </script>
    <script>
  $(function() {
    $( "#accordion" ).accordion();
  });
  </script>
</head>
<body>

<div id="accordion">
  <h3>Section 1</h3>
  <div>
    <p>
    Lorem ipsum dolor sit amet, consectetur adipiscing elit.
    Sed dictum tempus lacus ut gravida. Donec ut malesuada
    magna. Sed id lectus justo. Praesent at neque eget nulla
    porttitor auctor non a magna. Nullam interdum venenatis
    massa in rhoncus. Suspendisse potenti. Phasellus sit amet
    purus nec arcu faucibus sollicitudin vitae id ante. Duis
    viverra, elit ac aliquam facilisis, erat augue luctus nibh,
    eget fermentum nunc mi at tortor.
    </p>
  </div>
  <h3>Section 2</h3>
  <div>
    <p>
    Lorem ipsum dolor sit amet, consectetur adipiscing elit.
    Sed dictum tempus lacus ut gravida. Donec ut malesuada
    magna. Sed id lectus justo. Praesent at neque eget nulla
```

113

```
      porttitor auctor non a magna. Nullam interdum venenatis
      massa in rhoncus. Suspendisse potenti. Phasellus sit amet
      purus nec arcu faucibus sollicitudin vitae id ante. Duis
      viverra, elit ac aliquam facilisis, erat augue luctus nibh,
      eget fermentum nunc mi at tortor.
      </p>
    </div>
    <h3>Section 3</h3>
    <div>
      <p>
      Lorem ipsum dolor sit amet, consectetur adipiscing elit.
      Sed dictum tempus lacus ut gravida. Donec ut malesuada
      magna. Sed id lectus justo. Praesent at neque eget nulla
      porttitor auctor non a magna. Nullam interdum venenatis
      massa in rhoncus. Suspendisse potenti. Phasellus sit amet
      purus nec arcu faucibus sollicitudin vitae id ante. Duis
      viverra, elit ac aliquam facilisis, erat augue luctus nibh,
      eget fermentum nunc mi at tortor.
      </p>
    </div>
    <h3>Section 4</h3>
    <div>
      <p>
      Lorem ipsum dolor sit amet, consectetur adipiscing elit.
      Sed dictum tempus lacus ut gravida. Donec ut malesuada
      magna. Sed id lectus justo. Praesent at neque eget nulla
      porttitor auctor non a magna. Nullam interdum venenatis
      massa in rhoncus. Suspendisse potenti. Phasellus sit amet
      purus nec arcu faucibus sollicitudin vitae id ante. Duis
      viverra, elit ac aliquam facilisis, erat augue luctus nibh,
      eget fermentum nunc mi at tortor.
      </p>
    </div>
  </div>

</body>
</html>
```

Notice the lines of code highlighted in bold at the beginning of this code. By calling these two JavaScript files (the jQuery libraries), you then can do: $("#accordion").accordion(); and the jQuery user interface (UI) library defines that accordion should take what's in your <div> tags that has an id of accordion in your HTML and makes the accordion behavior you should be seeing. jQuery allows you to select elements by CSS selectors. As you can see here, the id with the value accordion was selected using #accordion. Remember in CSS that ids are selected with the "#" character, and classes are selected with the "." character. So to select a class in jQuery with the value accordion, you would use .accordion, and to choose the id with the value of accordion, you would use #accordion.

The basic way this accordion functionality works is that it looks for a pattern of HTML and then the accordion jQuery library knows to collapse the HTML at certain points in the HTML. The following pattern uses a <div> with an id of accordion and then includes a series of <h3> tags, <p> tags, and <div> tags in a specific order. The text between the tags (the content) can be anything you like.

Now, fire up the code in your browser and click the arrow next to Section 2 (see Figure 7-8). When you click Section 2, you'll see that Section 1 folds up, much like an accordion.

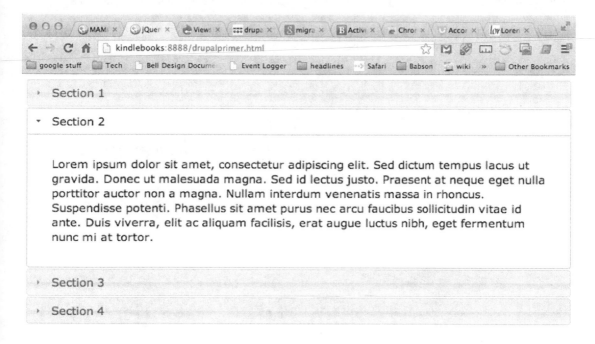

Figure 7-8. *jQuery accordion affect*

The accordion is a free effect you get from invoking the jQuery UI JavaScript library. Because the jQuery UI JavaScript library is dependent on code in the basic jQuery library, you see the following two lines in the preceding code:

```
<script src="http://code.jquery.com/jquery-1.9.1.js">
</script>
<script src="http://code.jquery.com/ui/1.10.2/
jquery-ui.js"></script>
```

It's important that you write these lines in *this* order because, as I said, the jQuery UI library depends on the core jQuery library.

■ **Note**   These query scripts are hosted at `http://code.jquery.com`. Microsoft, Google, and other content delivery networks (CDNs) also host jQuery for developers to invoke the JQuery code. You could download the JQuery code, host it locally, and call these JQuery scripts just like any other JavaScript files, or you can invoke them as shown here by referencing them from their CDNs.

Notice you had to wrap your code in the $(function() {});. You're establishing jQuery to be called with the $ character. Just remember you need to wrap your code with the $() characters to let the browser know you're going to use jQuery. $() is actually the most basic jQuery function—it is the function that invokes jQuery itself. To use jQuery you need to use the $ character a lot, but don't get confused. You can actually change from using the $ character to using any set of characters to wrap jQuery. Although I don't cover that here, you need to know this is possible because you'll likely come across it. You can read more about how to change how to invoke jQuery at http://learn.jquery.com/using-jquery-core/avoid-conflicts-other-libraries/.

Using the jQuery Library with Events

This section provides you with the basics about jQuery. Just as you were able to handle events in JavaScript, you can also use jQuery for events.

Consider the following, which contains HTML and JavaScript. Be sure to read the comments to understand how this code works.

```
<!doctype html>

<html lang="en">
<head>
  <title>jQuery UI Accordion</title>
  <link rel="stylesheet"
  href="http://code.jquery.com/ui/1.10.2/themes/smoothness/
  jquery-ui.css" />
  // First we include the JQuery libraries with the 2 lines
  // below as we've done previously.
  <script src="http://code.jquery.com/jquery-1.9.1.js"></script>
  <script src="http://code.jquery.com/ui/1.10.2/
  jquery-ui.js"></script>
  <link rel="stylesheet" href="/resources/demos/style.css" />
  <script>
  $(function() {
    // This line below says, when you click on the element
    // with the id of "click-me" you'll run the code listed
    // in the function that follows.
    $( "#click-me" ).click(function() {
    // After the user has clicked on the line with the
    // click me id, the punchline is placed after the HTML
    // element with the id of "click-me"
    // Remember an id in JavaScript is referenced with the
    // "#" sign, and a class would be referenced with a ".".
      $("#click-me").after("A penguin rolling down a hill!!!!!");
    });
  });
  </script>
</head>
```

```
<body>

<div id="click-me">What is black and white over and over
and over again? Click me for the punch line!!!</div></h2>

</body>
</html>
```

When you load this code into your browser, your page should look similar to the one shown in Figure 7-9.

What is black and white over and over and over again? Click me for the punch line!!!

Figure 7-9. *JavaScript events with jQuery*

If you click the text "Click me for the punch line!!!" you'll see the punch line, as shown in Figure 7-10. My kids find this hilarious!

What is black and white over and over and over again? Click me for the punch line!!!
A penguin rolling down a hill!!!!!

Figure 7-10. *Response on the screen after using jQuery to code a response to a user click event*

jQuery has many cool effects and behaviors that you can use to quickly and easily impress your clients and customers. To learn more about the other jQuery UI effects you now have at your fingertips, visit http://jqueryui.com/demos/.

Summary

This chapter covered some of the basics of JavaScript and jQuery. You first learned about variables, and the different values variables can hold: strings, integers, and Booleans. Next, you explored arrays and objects, which are variables that can hold one or many values, much like a filing cabinet can hold lots of information. You then took a look at events and how you can make your pages come alive for your users by responding to events. For example, JavaScript can respond to mouse clicks, mouse movement, page load events, and more. The chapter also covered jQuery, which is a bunch of JavaScript libraries packaged up so you can include really cool effects on your pages without needing to write much code. Because the difficult code has been written for you, all you need is to call the already-prepared jQuery functions. jQuery is a great example of how the programming community shares code and allows others to build on the backs of others to do great things. Building on the backs of others is a core idea of Drupal and all open source programming.

The next chapter continues the JavaScript discussion, showing you how to add JavaScript to your Drupal module.

CHAPTER 8

▚ ▚ ▚

Adding JavaScript to Your Drupal Module

In this chapter you will once again be adding to the hello_world module you created earlier. This time you add some basic JavaScript to the simple page you programmatically created in Drupal. You'll be using the basic JavaScript skills you just learned in Chapter 7. Being able to add JavaScript to your Drupal module will mean you'll be able to add click events, hover events, and all the other JavaScript goodness to make your pages dynamic and user friendly without needing to reload the page unnecessarily to get more information for your users (reloading the page takes about two to four seconds or more if poorly designed, depending on the web page). Enabling users to get the information they need with a great graphical user interface with dynamic JavaScript is in high demand in the marketplace today. The market is actually starting to value JavaScript skills as high or higher than back-end database and PHP skills, but knowing all these skills is ideally still very necessary.

▨ **Note**   The code for this Drupal module is on Github: `https://github.com/barnettech/drupal8_book/tree/with_css_jss`.

Adding JavaScript to Your Drupal Module

Following is the code for the hello_world module, but this time it contains the code to include some basic JavaScript. First, as always, is the info.yml file, which stays the same as in the first version of the module.

```
name:  Hello World
type:  module
description:  'A basic Drupal 8 Hello World Module.'
package:  Custom Modules
version:  1.0
core:  8.x
```

The hello_world.routing.yml file is also the same. Again, this file maps URLs (uniform resource locators) to what code to run and display on the page.

```
hello_world_settings:
  path:  '/hello/world'
```

```
defaults:
  _controller:  '\Drupal\hello_world\Controller\HelloWorldController::
myCallbackMethod'
  _title: 'Hello World'
requirements:
  _permission: 'view hello world'
```

The hello_world.module file also remains the same.

```php
<?php

/**
 * @file
 * A basic Drupal 8 Hello World Module.
 */

use Drupal\Core\Routing\RouteMatchInterface;

/**
 * Implements hook_permission().
 */
function hello_world_permission() {
  $permissions = array(
    'view hello world' => array(
      'title' => t('View Hello World module'),
      'description' => t('View the Hello World module page.'),
    ),
  );
  return $permissions;

}
```

Note, however, that unlike the other files, the HelloWorldController.php file now will include lines to add JavaScript to the file. In Drupal 8 you add your JavaScript and CSS by attaching a library defined in a file called your_module.libraries.yml. Add a new file hello_world.libraries.yml or your_module_name.libraries.yml, with the following code:

```
hello-world:
  version: 1.x
  css:
    theme:
      css/hello_world.css: {}
  js:
    js/hello_world.js: {}
```

This file and the code within define any CSS and JavaScript libraries you'll use in your module, you'll see how we include them in the highlighted code below in the HelloWorldController.php file. This file and the code within define any CSS and JavaScript libraries you'll use in your module, you'll see how we include them in the highlighted code below in the HelloWorldController.php file.

```php
<?php
/**
 * @file
 * Contains \Drupal\hello_world\HelloWorldController.
 */

namespace Drupal\hello_world\Controller;

/**
 * Provides route responses for the hello world page example.
 */
class HelloWorldController {
  /**
   * Returns a simple hello world page.
   *
   * @return array
   *   A very simple renderable array is returned.
   */
  public function myCallbackMethod() {
    $content = '
    <div class="myDiv">
      <div class="bg"></div>
        <div class="block-title">A basic Drupal page
        created programmatically, Hello World</div>

        Some random text to show off this transparent
        background ....
        Lorem ipsum dolor sit amet, consectetur adipiscing
        elit. Morbi nisi purus, gravida sit amet molestie
        et, facilisis vel nulla.
        Mauris faucibus augue eu quam feugiat at lacinia
        velit malesuada. Sed bibendum faucibus mattis.
        Maecenas quis ligula nibh, sit amet iaculis metus.
        Aenean lobortis massa ut nulla tristique eu
        vestibulum leo eleifend. Maecenas arcu lectus,
        facilisis in mattis sed, pretium et metus. Phasellus
        elementum, elit fringilla mollis sollicitudin ...
    </div>';
    $element = array(
      '#markup' => '<p><b>Saying Hello World in Drupal 8
      is cool!</b></p>' . $content,
      '#attached' => array(
        'library' => array(
          'hello_world/hello-world',
        ),
      ),
    );
    return $element;
  }
}
```

Drupal comes with several jQuery UI (user interface) libraries installed, as it turns out, so you don't need to download the draggable jQuery library, for instance. The draggable library allows you to click an element and drag it around the screen (a little like dragging a file you don't want any more to the trash bin on your Windows or Mac desktop). Because this library comes with Drupal, you can just invoke the draggable library with the following line: `$('.title').draggable();`. The code in this JavaScript example makes all the elements with a `title` class draggable.

■ **Note**   You can find the additional libraries that come pre-installed with Drupal here: `https://api.drupal.org/api/drupal/core!modules!system!system.module/function/system_library_info/8`. You'll have to wade through the code, but as you get to know the names of various jQuery libraries you'll come to recognize them (ui.accordion, datepicker, droppable, progressbar, etc.).

The line you added allowed you to add your own JavaScript file, `hello_world.js`, and in it you write to the Firebug console and make any text wrapped in the `title` class draggable.

If you load the page now, you'll be able to click the title and drag it around the screen. Instead of having to write out the whole path, you used the PHP: `drupal_get_path('module', 'hello_world')`. This code is a function to get the path to the module specified—in this case, `hello_world`—then you concatenate to that path, the path to your JavaScript file: `/js/hello_world.js`. Although could just write out the whole path, I find this method much easier.

The line you added in the preceding code looks in this module's js folder for the `hello_world.js` file. Make sure to create the js folder within your module's directory structure. Add the file `hello_world.js`, and add the following code to it:

```
(function($) {
    $(document).ready(function() {
      console.log('hello');
      $('.title').draggable();
    });
}(jQuery));
```

■ **Note**   The code used here is more standard JavaScript, and it will work in Drupal and outside Drupal. But there is another way to add JavaScript to Drupal. This particular method works only in Drupal (not in standard JavaScript files). For more information, visit `www.drupal.org/node/304258`.

You're now finished with this exercise. Figure 8-1 shows what the web page looks like. If you have any questions about what folders to make, and so on, take a look at the code and directory structure for the module at Github: `https://github.com/barnettech/ drupal8_book/tree/with_css_js`.

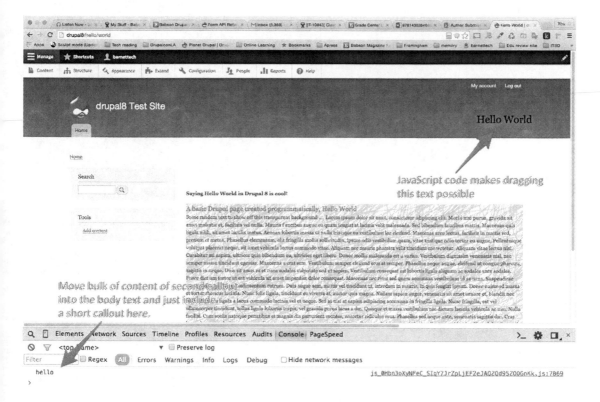

Figure 8-1. *The draggable jQuery library and a console.log message*

Summary

In this chapter you learned how to add the JavaScript you worked with in the previous chapter to your custom-created Drupal module. JavaScript can bring your page alive, allowing you to respond to user clicks and other events on the page, without ever needing to slow down the user to reload the page.

CHAPTER 9

■ ■ ■

A PHP Primer for Drupal

PHP is the programming language used in Drupal. As you may already know, Drupal uses a LAMP stack. The "P" in the word LAMP stands for PHP (the first letters stand for Linux, Apache, and MySQL). PHP is the programming language that does most of the work to make Drupal what it is—it is the guts of Drupal. This chapter teaches you the basics of the PHP programming language. It serves as a great primer for users new to the PHP language, and for users who have dabbled in PHP already, it serves as a good review of PHP. You need to understand this basic building block of Drupal if you want to become an expert in the Drupal content management system. This chapter gets you started.

■ **Note**   In presenting PHP to you for the first time, my first thought is to remind you once again that this book's aim is to teach you to fish. In this chapter I do my best to make sure you understand the basic concepts of PHP. Importantly, I also show you where to learn more about the details. A programmer's career involves quite a lot of "googling" when it comes to PHP syntax or how to do X, Y, or Z. Fortunately, the open source programming community—and the programming community in general—is generous about sharing code, examples, and troubleshooting tips.

Verifying Your Installation of PHP

First, make sure PHP is installed on your computer. To do this, open Terminal and type **php -v** at the command prompt. Your screen should display information about which PHP version you're using. Following is the output on my machine, which is running PHP version 5.36:

```
james-louis-barnetts-macbook-pro-2:js barnettech (master)$ php -v
PHP 5.4.10 (cli) (built: Jan 21 2013 15:12:32)
Copyright (c) 1997-2012 The PHP Group
Zend Engine v2.4.0, Copyright (c) 1998-2012 Zend Technologies
    with Xdebug v2.2.0-komodo, Copyright (c) 2002-2012, by Derick Rethans
```

If PHP is not installed, refer to Appendix A of this book for install instructions. The appendix includes directions for how to install Drupal. And if Drupal is working on your machine, then PHP is installed as well.

■ **Note**   If PHP is not installed, your install will differ depending on what operating system you have. Macs come with PHP installed, although I personally installed a different version called MAMP. If you google "MAMP," you'll easily find MAMP, which comes with an installer. If you use Windows, I've had a good experience with the Zend Server Community Edition: www.zend.com/en/products/server/downloads?src=greybar. There are many other LAMP installers out there for Macs, Windows, and Linux—all easily findable with a quick google for "LAMP Mac" (or whatever operating system you prefer).

Serving Up a Hello World Web Page with PHP

In this section you write your first bit of PHP. With this simple bit of code, you learn to use PHP to create a Hello World web page. As you may recall, the Hello World page in a programming language simply shows how to print out the words "hello world" in the programming language.

1. In your code editor, create a new file and call it hello_world.php.

2. In that file add the following simple line of code:

    ```php
    <?php echo 'HELLO WORLD!!!!!'; ?>
    ```

3. Now, at the command line (make sure you're in the same directory as your PHP script or you'll have to use absolute or relative paths to reference your PHP script), type the following:

    ```
    php hello_world.php
    ```

After you type the preceding line, the phrase "HELLO WORLD!!!!!" gets outputted to the terminal. Figure 9-1 shows what this output looks like on my screen (quite a simple program still).

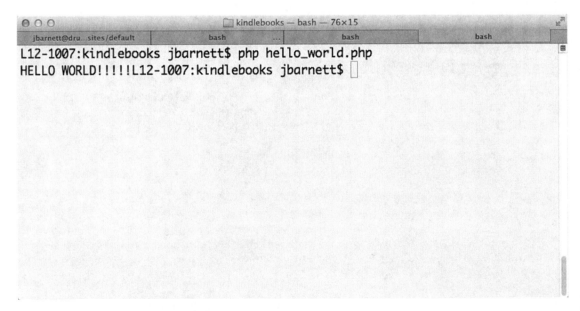

Figure 9-1. *Running the hello_world.php script on the command line*

4. Put the file `hello_world.php` in your "docroot" folder; you will navigate to `http://localhost/hello_world.php`. Now, bring up this extra simple PHP file in a web browser.

Recall from Chapter 4 that your Drupal docroot directory is the base, or "home," directory of your Drupal installation—it's where all your Drupal files and folders reside. To serve up PHP pages for a web browser, you'll want to put your files within this docroot folder. Here's where to find your docroot directory.

- If you change the configuration (in the Apache `configuration` file), you can really put it most anywhere. But out of the box, when you install LAMP, there will be a default place for the docroot. Often the name of the folder will be `htdocs`. If you use LAMP out of the box on a Mac, it will be in your `Sites` directory, which is within your user's home directory. For example, on my Mac it's here: `/Users/barnettech/Sites`. If you used Acquia Dev Desktop, the path would also be in your `Sites` directory; the path on my Windows machine is `C:\Users\James Barnett\Sites\acquia-drupal`.

- In Windows, you usually find the docroot by navigating to the `Program Files` directory, then find where Apache is installed, and then within the Apache directory you'll find the `htdocs` directory, which is the docroot.

- DAMP, the Acquia Drupal installer for Windows, puts the Drupal docroot within `C:/Users/your_username/Sites/acquia-drupal`.

Generally, you can access the file using the pattern I just described: `http://localhost/hello_world.php`. If you use subfolders, it would simply be `http://localhost/subfolder_name/hello_world.php`. Using MAMP (my Mac version of LAMP), it uses a different port (8888, but the default is usually 80 by the way—and it can be omitted from the URL (uniform resource locator) if using the default). Mine looks like `http://localhost:8888/hello_world.php`. Because it's a nonstandard port, I have to specify the port. If you cannot bring up the web page in your browser, it's probable that Apache is either not installed correctly or hasn't been started.

So you now have a PHP Hello World page. Now what? Well, recall from this book's introduction to JavaScript that you learned the concepts of variables and arrays. You'll also run into loop structures. These components are, in general, the basic building blocks of a programming language. You should feel comfortable with the fact that once you've learned one programming language, like JavaScript, the others you learn, like PHP, will be much easier. Time to meet some basic PHP.

Working with Some Basic PHP Code

To help you get comfortable with some PHP basics, this section provides a quick exercise that includes inline documentation, made-up comments that explain along the way what the code is designed to do. In this exercise you try out some basic PHP code, which shows usage of variables and the basic rand function, which is a PHP function that generates a random number.

■ **Note** When you work in programming, you often hear that the code is your documentation. Some people say this means that you should just be able to read the code and know what the programmer did. Others (and I am one of them), however, mean that you should be able to read the code to follow along. In this case the author of the code provides comments within the code itself to guide you along, especially for anything tricky or for anything so complex it would suck away your time trying to wrap your brain around it. The code in this chapter takes this approach, including comments throughout that explain what the code is doing.

---

1.   In your Apache docroot directory, create a new a file called basic_php.php and type the following code:

```
<!DOCTYPE html>

<html>
<head>
  <style>
    .background-image {
      width:1000px;
      height:500px;
      background:url(ocean.jpg) repeat;
      border:1px solid black;
    }
    .the-text {
      width:900px;
      height:360px;
      margin:30px 50px;
      background-color:#ffffff;
      border:15px solid black;
      opacity:0.6; /* We're playing with the opacity of the background
      image here so the text we put on top of it is more readable. */
      filter:alpha(opacity=60); /* For IE8 and earlier */
    }
    /* We're going to put all the output created with straight HTML
    colored with red text.*/
    .html {
      color: red;
      font-size: 35px;
    }
  /* We're going to put all the output created with PHP colored with
  green text.*/
    .php {
      color: green;
      font-size: 35px;
    }

  </style>

  <title>Basic PHP</title>
</head>
```

```
<body>
  <div class='background-image'>
  <div class='the-text'>
<div class='html'>Note how I can mix HTML with PHP programming. After
this bit of text, which is still within the "HTML mode," I'm going to
switch into using some PHP, wrapping all my PHP in the PHP tags as seen
below (red text on this page is in straight HTML and green text that
you see was done using PHP:</div>
<?php  // This is my tag signaling we're in "PHP Mode" now.
// Here below is a variable, an integer. An integer is a numeric value.
$age = 5;

// And here below is another variable, a string, which contains
// letter or numbers.
// I like the definition of a string on php.about.com
/*(http://php.about.com/od/programingglossary/qt/What-Is-A-String.htm):
"A string is a type of data. A string can contain letters, numbers or
characters. Although a string can contain numbers, it is not a numeric
value. A string can be short or long."*/

$name = "Jimmy Bo Bob";

/* See the PHP docs on how to generate a random number. PHP documentation
is quite good actually: http://php.net/manual/en/function.rand.php */
$random_number = rand(1,20);

echo '<div class="php">' . $name . ' who is ' . $age . ' years old,
received ' .
$random_number . ' dollars from the tooth fairy for losing his first tooth!
</div>';

?>  <!--And here is my closing PHP tag. After this line we'll be back
to using HTML programming. -->
  </div>
  </div>
</body>
</html>
```

Be sure to carefully review the comments in the preceding code, which begin with the characters //, because these comments explain what the various parts of the code are doing. Essentially, this code shows how to add PHP to your HTML. Save your code and display the file in your web browser (see Figure 9-2).

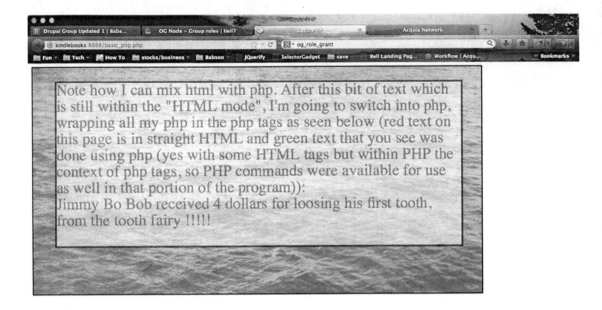

Figure 9-2. PHP code example in a web browser

Working with PHP Looping Structures

All programming languages have looping structures, structures allowing you to run one or more lines of code repetitively. This section looks specifically at what I'm referring to as "looping structures" and what they look like in PHP.

Using the foreach Loop

So you have an array with many elements in it. Recall that an array is one element, kind of like a filing cabinet, and it has many drawers. The beauty of an array is all those drawers fit into one variable, which you declare as an array. You learn soon how to pass an array to a function for the function to use the array. It's very convenient to have to pass just one variable around, rather than 10, 20, or even more variables.

```
$my_array = array('John', 'Curly', 'Moe');
// Now let's loop through the elements of the array and say hi to each
// member in this array.

foreach($my_array as $person) {
 // The </br> HTML element will force the cursor to the next line -
 // a line break.
  echo 'Hello' . $person . '</br>';
}
```

In plain English, this code says that for each element of the $my_array array, put each individual element in turn into the $person variable in the foreach statement. The first time the code's execution goes through this loop, it grabs the first element in the array, which is John, and puts the element into the $person variable. Then, it can operate on the $person variable (which at this point just contains the string John). In this case, it just prints out a greeting to John: Hello John. Then when it hits the closing parenthesis of the foreach structure, it goes to the top and grabs the next element in the array, in this case Curly. Then it runs through the code again within the curly braces of the foreach loop. Now it can operate on the $person variable again, but this time the $person variable contains the string Curly. When the foreach loop runs out of items in the $my_array variable, the foreach loop concludes and processing continues with whatever code comes next.

The output of the preceding code will be:

```
Hello John
Hello Curly
Hello Moe
```

Using loops, especially in conjunction with arrays, is as common as breathing in programming languages. This, I find, is the most common looping structure, but there are others, including the while loop.

Using the while Loop

Another looping structure is the while loop (www.w3schools.com/php/php_looping.asp), which looks like as follows:

```
x=1;
while(x<3) {
  x = x + 1;
  // This can also be written x++; which is just a shorthand way of writing
  //   this same code telling the processor to take x and add 1 to it.
  //   x is an integer in this case.
  echo 'Hello </br>';
}
```

So the code in the curly brackets will run for as long as x is less than 3. Thus the output will just be

```
Hello
Hello
Hello
```

You'll also see another basic "filing cabinet," which is used just like an array—it's called an *object*. You'll often have to loop through an object to get at all the elements inside of it.

```
$my_object->first_name = 'Jimbo';
$my_object->last_name = 'Bob';
echo 'Hello ' . $my_object->first_name . ' ' . $my_object->last_name;
```

The preceding code will give you the following output:

```
Hello Jimbo Bob.
```

The use of echo in PHP tells the system to print the following string to the screen. The "." character concatenates (adds to the output) what follows, which is the variable $my_object->first_name. In this case the output will be Jimbo because that is the value of the variable $my_object->first_name. Then you concatenate (add to the output) a space and then you concatenate (add to the output echoed to the screen) the value of the variable $my_object->last_name, which is set to Bob.

You can also loop through the object in PHP with foreach in PHP. "Looping through the object" refers to the code one at a time going through the object and grabbing each element, as shown here.

```
$x = 1;
foreach($my_object as $property) {
    echo 'property ' . $x . ' in the object is : '. $property . '</br>';
    $x = $x + 1;
}
```

The output will be

```
property 1 in the object is : Jimbo
property 2 in the object is : Bob
```

Here, the foreach statement steps through (loops through) the object, and the code prints out each element of the object.

Printing to the Screen

As shown in the preceding code, the basic method to print to the screen in PHP is to use the echo or print commands. For instance, consider the following code:

```
$my_message = "Hello, I hope you are having a good day!";
echo $my_message;
```

This code will print your message to the screen as output. Likewise, the print command will, like the echo command, print the same output to the screen. Consider the following block of code:

```
$my_message = "Hello I hope you are having a good day!";
print $my_message;
```

There you have it—two simple ways to print to the screen: the PHP echo and print commands.

Using If, If Else, and Else If Statements

The if statements and if else statements allow us to conditionally execute some code, which is extremely useful and is used daily by programmers. Take a look at the following code:

```
$my_name = "James";
if ($my_name == "James") {
  echo 'Hello James';
}
else {
  echo 'Hello ' . $my_name . '. You are not James, but it sure is nice
  to meet you!';
}
```

In this case the $my_name variable is, in fact, equal to "James", so the output is

```
Hello James
```

Consider what would happen if you set the first line in the earlier code to the following:

```
$my_name = "Rob";
```

Then it will print out the following:

```
Hello Rob. You are not James, but it sure is nice to meet you!
```

Notice that a single equal sign assigns a value to a variable, and a double equal sign checks if the variable is equal to some value. The double or triple equals sign is a comparison operator. Other comparison operators can be seen as follows:

```
x = 5;
y = 10;
if (x < y) {
  echo 'x is in fact less than y';
}
if (y > x) {
  echo 'y is in fact greater than x';
}
```

You can also use <= or >= to evaluate if a value is less than or equal to another value or to see if a value is greater than another value or equal to said value.

There is also the elseif statement to consider.

```
$my_name = "James";
if ($my_name == "James") {
  echo 'Hello James';
}
elseif ($my_name == "Rob") {
  echo 'Hello Rob ' . 'Thanks for drawing the original cover art for
  version 1 of this book!';
}
else {
  echo 'I am not sure who this is really, but thanks for coming to the show,';
}
```

You can see that this code does an elseif and checks if the value of $my_name is equal to "Rob". You can add as many elseif statements to check for other specific values. Often, if there are a lot of cases to check, then you'll use a switch statement, covered next.

Switch Statements

A switch statement is just like an if statement. It lets you conditionally execute some code; typically, I use a switch statement when I have more than three cases to check. The following code shows an example:

```
$name = "James";
// Check the name variable for different values.
switch ($name) {
  // In the case that the name variable is equal to "James" or "Jimmy",
  // execute this code.
  case "James":
  case "Jimmy":
    echo "This is the author of this book.";
    break;
  // In the case that the name variable is equal to "Jack", execute this code.
  case "Jack":
    echo "I actually don't know a Jack. Who are you?";
    break;
  // In the case that the name variable is equal to "Josh", execute this code.
  case "Josh":
    echo "I know a Josh. Yes, that is you. Nice to see you again!";
    break;
  //  In the case that there are no previous matches in the case
  // statement, then for all other cases execute this code.
  default:
    echo "If your name is anything else, well, nice to meet you as well.";
}
```

As you can see, using a switch statement keeps your code looking cleaner looking than using many if statements. It is a bit more efficient (less typing) and easier to read.

Working with Strings

When working with strings, there are some great commands, such as `strlen`, `strpos`, and `stripos`.

■ **Note**   Remember that a string can be any number of alphabetic, numeric, or other characters that will not be operated on using math. Strings are usually for humans (not computers) to read; to a computer, a sentence or paragraph is just a string of characters.

---

strlen

The `strlen` command will give you the length of the string. Take the following code as an example:

```
echo 'the length of my last name "Barnett" is ' . strlen("Barnett").;
```

The output of this code is

```
The length of my last name "Barnett" is 7.
```

Here is a link to the PHP documentation for `strlen`: `http://us2.php.net/strlen`.

strpos and stripos

The `strpos` and `stripos` commands will find the first occurrence of whatever you're looking for in another given string. Note that `stripos` is the same as `strpos`, except that when searching the second string for an instance of the first string, `stripos` is case insensitive (it will find a match even if the capitalization of the letters doesn't match); `strpos` is case sensitive.

Take a look at the following code:

```
$haystack = 'abcdefghi';
$needle   = 'a';
$pos = strpos($haystack, $needle);
echo '------';
echo 'needle was found at location ' . $pos . ' in the haystack string';
echo '-----';
```

The output of this code is

```
: ------needle was found at location 0 in the haystack string-----
```

Notice that in the preceding code the counting starts with zero. In the larger string abcdefghi, the a character is at position 0, b is at position 1, and c is at position 2.

The following code shows how strpos and stripos can be useful:

```
$haystack = "This is the string we will be searching";
$pos = stripos($haystack, "STRING");
if ($pos === FALSE) {
  print "The string was not found in the haystack variable\n";
}
else {
  print "Found the string at position $pos!\n";
}
```

Running this code produces the following output. Note that the use of \n forces a line break to be printed to the screen.

```
Found the string at position 12!
```

But consider what happens when you change the code to the following:

```
$haystack = "This is the string we will be searching";
$pos = stripos($haystack, "STRRRING");
if ($pos === FALSE) {
  print "The string was not found in the haystack variable\n";
}
else {
  print "Found the string at position $pos!\n";
}
```

In this case the string doesn't exist, because I obviously spelled the word STRING as STRRRING. In this case, this is the output.

```
The string was not found in the haystack variable
```

Notice that the code checked if $pos === FALSE with a triple equals sign. This approach is used because if the position found is at position 0, then 0 within PHP is evaluated as FALSE and 1 is evaluated as TRUE. (Remember, computers think in zeros and ones after all.) So the triple equals sign also checks that you're comparing the same types of values. In this case you are looking for an actual Boolean value of FALSE. If $pos really is FALSE and not a value of 0, which is an integer, then you don't want to evaluate to FALSE. The triple equal sign ensures you get an actual Boolean value to evaluate, not an integer.

Using Functions

Functions are a way to package up logic or functionality into reusable blocks. A function to check if a user is a class instructor or teacher's assistant, for instance, might go into a function and get called over and over again throughout your code. Functions are very useful and very common in PHP programming. Consider the following code, which includes an explanation of what is happening at key points:

```
// Notice the name of the function is name_check and it takes a variable
// as an argument, $my_name.
function name_check($my_name) {
```

```
  if ($my_name == "James") {
    $content = 'Hello James';
  }
  elseif ($my_name == "Rob") {
    $content = 'Hello Rob ' . 'Thanks for drawing the original cover art
    for version 1 of this book!';
  }
  else {
    $content = 'I am not sure who this is really, but thanks for coming
    to the show.';
  }
  return $content;
}

// Notice here we call the name_check function and pass in the
// value 'Walter' into the function which becomes the value of
// the $my_name variable in the function.
$return = name_check('Walter');
echo $return;
```

This code puts the value returned after executing the code in the name_check function into the $return variable. The code then prints out the value of the $return variable:

```
I am not sure who this is really, but thanks for coming to the show.
```

You passed the value 'Walter' into the name_check function and into the $my_name variable. It is also possible to pass multiple variables into a PHP function. Consider the following code:

```
function name_check($my_name, $evaluation) {
  if ($my_name == "James") {
    $content = 'Hello, James';
  }
  elseif ($my_name == "Robert") {
    $content = 'Hello Rob ' . 'Thanks for drawing the original cover
    art for version 1 of this book! ';
    $content .= ' ' . $my_name . ' ' . $evaluation;
  }
  else {
    $content = 'I am not sure who this is really, but thanks for coming
    to the show.';
  }
  // Below we return the value of the $content variable, which will get
  // stored in the $return variable;
  return $content;
}

$return = name_check('Robert', 'is awesome');
echo $return;
```

In this case you call name_check, put the results into the $return value, and print out the $return variable contents. But this time you pass in two values: 'Robert' and 'is awesome'. These values get sent into the first line of the name_check function:

```
function name_check($my_name, $evaluation) {
```

The $my_name variable takes the value of the first value passed in, which is 'Robert', and the $evaluation variable takes on the value of the second value passed in, which is 'is awesome'.

You can also set default values for variables by declaring a function, as follows:

```
function name_check($my_name = 'John Doe', $evaluation = 'is ok') {
```

In this case, if you do not set $my_name variable when you call the function, it takes on a default value of 'John Doe', and the $evaluation variable takes on the value 'is ok' if you do not set when the function is called.

By using functions you have to write a block of complex code only once, and then you can easily call the code whenever you like. This approach also provides abstraction so that you and other programmers don't need to get involved in the complexities of the block of code in a function and can just use said code, making life easier for whomever needs to use that function. Object-oriented code, beyond the scope of this book, is often used primarily to take advantage of this concept. My favorite book about PHP object-oriented code structure is *PHP Objects, Patterns, and Practice* by Matt Zandstra (Apress, 2005) (www.apress.com/9781590599099). The book does a nice job of making a complex subject easy to read about.

Functions Operating on Arrays

Arrays are extremely useful in PHP, and there are many functions in PHP that allow you to work with arrays. The list of functions is quite long, and you can find the full list at www.php.net. The official site for PHP documentation is www.php.net/manual/en/ref.array.php. The following sections look at a few of my favorites.

array_search

The array_search function searches through an array for a value and returns the key of where it's found in the array. If the value is the first element in the array, the key will be 0; if it's the second item in the array, it will return the integer 1; if it's the third element of the array, it returns the integer value 2. (Remember, the computer often starts counting from 0, not 1.) If the array_search function doesn't find what it's looking for in the array, it returns the Boolean value FALSE. Consider the following code:

```
$array = array('blue', 'purple', 'green', 'red');
$key = array_search('green', $array); // $key = 2;
echo $key;
```

The output from this small bit of code is the integer 2 because in the list, green is, in fact, at position 2. Notice that you don't have to define the keys in the following line:

```
$array = array('blue', 'purple', 'green', 'red');
```

The first element key by default is 0, then 1, 2, 3, and so on. Each key corresponds with the value in the array; these are known as *key/value pairs*. You can reference a value by referencing the key. For instance, you can do the following:

```
$array = array('blue', 'purple', 'green', 'red');
echo $array[3];
```

This code prints out red to the screen because you printed out the third element of the array (again, counting in an array starts from 0, not 1).

You can also define the names of keys in an array. Look at the following code, which contains an array with these key/value pairs:

```
$array = array('positon-one' => 'blue', 'position-two' => 'purple',
'position-three' => 'green', 'position-four' => 'red');
echo $array['position-two'];
```

Running this code prints out purple to the screen. It is useful to define the names of your array's keys for easier reading and organization of your code. When doing more complex things, you can use variables as the key names, so you can dynamically create arrays. The key names can vary depending on the flow of your code.

You can also put arrays or objects within an array. Think of it as putting a filing cabinet within a filing cabinet. Drupal is known for having enormous arrays, and you'll often see arrays and objects within arrays, or arrays within objects. For documentation on the array_search command, visit http://www.php.net/manual/en/function.array-search.php.

array_push

The array_push command adds an array element to the end of the array. Take the following code as an example:

```
$my_array = array("orange", "banana"); array_push($my_array, "apple", "raspberry", "pear");
// print_r prints out whatever is in a variable and it handles printing
// out of arrays and objects better than an echo or print command.
print_r($my_array);
```

This code prints out the new array with its new elements: apple, raspberry and pear are now added to the end of $my_array. Following is the output:

```
Array
(
    [0] => orange
    [1] => banana
    [2] => apple
    [3] => raspberry
    [4] => pear
)
```

You can see that the array now has the new fruits appended to the end of the array. The print_r command printed out the array, nicely formatting the array's key/value pairs. For documentation on the array_push command, visit www.php.net/manual/en/function.array-push.php.

asort, arsort, ksort, and krsort

The assort, arsort, ksort, and krsort commands sort your arrays alphabetically by values or by keys. asort sorts your array's values; arsort sorts your array's values in reverse order. ksort sorts your array by the array's keys in alphabetical order; krsort sorts your array's keys in reverse alphabetical order.

array_keys and array_values

The commands array_keys and array_values let you put just either the array's keys or its values alone into an array, which can be useful. Take the following code:

```php
$array = array('position-one' => 'blue', 'position-two' => 'purple',
'position-three' => 'green', 'four' => 'red');
$keys = array_keys($array);
$values = array_values($array);

echo 'The arrays keys are: ';
print_r($keys);
echo 'The arrays values are: ';
print_r($values);
```

This code returns the following output:

```
The arrays keys are: Array
(
    [0] => position-one
    [1] => position-two
    [2] => position-three
    [3] => four
)
The arrays values are: Array
(
    [0] => blue
    [1] => purple
    [2] => green
    [3] => red
)
```

More documentation on array_keys and array_values is available at www.php.net/manual/en/function.array-keys.php and www.php.net/manual/en/function.array-values.php.

TAKING ADVANTAGE OF THE OFFICIAL PHP DOCUMENTATION

I've made reference to the official PHP documentation in the section "Functions Operating on Arrays," but I want to call attention to the official PHP documentation on www.php.net. I've programmed using many different programming languages, and by far I find the PHP community's documentation to be the best. Generally, each function or concept in PHP has its own page (each PHP function has its own page). More important, there are multiple examples of how to use the function being discussed, so if the first or second examples confuse you, just move on to another example.

Summary

This chapter looked at how to use PHP. After creating a couple of web pages that made use of PHP, you studied some of the key logic behind PHP, which included looping structures and conditional code with `if` statements and `switch` statements. You then looked at PHP arrays, objects, string, integers, and Booleans. You looked at comparing strings and integers with ==, ===, <, > and <=, >= operators. In addition, you studied some key PHP functions such as `strlen`, `strpos`, and `stripos`. You looked at the value of packaging up some code into functions, which then can be called over and over again without recoding the same logic. Next, you looked at lots of functions for interacting with arrays: `array_search`, `array_push`, `asort`, `arsort`, `ksort`, `krsort`, `array_keys`, and `array_values`. Finally, you took a look at the great http://www.php.net documentation, where you can learn about the many more commands available to you to craft your web and command-line PHP applications. Now that you know some of the basics of PHP, the next chapter puts that knowledge to work, teaching you to add PHP-generated output to your Drupal module.

■ ■ ■

## CHAPTER 10

Adding PHP-Generated Output to Your Drupal Module

Now you can plug your knowledge of PHP into your basic Drupal module. The hello_world.module file itself in your module, of course, uses PHP as the essential piece of the module, the Controller, the class, and more. But also in this chapter you'll see how to use PHP to help construct the output on the screen for the user. Knowing PHP well will allow you to add dynamic content to your module, which would require variables, if statements, and other complex logic. PHP is used as the nuts and bolts of Drupal itself and all its modules, and it will be a staple for all of your custom module work.

■ **Note** The code for this Drupal module is on Github: https://github.com/barnettech/drupal8_book/tree/with_php/hello_world.

Adding Custom PHP to the hello_world.module File

In the new HelloWorldController.php file we use objects, a foreach loop, and some other PHP constructs to add to the module. The HelloWorldController.php file now should look as follows (newly added code is shown in bold):

```php
<?php
    /**
     * @file
     * Contains \Drupal\hello_world\HelloWorldController.
     */

    namespace Drupal\hello_world\Controller;

    /**
     * Provides route responses for the hello world page example.
     */
```

```
class HelloWorldController {
  /**
   * Returns a simple hello world page.
   *
   * @return array
   *   A very simple renderable array is returned.
   */
  public function myCallbackMethod() {
    $content = '
    <div class="myDiv">
    <div class="bg"></div>
    <div class="block-title">A basic Drupal page created
    programmatically, Hello World</div>';
    $x = 1;
    // Declare a new object called $my_object and per
    // https://drupal.org/node/1817878 you need to reset to
    // the global namespace by prefacing stdClass() with \stdClass()
    $my_object = new \stdClass();
    $my_object->first_name = 'Jimbo';
    $my_object->last_name = 'Bob';
    $content .= 'Hello ' . $my_object->first_name . '
    ' . $my_object->last_name . '</br>';
    foreach($my_object as $property) {
      $content .= 'property ' . $x . ' in the object is :
      '. $property . '</br>';
      $x = $x + 1;
    }
    $content .= '<br />
        Some random text to show off this transparent background ....
        Lorem ipsum dolor sit amet, consectetur adipiscing elit.
    Morbi nisi purus, gravida sit amet molestie et, facilisis vel
    nulla. Mauris faucibus augue eu quam feugiat at lacinia velit
    malesuada. Sed bibendum faucibus mattis. Maecenas quis ligula
    nibh, sit amet iaculis metus. Aenean lobortis massa ut nulla
    tristique eu vestibulum leo eleifend. Maecenas arcu lectus,
    facilisis in mattis sed, pretium et metus. Phasellus elementum,
    elit fringilla mollis sollicitudin, ipsum odio vestibulum quam,
    vitae tristique odio tortor eu augue. Pellentesque volutpat
    placerat neque, sit amet vehicula lectus commodo vitae. Aliquam
    nec mauris pharetra velit tincidunt consectetur. Aliquam vitae
    lectus nisi. Curabitur mi sapien, ultrices quis bibendum eu,
    mauris pharetra velit tincidunt consectetur. Aliquam vitae
    lectus nisi. Curabitur mi sapien, ultrices quis bibendum eu,
    ultricies eget libero. Donec mollis malesuada est a varius.
    Vestibulum dignissim venenatis nisl, nec semper massa tincidunt
    egestas. Maecenas a erat sem.
```

```
montes, nascetur ridiculus mus. Phasellus sed neque ante,
venenatis sagittis dui. Cras lorem ipsum, scelerisque tempor
aliquet quis, imperdiet in augue. Curabitur tellus est, ultrices
eu sagittis et, pellentesque id enim. Nunc lobortis mattis
viverra. Sed non purus ipsum. Aenean ac justo sed urna eleifend
consequat.
</div>';
$element = array(
    '#markup' => 'Saying Hello World in Drupal 8 is cool!' . $content,
    '#attached' => array(
      'library' => array(
          'hello_world/hello-world',
      ),
    ),
);
return $element;
  }
}
```

Figure 10-1 shows the resulting web page.

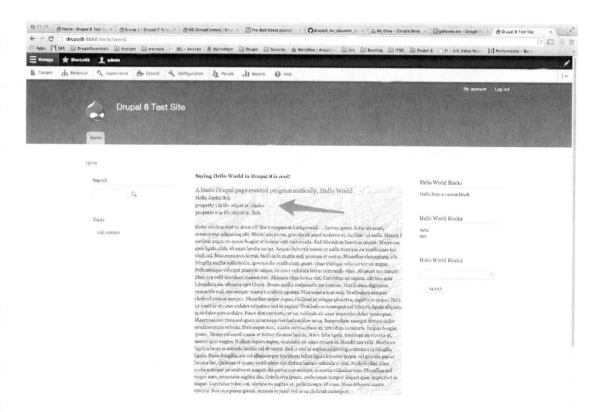

Figure 10-1. *The updated page that results from the custom Drupal module created using PHP code*

Summary

In this chapter you looked at how to use PHP in your custom module. PHP is the nuts and bolts of Drupal itself, its modules, and all custom modules. It is the programming logic that is the brains of the Drupal content management system. You also saw how you could enhance your own custom-created hello_world module by adding in some PHP to help generate output to the screen for the user. In the next chapter you'll learn how to create blocks programmatically and take an introductory look at the back-end MySQL database system, which is most often used as the back-end data store for Drupal.

■ ■ ■

## CHAPTER 11

Creating a Drupal Block Programmatically and Basic MySQL Usage

This chapter shows how you can have a Drupal module do more than one thing—in this case the hello_world module creates a custom page and you will now create a custom block. Rather than create a brand-new module to create the custom block, you'll just add code to the existing module. This chapter also explores how to construct basic queries to pull information out of Drupal's back-end datastore, which for most Drupal installations will be a MySQL database (although hooking up other database types to Drupal is possible).

■ **Note**   The code for this Drupal module is on Github: `https://github.com/barnettech/drupal8_book/tree/master/hello_world`.

The primary file of concern is the `HelloWorldBlock.php` file: `https://github.com/barnettech/drupal8_book/blob/master/hello_world/src/Plugin/Block/HelloWorldBlock.php`.

Creating Your First Block Programmatically

In this section you will create some code within the custom module that allows you to, with code, create a block that shows up within Drupal's block system. Then, through the block system (covered in Chapter 3), you can place the block you will create in code into a region of Drupal—the header, a sidebar, the footer, or any other region of the theme. Being able to create a block in a module makes it possible to use HTML, CSS, JavaScript, and PHP to construct any block imaginable. As in previous chapters, you can think of the code that follows as a template that you can copy, paste, and modify. Also, note that the PHP comments in Drupal 8 modules actually do matter and need to be syntactically correct just like the rest of the PHP code in the module.

1. Create all the necessary directories (check Github to get a better visual of the directory structure). On my local machine (a Mac) the directory structure looks as follows: /Users/jbarnett/Sites/drupal8/drupal/modules/custom/drupal8_book/hello_world/src/Plugin/Block.

2. Open your code editor and create the file HelloWorldBlock.php file within the Block directory. This step is most important. If you are creating your own custom block and name your module something other than "hello_world," replace the preceding directory name hello_world with your module's name. Type this code within your HelloWorldBlock.php file:

```php
<?php

/**
 * @file
 * Contains \Drupal\hello_world\Plugin\Block\HelloWorldBlock1
 */

namespace Drupal\hello_world\Plugin\Block;

use Drupal\Core\Block\BlockBase;
use Drupal\block\Annotation\Block;
use Drupal\Core\Annotation\Translation;

/**
 * Provides a simple block.
 *
 * @Block(
 *   id = "hello_world_block1",
 *   admin_label = @Translation("Hello World Block1"),
 *   module = "hello_world"
 * )
 */
class HelloWorldBlock extends BlockBase {

  /**
   * Implements \Drupal\block\BlockBase::blockBuild().
   */

  public function build() {
    $this->configuration['label'] = t('Hello World Block1');
    return array(
      '#markup' => t('Hello from a custom block'),
    );
  }
}
```

The preceding code provides for a simple block that displays the name Hello World Block 1.

3. Save the file.

4. Place the new block you created in the block system into a region on your site. Chapter 3 already covered how to do this, but as a refresher, click Menu in the black admin bar and then click the Structure link.

5. Click the Block layout option (see Figure 11-1).

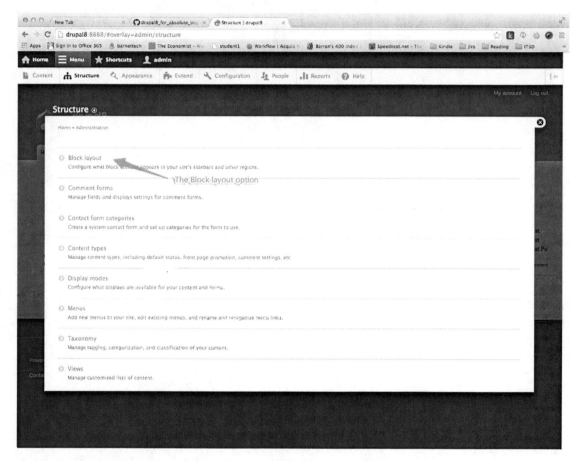

Figure 11-1. *Clicking the Block layout option places your custom block on the page*

6. With the screen shown in Figure 11-2 now displayed, click the "Place block" button next to the region where you would like to place your block.

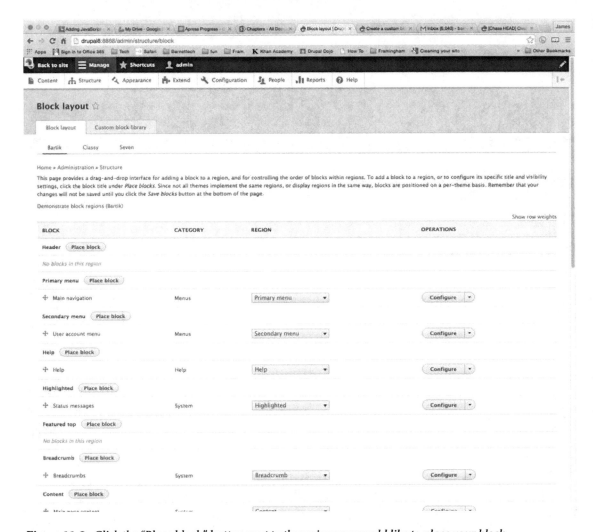

Figure 11-2. *Click the "Place block" button next to the region you would like to place your block*

7. A list of available blocks will appear, you'll then click the button "Place block" to the right of "Hello World Block 1". Then you'll see a screen (Figure 11-3) where you can choose to restrict visibility of the block, by content type, to only certain pages, or roles.

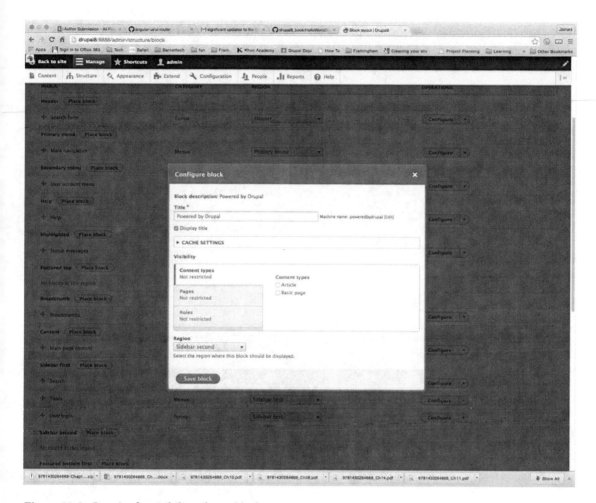

Figure 11-3. *Restrict the visibility of your block*

8. Click the Save block button.

Figure 11-4 shows how the blocks look after I place the new block in the right sidebar using the block system.

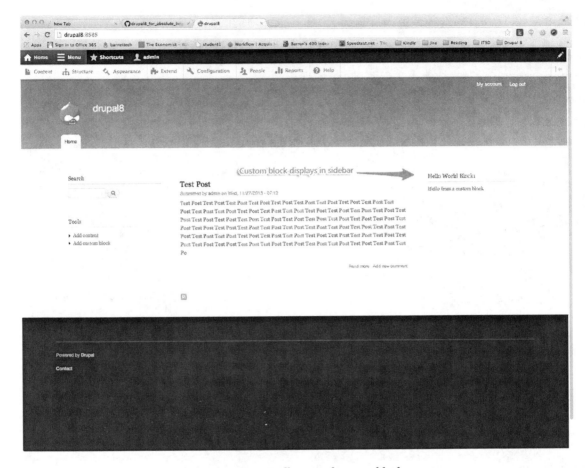

Figure 11-4. *The result of your first programmatically created custom block*

You just learned how to create a block in your custom module. In the next section, you find out how to grab data from Drupal's back-end datastore, the MySQL database. To grab data from the database, you use what is known as a "query."

Learning about the Drupal Database and Using a MySQL Query in a Custom Block

Now it's time to have fun and run some MySQL queries in the Drupal database. In this case, you will list all recent blog titles in one of the blocks. To do that, you need to query the database, which is the store of information behind the scenes of Drupal, to get a list of the five most recently created blog posts. First, you need to access the Drupal database via a tool called phpMyAdmin (there are many other tools out there as well to help you directly access the database, which is a MySQL database). Then you can display the results of your query in Drupal within a block you create programmatically.

1. If you installed Drupal using DAMP (covered in Chapter 1), go to the Acquia
    Dev Desktop Control Panel and click "Manage my database" to open the
    phpMyAdmin tool, which allows you to manage the MySQL database. I'm
    using MAMP (not DAMP) on my Mac; if I click "Open start page" from the
    MAMP control panel, I see a link for phpMyAdmin in an upper left tab on
    the page. However you installed Apache and MySQL, read your installation's
    documentation and open the phpMyAdmin tool.

2. Choose the database you installed Drupal within (see Figure 11-5). Out of the
    box, DAMP creates a database called `acquia_drupal`—click that one. I called
    mine `drupal8` for the sake of this demo.

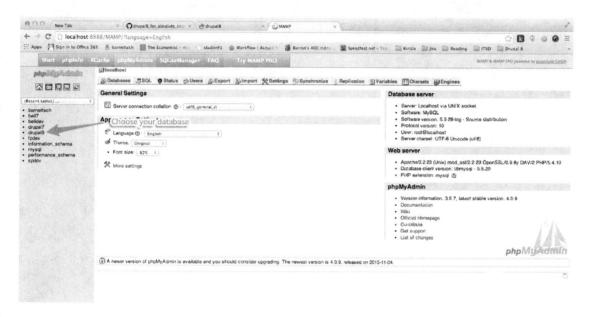

Figure 11-5. *A screenshot of phpMyAdmin*

Once you click the name of your Drupal database, a screen like the one shown in Figure 11-6 displays.

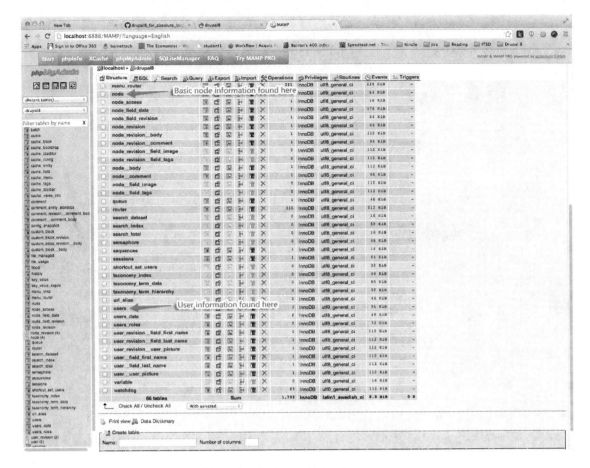

***Figure 11-6.** The node and users table within the Drupal8 database*

Before continuing, remember that "nodes" are what Drupal programmers call "pieces of content" in the Drupal system. You create your content types (or use the default content types that install with Drupal) to create articles, basic pages, blogs, wikis, events, or other types of content. These pieces of content are stored in the database as what we call "nodes."

Each node has its data stored in the MySQL database in various tables. You will now look at some of these tables that comprise the node data. First, you will look at the node and node_field_data tables in phpMyAdmin to take a peek under the covers and see what the data looks like in the database.

3. Click the node_field_data table (see Figure 11-7). You should be able to see some basic information stored here about each of your pieces of content, including titles and other basic information.

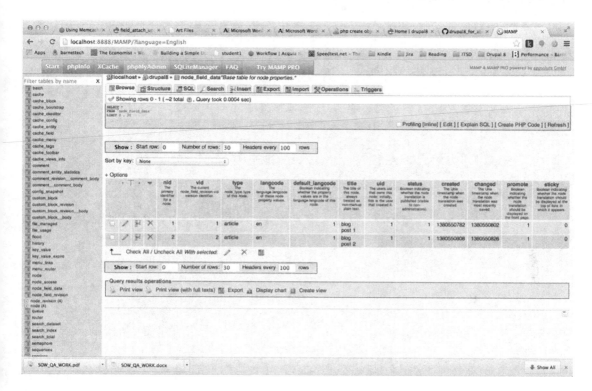

Figure 11-7. *The node_field_data table within phpMyAdmin*

■ **Note** If you're a Drupal veteran, you'll notice the title for nodes is no longer stored in the node table but instead is in this node_field_data table. There is still a node table, but it stores much more basic info than Drupal 7 did.

The node and node_field_data table are connected by the nid (node id) column. So if, for example, the content's unique node id (nid) was 5, then in the node table and the node_field_data table, both columns with a nid of 5 are related. That means the system will draw information from both tables (and many other tables with the unique nid of 5) to piece together all the data it needs to display the piece of content stored with the unique node id (nid) of 5. (This is why databases are often called relational databases. Databases stitch together all the data they need via these relationships the data tables have.)

Notice in Figure 11-7 that the node table has columns and rows. Each column is referred to by what you see at the top, in row 1. There are nid, vid, type, langcode, and title columns. The nid is the unique id of the piece of content (the node); the title is the title of the node; and langcode refers to what language the node is written in (English is represented in the database as *en*, for example), and so on. The type column shows what content type the node is (recall the discussion of Drupal content types in Chapter 3: every node belongs to one of the content types defined in your Drupal installation). This exercise focuses on the column we're most interested in: the title column.

4. Click the SQL tab toward the top of the page (shown in Figure 11-8).

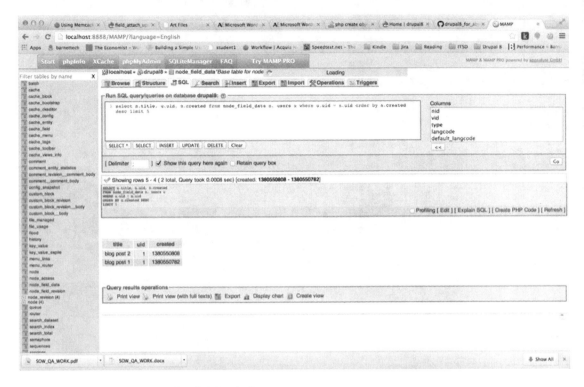

Figure 11-8. *Running a query in phpMyAdmin*

5. In the text area, type the following MySQL query to get information from the database on the five most recent articles (nodes) entered into Drupal. After typing the query (see Figure 11-8), click the Go button in the lower right corner of the page to run your query.

```
select n.title, u.uid, n.created from node_field_data n,
users u where u.uid = n.uid order by n.created desc limit 5
```

Because there were only two blog posts in my database (see Figure 11-8), that's all the posts that are returned.

You see that the results returned the blog post title, the unique user id (UID) of the user who submitted the article (his or her UID), and the time the article was created in Unixtime.

■ **Note** Unixtime is a common way (in programming languages) to measure time. It's the number of seconds since midnight Coordinated Universal Time (UTC), 1 January 1970. To read more about Unixtime, visit http://en.wikipedia.org/wiki/Unix_time.

Here's an explanation of the query. You'll notice that node is followed by n. which is an alias for the node_field_data table.

The first part of the query says `select n.title`. This could have been written as `select node_field_data.title`, but `n.title` is easier and allows you to learn about aliases, because they're so common. So this code says, "Select the title, uid (unique user id), and created time for these nodes."

The alias before these column names refers to which table to find the column. To ensure that the system finds the exact column you're looking for, you must be explicit. Although you can omit the alias in MySQL if there is no ambiguity as to which columns you're referring to (i.e., different tables don't have duplicate column names), I recommend that if you're dealing with more than one table to always prefix columns with a table alias. Note that this code also gives the users table an alias of u.

After the query selects which columns it would like returned (title, UID, and created), it has the "WHERE" clause. In this case the "WHERE" clause is `where u.uid = n.uid` and tells the database tool you're using that the `user` and `node_field_data` tables are related when the uid in the two columns match. If a UID of 1 wrote the node, then you can also give me info from the `users` table for the user with uid of 1. In this way you can select information from multiple tables with one query statement.

■ **Note**   When two tables (or more) are related, they have something in common. In this case the node was written by a user with a given unique UID, and the `users` table also lists all users with their unique UIDs. This means we can relate the `node` table to the `users` table when looking at any given node, and we can see which UID wrote the node. Then, by relating the `node` table to the `users` table by the UID, we can pull up more information about the user who wrote the node by pulling more information from the `users` table. This is the heart of how databases work, and it is why MySQL is called a *relational* database.

Note that the query also includes `order by n.created desc`. This part of the code orders the results by the `created` column (which you know is from the node table because it has the alias n. prefacing it) in descending order. This will display the titles in reverse chronological order, with the newest content at the top. Note that `asc` stands for ascending and would be another way to sort data.

There are much fancier queries for sure, but these are the basics and can take you very far—you can relate as many tables as you like to assemble the data you need. Now, you're ready to practice running a basic query in your phpMyAdmin web tool.

Using a Query to Display Data in a Custom Programmatically Created Block

Now, get ready to use a basic query within your custom Drupal module. Because you're going to make a second custom block, you'll need the file called `HelloWorldBlock2.php` to add in your query. You can create this second block by copying the `HelloWorldBlock.php` file.

1. Open your `HelloWorldBlock.php` file. Save a copy of it named `HelloWorldBlock2.php` in the same directory. So, for example, within my directory (`/Users/jbarnett/Sites/drupal8/drupal/modules/custom/drupal8_book/hello_world/src/Plugin/Block`) on my Mac, I now have two files: `HelloWorldBlock.php` and `HelloWorldBlock2.php`.

2. Modify HelloWorldBlock2.php as shown here in bold.

```php
/**
 * @file
 * Contains \Drupal\hello_world\Plugin\Block\HelloWorldBlock2
 */

namespace Drupal\hello_world\Plugin\Block;

use Drupal\Core\Block\BlockBase;
use Drupal\block\Annotation\Block;
use Drupal\Core\Annotation\Translation;
/**
 * Provides a simple block.
 *
 * @Block(
 *   id = "hello_world_block2",
 *   admin_label = @Translation("Hello World Block2"),
 *   module = "hello_world"
 * )
 */
class HelloWorldBlock2 extends BlockBase {

  /**
   * Implements \Drupal\block\BlockBase::blockBuild().
   */
  public function build() {
    $this->configuration['label'] = t('Hello World Block2');
    // You wrap your query in the db_query function and put
    // the results in the $result variable
    $result = db_query("select n.title, u.uid, n.created
    from node_field_data n, users u where u.uid = n.uid order
    by n.created desc limit 5");
    $content = "";
    // The result variable is an object with as many rows in
    // it as there were rows of data returned from your query,
    // you're going to loop through these rows with the foreach
    // statement, put the individual row data into the $row
    // variable, add the title from that $row into the $content
    // variable, continue the loop, add the next title, and so
    // on until all the titles are listed in the $content
    // variable.
    // Then you assign $block['content'] to be equal to
    // $content and tada! Your titles from your query end up
    // in the first block on your screen.
    foreach($result as $row){
      // The ".=" rather than just "=" means take whatever
      // was already in the content variable and then
      // concatenate it with what comes after ".="
    $content .= $row->title . '</br>';
    }
```

```
        return array(
          '#markup' => $content,
        );
    }
}
```

The preceding code provides for a simple block that displays the name Hello World Block 2. To begin, you wrap your query in the db_query function and put the results in the $result variable. The $result variable is an object with as many rows in it as there were rows of data returned from your query. You're going to loop through these rows with the foreach statement, put the individual row data into the $row variable, add the title from that $row into the $content variable, continue the loop, add the next title, and so on until all the titles are listed in the $content variable. Then you assign $block['content'] to be equal to $content and—ta-da!—your titles from your query end up in the first block on your screen.

3. Save your file and display your page. Your screen should look similar to that in Figure 11-9.

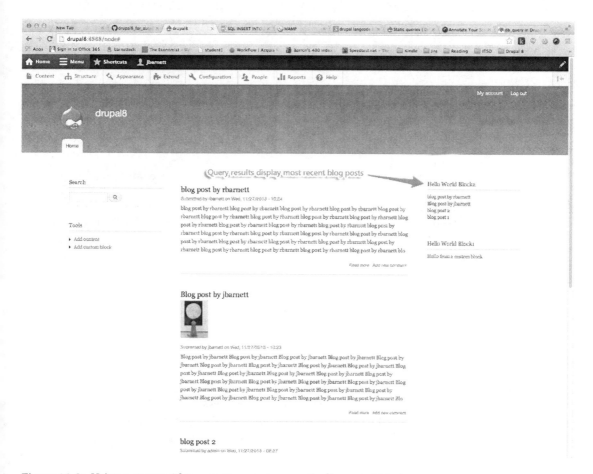

Figure 11-9. *Using a query within a custom programmatically created block*

To modify the query in the preceding code example, you could add variables into the query, say, to show only titles of articles of type `article` (as opposed to type `wiki` or any other content type). The query would look as follows in Drupal:

```
$result = db_query("select n.title, u.uid, n.created from
node_field_data n, users u where u.uid = n.uid and n.type = :type
order by n.created desc limit 5", array("type" => "article"));
```

Notice that `:type` is a placeholder for a variable, and in the array following the query, you define what `"type"` is. In this case, you put in a hard-coded `"article"` to define the placeholder (variable in the query), but more often you would use `array("type" => $article)` where `$article` would dynamically be defined based on what was happening in the code at the time of execution.

■ **Note**   You use the placeholders in Drupal to avoid SQL injections attacks. (For a formal definition of this vulnerability, see `http://en.wikipedia.org/wiki/SQL_injection`.) Because a variable can contain user-created data, you don't want to insert any malicious code into your system. The placeholder system allows Drupal to know what data to "scrub" and make sure a SQL injection attack cannot occur.

Often, queries return multiple results, as in the preceding case. Those results are stored in the `$results` variable (the variable name doesn't matter), and then you loop through the results like you did earlier, using the following code:

```
foreach($result as $row){
        $content .= $row->title . '</br>';
    }
```

But if you know there will be just one piece of data returned, like a nid, which is common, you can write code to just put the one piece of data (like the nid) into the variable directly. In doing so, you don't need to loop through results to get to that one bit of data. The code looks as follows:

```
$nid = db_query("SELECT n.nid from node where title = 'Drupal
Web Programming Essentials'")->fetchField();
```

In the preceding code, the single value is returned and is put within the `$nid` variable, preventing the need to loop through the data in a foreach statement. Notice that fetchField()fetches the single piece of data for you; there is no need to loop through the result for just one piece of data returned. This method only works when there is just one piece of data being returned.

■ **Note**   You'll hear the term "CRUD" operations with respect to databases. CRUD is short for all the basic database operations you'll be using: create, retrieve, update, and delete. To create a new record in a database table, you'll use an INSERT statement, to update data you'll use an UPDATE statement, and to delete data you'll use a DELETE statement.

We've breezed through learning some SQL, which can be immediately useful for you. The rest of the chapter gives you more basic knowledge of MySQL and reviews basic essential SQL usage. Understanding SQL is essential to programming and this coverage of basic SQL should provide a solid foundation on which to continue building your knowledge of databases.

MySQL Primer

MySQL uses the query language SQL (structured query language), which, as you've gathered by now, allows you to access data and make changes to back-end stored data. SQL has some variation when seen in different database systems (Oracle, SQL Server, MySQL), but it's mostly the same. This SQL primer goes over the primary must-know syntax to get you going.

Wildcard Character in Queries

You can use the wildcard character (*) in your SQL select statement to return data for all columns in a given table. For example, consider the following query:

```
select * from node;
```

You'll see that the result is all the rows from the node column and data from every column (see Figure 11-10). In contrast to the wildcard character, you could use this query to return all rows from the node table but *only* information from the nid column.

```
select nid from node;
```

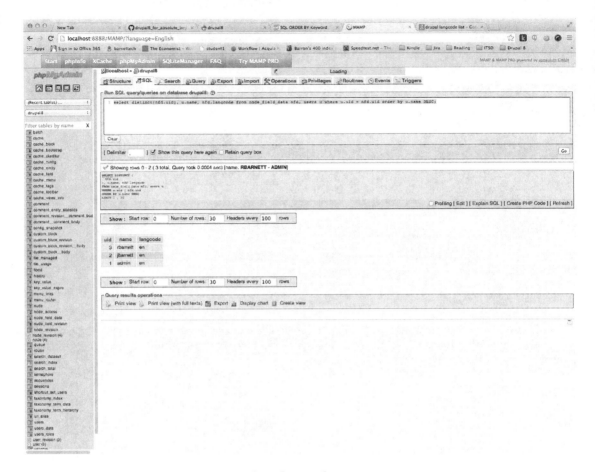

Figure 11-10. *The results of the SQL query select * from node*

Distinct

The distinct keyword in a select query allows you to ensure that all results in a particular column have no duplicate values. Let's say you want to see a list of all the contributors to your web site—a list of all UID numbers of those who've contributed—but you don't want to see any duplicates. Each user in the Drupal system has a unique UID. Following would be the query to use:

```
select distinct(uid) from node_field_data;
```

This query would ensure a list of results that does not show duplicate uid values in the list. You can still add other columns to the select statement, but you won't receive any rows with duplicate UIDs.

Now consider the following query:

```
select distinct(uid), langcode from node_field_data;
```

This query will show a list of UIDs and what languages the user wrote their node in. A result of "en" in the langcode column means the node is in English.

WHERE

Recall that you encountered the where keyword earlier in this chapter. The where keyword allows you to filter your results or join with another table. Take the following query, which uses a where clause to limit the results, showing only the posts written by the user with the uid of 356:

```
select * from node_field_data where uid = 356;
```

Or you can join two (or more) tables to stitch together information from related tables to provide the results. Take the following query, which shows us a list of unique usernames that contributed to the site (rather than just a list of UIDs):

```
select distinct(nfd.uid), u.name from node_field_data nfd,
users u where u.uid = nfd.uid;
```

The preceding code joins the node_field_data and users tables. You do this because you want more information about the user referenced in the node_field_data table. In the node_field_data table, you had only the user's UID, and joining (adding) the users table to the query allows you to grab more information about the user.

When you get to know your database's schema (layout), you get to know what columns are related. In this case, the UID in the node_field_data table is a "foreign key" that can map to the users table, which also has a UID column. A foreign key implies that a column is identical in another table and the tables can be joined on this foreign key column. You'll notice that table aliases are used once again. The users table has an alias of u, and u. prefaces the name column. This makes it clear to the system that you're referring to the name column within the users table. The node_field_data table is given an alias of nfd. Notice the columns that are prefaced with the nfd alias. Remember, all columns in the query should be prefaced with the table's alias name so it's clear which columns are being referenced. See Figure 11-11.

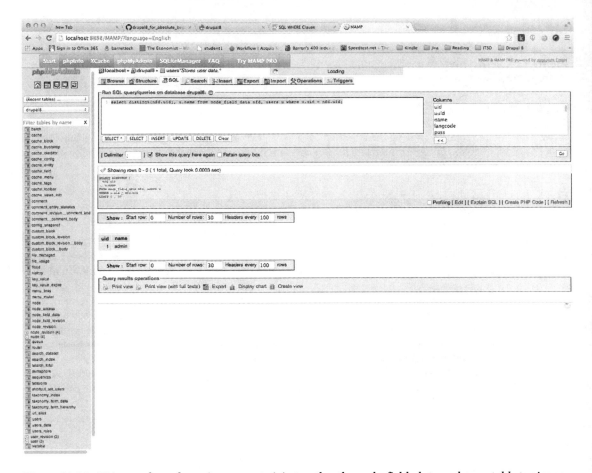

Figure 11-11. *Using a where clause in a query to join together the node_field_data and users table to give us the information we're looking for*

AND and OR

You can use the AND and OR keywords in your SQL queries to further limit, or qualify, your results. Take the following query, which shows only results written by user 'jbarnett' *and* written in either English ('en') *or* with a language of undefined ('und'):

```
select distinct(nfd.uid), u.name, nfd.langcode from
node_field_data nfd, users u where u.uid = nfd.uid
and u.name = 'jbarnett' and nfd.langcode = 'en' or
nfd.langcode = 'und';
```

As you can see, using AND and OR keywords in a SQL query is extremely helpful in returning the desired results.

ORDER BY

Using order by in your query allows you to sort by a column either alphabetically or numerically; you can also sort them in order or reverse order. For example, the following query lists all of the site's contributors sorted by the name column:

```
select distinct(nfd.uid), u.name, nfd.langcode from
node_field_data nfd, users u where u.uid = nfd.uid order
by u.name;
```

You can use the DESC or ASC keywords to specify if you want to order in descending order or ascending order. By default, if you don't use these keywords (DESC or ASC), your results will sort in ascending order when you use order by.

```
select distinct(nfd.uid), u.name, nfd.langcode from
node_field_data nfd, users u where u.uid = nfd.uid order
by u.name DESC;
```

You can see the results of the preceding query in Figure 11-12.

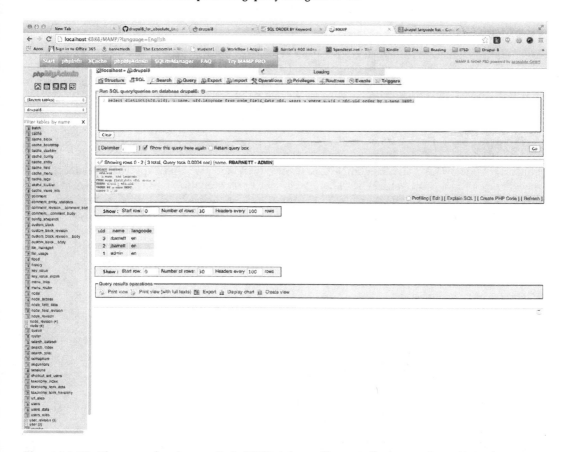

Figure 11-12. *The query showing results in DESC order and because the name column is a string type (alphabetical) the data is sorted in reverse alphabetical order. If the column specified by our order by clause was an integer we would be sorting numerically or in reverse numerical order*

Using SQL in Drupal

I did not introduce this in the preceding code, so that there would appear to be very little difference between using SQL in phpMyAdmin and using SQL in your Drupal code, but something to remember is that every time you reference a table in your SQL within your Drupal code you'll be wrapping the table name in brackets: {table_name}. This convention allows for other Drupal functions to override queries.

As well, remember that where you would put a variable in a query, you use placeholders rather than putting the variables directly in your SQL, which would create a security hole allowing for user-provided values to be injected into the query (which could allow for malicious code to be injected into our queries, called a SQL injection attack). Further documentation on placeholders is available at https://drupal.org/node/310072.

For more documentation on the Drupal way to create Drupal queries, consult these drupal.org documentation pages: http://drupal.org/developing/api/database.

Finally, here are some links to drupal.org pages to get into more details on how to do CRUD within Drupal: these pages also go into much more depth than this Drupal primer, but feel free to peruse the more advanced concepts so you know to look for them someday when they may come in handy.

- More on queries: http://drupal.org/node/310072

- More on inserts: http://drupal.org/node/310079

- More on updates: http://drupal.org/node/310080

- More on deletes: http://drupal.org/node/310081

Chapter 16 delves into more advanced MySQL usage, covering insert statements, update statements, delete statements, and many other SQL keywords to help you do what you need to get done.

Summary

This chapter covered how to create a custom programmatically created block in Drupal that you placed into a specific region of your Drupal site. In addition, this chapter covered how to use basic MySQL queries to obtain the data results you would like to display to your users from the back-end database. Next, the chapter showed you how to use a query in another block you created programmatically to display a list of the most recent blog posts on your site. The chapter continued with a MySQL primer, showing how to use phpMyAdmin to browse your back-end database. Finally, you learned basic SQL to learn how to use SELECT and get the data you're looking for in your MySQL database—the back-end datastore for Drupal.

■ ■ ■

## CHAPTER 12

Theming Your Site Part 1: Theme Functions and a Twig Primer

This chapter focuses on the proper way to theme your site, using a markup language called Twig, using theme functions, using theme template files, and using subthemes. Within the pages of this chapter, you'll take a look at theming the output from a module by using theme functions and a theme template. This chapter also includes an in-depth Twig primer. (Chapter 13 will introduce you to creating a new theme and a subtheme.) Knowing Drupal programming without knowing how to make your web site look good is not going to go over so well with your clients, employer, or end users. Giving users a great-looking site with a great user experience is why theming your site is an important skill set.

Theming Output from a Module

Theme functions provide a way to customize any module's output. Lets look again at the output you produced with the Hello World module up to this point. You created the output just fine, but you did not yet put the output of the module into a theming function, which allows your users to "override" the output without hacking your module. Overriding the output refers to tailoring how the module's output looks for your site, so you can pick your own layout, colors, and other CSS (Cascading Style Sheets) to your liking.

First, let's look at where we left the custom .../hello/world page, the code from HelloWorldController.php from the with_install_file branch's version.

■ **Note** The code for this Drupal module is on Github: https://github.com/barnettech/drupal8_book/blob/with_install_file/hello_world/src/Controller/HelloWorldController.php.

```php
<?php
/**
 * @file
 * Contains \Drupal\hello_world\HelloWorldController.
 */

namespace Drupal\hello_world\Controller;
/**
 * Provides route responses for the hello world page example.
 */
```

```
class HelloWorldController {
  /**
   * Returns a simple hello world page.
   *
   * @return array
   *   A very simple renderable array is returned.
   */
  public function myCallbackMethod() {
    $element = array(
      '#markup' => '<p><b>Saying Hello World in Drupal 8
      is cool!</b></p>',
    );
    return $element;
  }
}
```

At the end of the function `public function myCallbackMethod`, the value of `$element` array is returned. The array has the entire markup, which spits out directly to the screen.

Now let's look at what the module will look like with proper theme functions (see Figure 12-1).

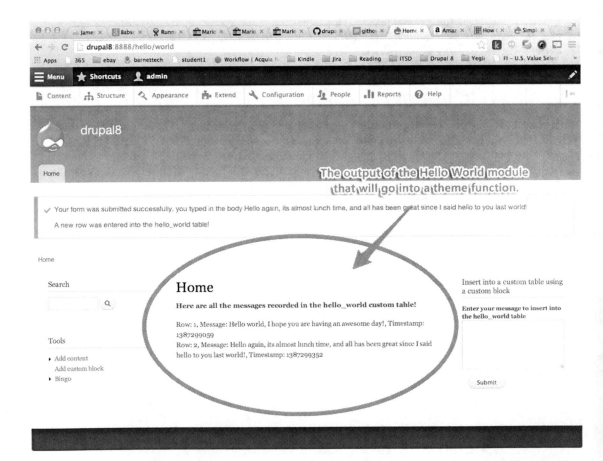

Figure 12-1. *The output of the Hello World module at the URL ...hello/world, which will go into a theme function*

Using a Theme Function

Here is the code for Hello World with the theme function. Notice the `hello_world.module` file now has a new function called `hello_world_theme`, which implements `hook_theme`. Remember, whenever implementing a hook, just replace the word "hook" with your module's name.

■ **Note**   The code for the Hello World module with a theme function in place lives in Github at
https://github.com/barnettech/drupal8_book/tree/with_theme_function/.

```php
<?php

/**
 * @file
 * A basic Drupal 8 Hello World Module.
 */

/**
 * Implements hook_permission().
 */
function hello_world_permission() {
  $permissions = array(
    'administer hello world' => array(
      'title' => t('Administer Hello World module'),
      'description' => t('Change the settings for Hello
      World module.'),
    ),
  );
  return $permissions;
}

/**
 * Implements hook_theme().
 */
function hello_world_theme() {
  return array(
    'hello_world_primary_page' => array(
      'function' => 'theme_hello_world_primary_page',
      'variables' => array(
        'items' => NULL,
      ),
      'file' => 'hello_world.theme.inc',
    ),
  );
}
```

You can see in the function `hello_world_theme` that you declare the theme function `hello_world_primary_page` for use later in the function. The actual definition of the function is located in the file `hello_world.theme.inc` and you set up a variable named `items` to pass to the function. You'll pass in as many rows from the `hello_world` table you'd like to have returned from the theme function.

Next let's take a look at the theme function itself in the `hello_world.theme.inc` file. You could have put the theme function in the `hello_world.module` file, but it clutters the primary module file to do this. Also the system will need to parse through the whole `hello_world.module` file often looking for hooks, so it just slows things down. Because this function will do just fine in the separate file `hello_world.theme.inc`, following is `hello_world.theme.inc`:

```php
<?php

/**
 * Generates the output for the hello/world page.
 *
 * @param $item
 *   How many items to show from the hello_world database.
 *
 * @return
 *   HTML-formatted output from the hello_world table
 *   in the database.
 */
function theme_hello_world_primary_page($items) {
  $content = '<p><b>Here are all the messages recorded in
  the hello_world custom table!!!!! </b></p>';
hello_world custom table!!!!! </b></p>';
  if (isset($items['items'])) {
    $results = db_query('SELECT * from hello_world
    limit ' . $items['items']);
  }
  else {
    $results = db_query('SELECT * from hello_world');
  }
  foreach($results as $row) {
    $content .= 'Row: ' . $row->hid . ', Message: ' .
    $row->message . ', Timestamp: ' . $row->timestamp . '</br>';
  }
  return $content;
}
```

■ **Caution** In `hello_world.theme.inc`, the theme function has the function name `theme_hello_world_primary_page`, but when defining the theme function name, the `theme_` part of the function name was omitted. You need to follow this convention to get your theme function "wired up" and working correctly.

The preceding code, with its comments, is simple enough to understand—we put our theme function named `theme_hello_world_primary_page` in the `hello_world.theme.inc` file. This theme function takes the variable `$items` as an argument, as mentioned earlier, so you can limit the number of rows returned from the theme function from the `hello_world` table in the database.

Then, in `HelloWorldController.php`, you can see that the `hello_world_primary_page` theme function is invoked, returning its output as the result instead of returning the contents of the variable `$content` as we did previously, which had been directly defined with the HTML results. I include the version of `HelloWorldController.php` here for your convenience.

▓ **Note**   You can find this code on Github: https://github.com/barnettech/drupal8_book/blob/
with_theme_function/hello_world/src/Controller/HelloWorldController.php.

```php
<?php
    /**
     * @file
     * Contains \Drupal\hello_world\HelloWorldController.
     */

    namespace Drupal\hello_world\Controller;

    use Symfony\Component\DependencyInjection\ContainerAware;

    class HelloWorldController extends ContainerAware {

      /**
       * Page Callback Method to Print out Hello World Text
         to the Screen.
       */
      public function myCallbackMethod() {
        return array(
          '#theme' => 'hello_world_primary_page',
          '#items' => 100,
        );
      }
    }
```

The preceding code provides a theme function to be called to produce the output for the module.
The hello_world_primary_page theme function will be called to produce the output on the page for the
end user (see Figure 12-2).

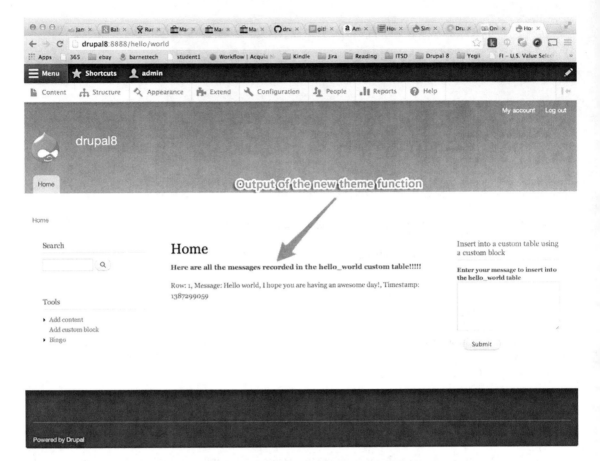

Figure 12-2. *The output of the theme function on the hello world page, limiting the number of rows to return from the hello_world table to just 1 by passing an argument to the theme function*

You have now completed one version of the theme function. Next, you will add a template to the theme function.

Using a Theme Template

In this section you add a template to the theme function.

■ **Note**   The version of Hello World that uses a theme template lives here on Github: `https://github.com/barnettech/drupal8_book/tree/with_theme_template`.

The hook_theme function now has a template file defined as hello_world_primary_page. This means that you need to create a `templates` directory within the `hello_world` root directory. Then, within the `templates` directory, you will place the template file, which will be named `hello_world_primary_page.html.twig`.

Here is the modified hello_world.module file, with the modified hook_theme function adding the template.

```
/**
 * @file
 * A basic Drupal 8 Hello World Module.
 */


/**
 * Implements hook_permission().
 * Hook permission sets up a permission to gate content
 * on the admin/people/permissions page.  In the
 * hello_world.routing.yml file you'll see we gate our
 * content by requiring the user's role have the 'Administer
 * Hello World module' permission to view the content
 * the module creates.
 */
function hello_world_permission() {
  $permissions = array(
    'view hello world' => array(
      'title' => t('View Hello World module'),
      'description' => t(View the Hello World module page.'),
    ),
  );
 return $permissions;
}

/**
 * Implements hook_theme().
 */
function hello_world_theme() {
  return array(
    'hello_world_primary_page' => array(
      'template' => 'hello_world_primary_page',
      'variables' => array(
        'items' => array(),
      ),
    ),
  );
}

/**
 * Preprocess variables for the primary hello world page.
 *
 * @param array $variables
 *   An associative array containing:
 *   - items: Array of participant names.
 */
```

```
function template_preprocess_hello_world_primary_page
(&$variables) {
  if (isset($variables['items'])) {
    $results = db_query('SELECT * from hello_world limit ' .
    $variables['items']);
  }
  else {
    $results = db_query('SELECT * from hello_world');
  }
  $variables['results'] = $results;
  $variables['test_var'] = 'We can set as many variables in
  the preprocess function as we like, this variable called
  test_var simply passes this text itself to the theme template';

}
```

The preceding code implements the hook_permission() function, which sets up a permission to gate content on the admin/people/permissions page. The code then implements hook_theme and preprocesses the variables for the primary Hello World page.

I've also added the preprocess function (covered in just a bit) in the preceding code, but for now, focus on the following function:

```
/**
 * Implements hook_theme().
 */
function hello_world_theme() {
  return array(
    'hello_world_primary_page' => array(
      'template' => 'hello_world_primary_page',
      'variables' => array(
        'items' => array(),
      ),
    ),
  );
}
```

You can now see in the array that you defined the template filename in the array with the following line:

```
'template' => 'hello_world_primary_page',
```

Next, and already introduced in the preceding code, you'll see the preprocess function template_preprocess_hello_world_primary_page.

```
/**
 * Preprocess variables for the primary hello world page.
 *
 * @param array $variables
 *   An associative array containing:
 *   - items: Array of participant names.
 */
```

```
function template_preprocess_hello_world_primary_page
(&$variables) {
/* In the preprocess function we establish values in the
$variables array which we'll be able to use within the
 hello_world_primary_page. */
  if (isset($variables['items'])) {
    $results = db_query('SELECT * from hello_world limit ' .
    $variables['items']);
  }
  else {
    $results = db_query('SELECT * from hello_world');
  }
  $variables['results'] = $results;
  $variables['test_var'] = 'We can set as many variables
  in the preprocess function as we like, this variable
  called test_var simply passes this text itself to
  the theme template';

}
```

This function is a preprocessor for the template, and it is here that you should do any of the logic, database queries, and complexities that would require PHP. The template itself should just be for the presentation layer, and within the template you can use the defined variables created in the preprocess layer. Consider the following function: template_preprocess_hello_world_primary_page.

Here you define two variables for use by the theme template: the results array and the string test_var. In the results array, you put the results of the query of the hello_world table. In the test_var string, you just put in a text message that you will later display on the screen.

Next, in the templates directory, you look at the template file you registered in the hook_theme function hello_word_theme. The template's name, as was defined in hello_world_theme, is hello_world_primary_page.html.twig. You defined the name as hello_world_primary_page in the hello_world_theme function, but in Drupal 8, which uses Twig, the filename then, by convention, becomes hello_world_primary_page.html.twig.

■ **Note**   The contents of the hello_world_primary_page.html.twig file are on Github: https://github.com/barnettech/drupal8_book/blob/with_theme_template/hello_world/templates/hello_world_primary_page.html.twig.

```
<div class="hello_world">

  <ul class="hello-world-items">
    {% for item in results %}
      <li class="hello-world-item">{{ item.message }} This
      message was written by the user with a uid of
      {{ item.uid }} </li>
    {% endfor %}
  </ul>
```

```
Here is another variable I created in the theme
preprocessor function called test-var:
{{ test_var }}
```

```
</div>
```

Twig Explained

Before diving into understanding the code in ...templates/hello_world_primary_page.html.twig, let's talk about Twig, which is new to Drupal 8.

Drupal 8 has moved toward using a Twig-based template engine. Twig is its own markup language for templating. Twig is also from the Symphony project that Drupal 8 has incorporated into many layers of Drupal 8 core. Using Twig means not putting PHP directly into templates. The modern paradigm MVC ("Model," "View," "Controller") aims to put the logic and data model into the controller and model layers of a project and then the view should not contain these pieces—and the view in this case is the Twig template file. By having a view without PHP, logic, and database calls, themers can just work on the theming side, and developers can hand off all the logic and data encapsulated into the variables passed to the Twig templates. This approach creates a more pure separation between developers and themers. Themers generally have more skills in tweaking the front end and developers generally are stronger with the back-end logic and programming. Without Twig, as it was in Drupal 7 and prior versions, it is very easy to start putting lots of PHP code directly in templates. I have committed this sin as well, but now Twig is here to keep the peace.

The hello world Twig Template Explained

In the ...templates/hello_world_primary_page.html.twig file, you can see that some HTML markup remains—you can still use straight HTML. The first two lines of the file use of some basic HTML elements, including a <div> tag and an unordered list tag.

```
<div class="hello_world">
```

```
  <ul class="hello-world-items">
```

Then this line

```
{% for item in results %}
```

This is Twig's syntax for looping through what's in the results array. Each row of results is put into the item variable within each iteration through the loop.

Then you have the following line:

```
<li class="hello-world-item">{{ item.message }}  This
message was written by the user with a uid of
{{ item.uid }} </li>
```

Here you see that Twig, to spit out the value of a variable, wraps the variable name not with a dollar sign but with double curly brackets. So you see that you output the value of item.message variable with {item.message}. In PHP you would output an array with this syntax $item['message'], and in PHP you would use this syntax for an object $item->message. In Twig you have the same syntax whether the variable passed into the Twig template was an array originally or an object: you use the dot syntax. In this case, with item.message, it didn't matter if in the preprocessor, the results variable was an object or an array.

You next access the element of the array results from the preprocessor, uid, with the same dot syntax with {{item.uid}}. Later in the hello_world_primary_page.html.twig file, you access a standard variable (an array) with {{ test var }} to output the value of this string in the template. Following is the line in the file that outputs the value of {{ test var }}:

```
Here is another variable I created in the theme preprocessor
function called test-var:
{{ test_var }}
```

Accessing all the elements of the results array, we end the loop with the following line:

```
0
```

I'll speak more about Twig and what you'll need to know shortly, but with the lines of the new Twig template explained, let's take a look at the output the browser, as seen in Figure 12-3.

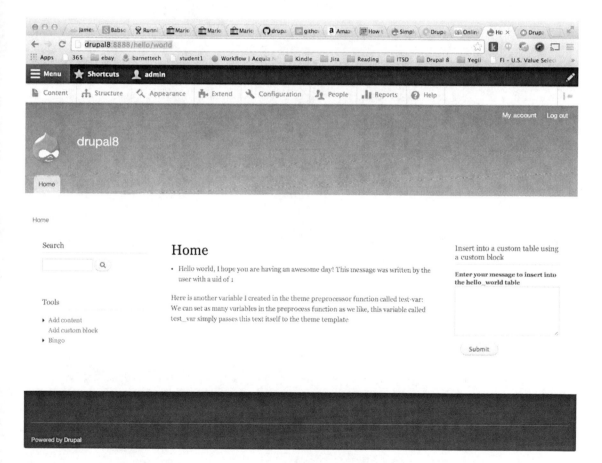

Figure 12-3. *The output of the hello_world module using a Twig template file*

In Depth with Twig: A Twig Primer

Twig has its own markup language, and it forces you to keep PHP out of your templates. By allowing PHP in templates, it was just too tempting to quickly put logic right into the view of our data. Instead, Drupal 8 forces us to put our logic in the preprocessor functions, something we were supposed to all be doing in Drupal 7 and prior. John Albin, who created the Zen theme in Drupal and has created lots of other great code for the Drupal project, was at the Drupalcon Denver conference and said, "We hand themers a loaded gun and tell them to hammer in a nail with it. Oh, and be careful."

One of the primary benefits of using Twig is security. By keeping PHP of the templates, there is less of a chance of injecting code through the theme layer. Often templates are written by developers, but often they are written by themers and folks who lack in-depth programming knowledge and are just trying to tweak the visuals of the web site. Separating PHP from the templates will keep nonprogrammers out of trouble and will allow for better separation of roles, allowing themers to be hired to muck around in the theme without needing to know PHP or programming, This will help with team morale, as themers aren't as able to break the complex logic that programmers have laid as a framework for the themers to utilize.

Here is the Twig home page: http://twig.sensiolabs.org/ (see Figure 12-4).

Figure 12-4. *The TWIG home page at http://twig.sensiolabs.org/*

The Twig documentation home page lives here: `http://twig.sensiolabs.org/documentation`. Some of the documentation is for using Twig directly in the Symphony framework. Drupal has incorporated some pieces of Symphony as I've said, and looking through the documentation we'll need to just focus on understanding Twig markup. The page `http://twig.sensiolabs.org/doc/templates.html` explains some of the basics of Twig, and the rest of this chapter gives you a tour of this documentation. I encourage you to go directly to the Twig documentation on the Internet for the complete documentation.

Twig Variables

A string or integer variable would be expressed in double curly brackets as follows:

```
{{ foo }}
```

An object or array is expressed with dot syntax "." as we spoke of before, as follows:

```
{{ foo.bar }}
```

This code will allow access to an array element defined in a Drupal preprocessor function as, say, `$foo['bar']` or `$foo->bar`—the first being an array element in PHP, the second being an object property.

If you use special characters in the variable name, with Twig you need to access the variable a bit differently, as follows (to access the variable `$data-foo` which has a dash in the variable name which is considered a special character):

```
{{ attribute(foo, 'data-foo') }}
```

You can set the values of variables directly in your Twig template. Look at the following three examples from the Twig documentation:

```
{% set foo = 'foo' %}
{% set foo = [1, 2] %}
{% set foo = {'foo': 'bar'} %}
```

Twig Filters

You can use the pipe symbol to act directly on data and filter it. Consider the following example from the Twig documentation:

```
{{ name|striptags|title }}
```

The preceding line will take the name variable and then strip any HTML tags from it. Then it will apply title casing to the text of the name variable. In the following example, the list array will be filtered, changed into a list separated by commas:

```
{{ list|join(', ') }}
```

This page has more on the join filter `http://twig.sensiolabs.org/doc/filters/join.html`. Take a look at the following example, taken from this documentation page:

```
{{ [1, 2, 3]|join('|') }}
{# outputs 1|2|3 #}
```

This code shows another example of an array of values being transformed into a list separated by the pipe character, |.

The following snippet of code wraps the text "This text becomes uppercase" in the filter upper filter, making the text, as you are guessing, in uppercase letters:

```
{% filter upper %}
    This text becomes uppercase
{% endfilter %}
```

Twig Control Structures

In this section I introduce you to some control structures you can use in your Twig files. These include for loops, if statements, and such—concepts you'll already be familiar with from studying JavaScript and if statements.

For Loops

Twig has some built-in functions, like the Twig equivalent of the foreach loop in the hello_world module earlier in this chapter. You saw how to use the following snippet of code to loop through the results array:

```
{% for item in results %}
    <li class="hello-world-item">{{ item.message }} This
    message was written by the user with a uid of
    {{ item.uid }} </li>
{% endfor %}
```

Looping through the results array, each row is placed in the item variable for Twig to use in the template.

If Statements

You can use if statements in Twig, just like in PHP. Here's an example.

```
<ul>
{% if message|length > 5 %}
  <li>A message with a character length of greater
  than 5 is: {{ message }}</li>
{% endif %}
</ul>
```

Twig Functions

This section describes some essential Twig functions, including dump, date, and include.

Dump Function

There's a dump function in Twig to dump (or look at) the content of a variable, which is very helpful in debugging. Here's how it works.

```
<pre>
    {{ dump(user) }}
</pre>
```

This snippet of code will dump the contents of the user variable to see on the screen. Wrapping the output in the <pre> HTML tag makes it more readable.

Date Function

You can compare dates using the Twig date function. Here's an example.

```
{% if date(user.modified) < date('-5days') %}
    {# do something #}
{% endif %}
```

Include Function

You can use the include function to include another template, and the output of the included template will get inserted into the template that uses the include statement. By default variables in the included template will be available to the template issuing the include statement. Following is an example:

```
{% include 'sidebar.html' %}
```

The include function documentation page is located here: http://twig.sensiolabs.org/doc/functions/include.html. This page includes more information on how to choose to include or exclude variables in the included template. More Twig functions can be found in the official Twig documentation: http://twig.sensiolabs.org/doc/functions/index.html.

Twig Comments

Twig comments will not get rendered in the output on your web page; they serve merely as documentation for yourself or others. To create comments in Twig, use the syntax in the following example:

```
{# We are within comment tags so nothing will get rendered
    that I put within the comments tag.
    {% for winner in winners %}
        the winner is {{ winner }}
    {% endfor %}
#}
```

Even though I had some legitimate Twig markup within the comment tags, it doesn't get rendered. Comments, besides allowing a place to put in documentation (which is very important), allows you to comment out some code to try out how a page looks or works with or without the commented-out section of code.

Twig Template Inheritance

A really cool feature of Twig is template inheritance. You can have a base template, then have another template that inherits and extends the base template. Take the following example from http://twig.sensiolabs.org/doc/templates.html.

In the following code example, base.html is the base Twig template.

```
<!DOCTYPE html>
<html>
    <head>
        {% block head %}
            <link rel="stylesheet" href="style.css" />
            <title>{% block title %}{% endblock %} - My Webpage</title>
        {% endblock head %}
    </head>
    <body>
        <div id="content">{% block content %}{% endblock %}</div>
        <div id="footer">
            {% block footer %}
                &copy; Copyright 2011 by <a href=
                "http://domain.invalid/">you</a>.
            {% endblock footer %}
        </div>
    </body>
</html>
```

Another Twig template is defined, as shown.

```
{% extends "base.html" %}

{% block title %}Index{% endblock %}
{% block head %}
    {{ parent() }}
    <style type="text/css">
        .important { color: #336699; }
    </style>
{% endblock head %}
{% block content %}
    <h1>Index</h1>
    <p class="important">
        Welcome to my awesome homepage.
    </p>
{% endblock content%}
```

Notice the following line:

```
{% extends "base.html" %}
```

This is the key line that sets base.html as the base template. Any block that isn't defined in the template that extends base.html gets inherited from the base template. This way you can use the base.html template and override any block you like. You can also, using the parent() function, bring in the content of the parent base template any time you like. Following is an example:

```
{% block main_content %}
    <h1>Here is my content</h1>
    ...
    {{ parent() }}
{% endblock main_content %}
```

The official Twig documentation on template inheritance can be found at http://twig.sensiolabs.org/doc/tags/extends.html.

Blocks can be nested, and blocks in a template have access to variables even from other blocks.

Twig Dynamic Inheritance

Blocks can be called with the use of variables.

```
{% extends some_var %}
```

If the some_var variable is defined as sidebar_right, then the template will extend the sidebar_right base template.

You can provide a list of templates to extend, and the first in the list that exists will be used.

```
{% extends ['first_layout.html', 'second_layout.html'] %}
```

Twig Conditional Inheritance

You can also conditionally extend a template:

```
{% extends mytemplate ? "base1.html" : "base2.html" %}
```

In this example, if the variable mytemplate evaluates to true, then you use the base1.html template; otherwise you use base2.html.

Twig Blocks

To clarify, if a template extends a template and the base template had blocks within it, and the template extending the base template has a block or blocks named the same as in the parent template, then the child blocks are named the same as the parent's and will override the blocks with the same name in the parent. Blocks are a way to allow child templates to use the parent template, parent template logic, and markup, while making certain sections (the block) overrideable. For more information see the section "How Blocks Work" in the official Twig documentation pages: http://twig.sensiolabs.org/doc/tags/extends.html#how-blocks-work.

Escaping Characters in Twig

Whenever you use a variable in Twig, there's the chance that the variable value might affect the output of your HTML. You can escape just one variable like the following:

```
{{ myvar|e }}
```

By default the " | e " way of escaping a variable in Twig converts all characters that could affect the HTML markup of your web page. You can also escape characters that would affect your JavaScript, CSS, URL, or HTML attribute coding respectively, as follows:

```
{{ myvar|e('js') }}
{{ myvar|e('css') }}
{{ myvar|e('url') }}
{{ myvar|e('html_attr') }}
```

You can also autoescape everything in a section of your template, as follows:

```
{% autoescape %}
    Everything in between the autoescape tags will be escaped
    with the default mode of preventing HTML conflicts.
{% endautoescape %}
```

You can also use the autoescape tags to prevent conflicts with JavaScript or any of the other possible conflicting markup.

```
{% autoescape 'js' %}
    Everything in between the autoescape tags will be escaped
    with the JavaScript mode of preventing JavaScript conflicts.
{% endautoescape %}
```

Likewise you can replace 'js' with 'css', 'url', or 'html_attr' to prevent conflicts with autoescape tags.

You can also mark a whole block of text as "just text," and it ends up escaping the whole block. So what usually would be parsed as a variable, or a control loop, and so on, is just treated as plain text. You use the following verbatim tag for this:

```
{% verbatim %}
    <ul>
    {% for item in items %}
        <li>{{ item }}</li>
    {% endfor %}
    </ul>
{% endverbatim %}
```

Hashes and Arrays, Strings, Integers, and Null and True/False Values

To create an array in Twig, you use the following syntax:

```
["foo", "bar"]
```

To create a hash (an "associative array" in PHP speak), you use the following syntax:

```
{"foo": "bar"}
```

You can have hashes within an array and or an array within a hash. That is, you can nest these elements. Here are some more examples that work.

```
{ 'one': 'foo', 'two': 'bar' }
```

```
{ foo: 'foo', bar: 'bar' }
```

```
{ 1: 'foo', 2: 'bar' }
```

```
{ (1 + 1): 'foo'}
```

The Booleans true and false are used as they are in other languages. You can also use the null keyword to define something as undefined.

Twig Math

You can do math in Twig:

```
{{ 1 + 1 }}
```

The result is, of course, 2.

Twig Comparisons

The normal comparison operators, ==, !=, <, >, >=, and <=, all work as would be expected, but in addition you can use "starts with" or "ends with," as follows:

```
{% if 'Drupal' starts with 'D' %}
{% endif %}
```

```
{% if 'Drupal' ends with 'l' %}
{% endif %}.
```

Regular Expressions

You can use regular expressions as in other programming languages.

```
{% if cellphone matches '{^[\d\-]+$}' %}
{% endif %}
```

In and Not In

You can check if something contains or doesn't contain another value.

```
{% if 2 not in [2, 3, 4] %}
```

```
{{ 1 in [1, 2, 3, 4] }}
```

```
{{ 'de' in 'abcdefghi' }}
```

All three of the preceding examples will return true.

Twig Tests

There are some built-in tests in Twig, testing if something is null, odd, even, same as, iterable, empty, divisible by, defined, or constant.

You can read the official documentation on the test functions at http://twig.sensiolabs.org/doc/tests/index.html. Following is an example from these documentation pages:

```
{# evaluates to true if the foo variable is null, false,
an empty array, or the empty string #}
{% if foo is empty %}
    ...
{% endif %}
```

String Interpolation

If you put a variable or math, for example, within a double quoted string, Twig will allow you to use a variable, math, and so on. Here's the syntax.

```
{{ "foo #{bar} baz" }}
{{ "foo #{1 + 2} baz" }}
```

In the first case the variable bar is inserted into the text of the string. In the second case the result of the advanced addition 1 + 2 is inserted into the text of the string.

Twig Extensions

Twig can also be extended and new tags, functions, and filters can be found at https://github.com/fabpot/Twig-extensions. You can also learn to create your own extensions by going to the following page: http://twig.sensiolabs.org/doc/advanced_legacy.html.

Summary

This chapter covered quite a bit. You learned to add theme functions to your custom modules. Knowing how to do this is quite useful even if you're just learning how to override a function from another contributed module you downloaded from `drupal.org`. You also learned how to create templates for your theme functions, and you learned that Drupal 8 now uses a Twig-based template engine. Twig has its own markup, and by using Twig in Drupal 8, you keep PHP out of your theme templates, allowing your logic to be encapsulated by programmers and your view and front-end look and feel of the site to be worked on by themers, who don't necessarily need to be programmers. This separation of theming and programming logic provides for more security and prevents front-end work from breaking complex business code and logic.

■ ■ ■

## CHAPTER 13

Theming Your Site Part 2: Creating a Custom Theme and Subtheme

Making your site look great is very important—to attract customers, to keep users engaged on your site, and more. This chapter dives down deep in how to knock your design out of the park, showing you how to properly approach theming in Drupal 8. In Drupal, the look of your site is referred to as the *theme* for your site, and you can easily switch between different Drupal themes to change the design of your site. This chapter teaches you how to create both themes and subthemes. You will create a custom subtheme using Bartik, which ships with Drupal 8, as the base theme.

■ **Note**   Actually, Bartik uses the Classy theme as its base theme; Bartik is just a subtheme itself. Although we're using Bartik as the basis for our new subtheme, the true base theme of both the Bartik theme and our new theme will, in fact, be "classy."

Creating a Subtheme

There are many Drupal 8 themes that can serve as a great base theme, from which you can then start creating subthemes. A Drupal subtheme allows you to declare an existing theme as the "base" theme. Then, by changing the subtheme, you can override certain aspects of the base theme. That means you can safely customize your theme to your heart's delight to get the look your want for your web site. The base theme is helpful in not forcing you to re-create the wheel, while still allowing you to create a subtheme so you can get the exact final theme presentation you're looking for.

■ **Note**   Technically speaking, you could just start hacking the base theme itself to your liking, but doing so means you will no longer be able to get updates to the base theme. And the base theme's updates may contain security updates or other improvements you may want to adopt into your site. Therefore, when you want to customize a theme, it's recommended that you work with a subtheme instead.

Let's take a look at how to create a subtheme using the Bartik (classy) theme as the base. First, go to the ...core/themes directory and do an **ls**. You'll see that out of the box Drupal 8 includes the Bartik, Classy, Seven, and Stark themes.

You need to make a copy of the Bartik theme to make it your new subtheme. Type the following at your Linux command prompt:

```
cp -r bartik ../../themes
```

You've now made a copy of the Bartik theme out of `...core/themes` into the `themes` directory. Note that you can still also put themes in the `...sites/all/themes` directory.

You'll find a `README.txt` file in the `themes` directory, which says the following:

> *Place downloaded and custom themes that modify your site's appearance in this directory to ensure clean separation from Drupal core and to facilitate safe, self-contained code updates. Contributed themes from the Drupal community may be downloaded at* http://drupal.org/project/themes.

> *It is safe to organize themes into subdirectories and is recommended to use Drupal's subtheme functionality to ensure easy maintenance and upgrades.*

> *In multisite configuration, themes found in this directory are available to all sites. In addition to this directory, shared common themes may also be kept in the* sites/all/ themes *directory and will take precedence over themes in this directory. Alternatively, the* sites/your_site_name/themes *directory pattern may be used to restrict themes to a specific site instance.*

> *Refer to the "Appearance" section of the* README.txt *in the Drupal root directory for further information on theming.*

You can see from this `README.txt` file that there are two places you can choose to put your themes: in the `themes` directory or in the `...sites/all/themes` directory. In Drupal, one code base can service multiple web sites. This is known as a multisite Drupal instance. As the `README.txt` file says, you can employ a theme to be available for only one particular site within the multisite Drupal installation by placing your theme in the appropriately named directory, but by placing the theme in the `...sites/all/themes` directory, the theme will be available for all Drupal sites even if within a multisite installation.

Note You can read more about multisite installations at `https://drupal.org/documentation/install/multi-site`.

Once you copy the Bartik theme into the `themes` directory, you can start to modify it to become the Bartik subtheme. By creating the Bartik (classy) subtheme (shown in Figure 13-1), you'll still be able to update Bartik (and Bartik's base theme called Classy), which means you'll still get all the fixes and updates—and, most important, all security updates. Doing so also keeps your subtheme modifications intact—that is, you won't override your changes to the subtheme when you update the Bartik and Classy themes.

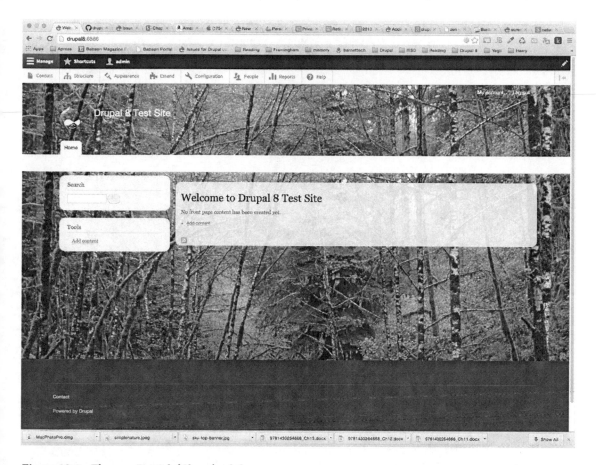

Figure 13-1. *The new Bartick (Classy) subtheme*

Before you can customize the subtheme, you need to do a bit of housekeeping. I've copied all the files from Bartik in the … core/themes/bartik folder into a new folder I've called barnettechetJLB in the `themes` directory. This barnettechetJLB folder then houses my new Bartik subtheme. However, there are some filename changes that need to be made.

Every filename in the barnettechetJLB folder that has the word "bartik" in it needs to be changed to the new subtheme's name: barnettechetJLB. (You can name your subtheme anything you like.) This means changing function names, which need to start with the theme's name to be the new subtheme's name (this occurs in the `barnettechetJLB.theme` file). That means that in the main `barnettechetJLB.info.yml` file, I declare the subtheme's name as "barnettechetJLB." Any file in this directory now belongs to the bartikJLB subtheme and not to the Bartik base theme.

It's easy enough to go through all the files and change "bartik" to "barnettechetJLB." To find any instance of the word "bartik" within the files, go into the `barnettechetJLB` directory and type the following command:

```
grep -lri "bartik" *
```

This command will recursively search (through all directories) through all files, look for the word "bartik," and print a list of all files that need to be edited.

You'll notice that this grep command, which is a search command really, includes the arguments -lri. The l means "don't show the context of where the match was found—just tell me the filenames." You can omit this argument (omit the l) if you prefer to see the context where the match was found. The r in the argument list says to look recursively through all subdirectories. The last argument, i, says to make the search case insensitive, so even if there's an instance of the word "Bartik" with a capital "B" or any other letter in "bartik" capitalized, it will still show a match. The dash (-) after the grep command signifies that the argument list follows. You will need to keep the dash in there to use any of the arguments, although you can omit the dash if you are going to omit all the arguments.

■ **Note** You can find these files on Github: `https://github.com/barnettech/drupal8_book/tree/subtheme`. I've also uploaded this basic Bartik subtheme to `drupal.org`: `www.drupal.org/project/barnettechetjlb`. I decided to use the same Github repository to store the example subtheme that I used for the Hello World example module files. You can clone the branches of the repository with the Hello World module into your `...modules/custom` directory and then also clone the same repository into your `themes` directory (or `...sites/all/themes` directory). Then, to look at the barnettechetJLB theme, just make sure you change branches to the "subtheme" branch to get the theme, or any of the other branches you like to see that version of the Hello World module.

After copying the files from the Bartik theme to create the barnettechetJLB subtheme, you need to identify a few of the templates that you will most likely want to override (i.e., templates where you don't want to use the default look and feel that the Bartik base theme provides). So in the `templates` directory, you need to copy over the following files (see Figure 13-2):

- `page.html.twig`
- `node.html.twig`
- `maintenance.html.twig`
- `comment.html.twig`

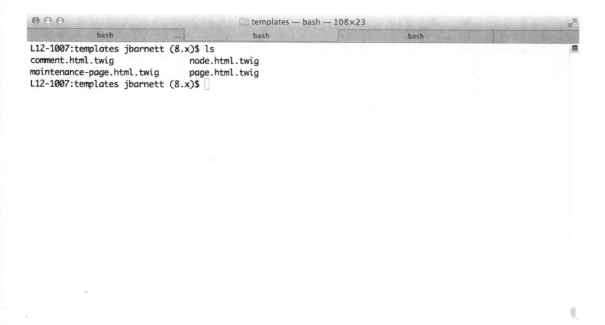

Figure 13-2. The template files copied from the bartik theme into the barnettechetJLB theme. These new template files will override those in the Bartik base theme `templates` *folder*

Now, when you want to override the look and feel for your own subtheme, you can make my changes directly to the copied files. The templates in the subtheme will always take precedence over the base theme template files. So a subtheme can allow you to use a base theme for the look of non-overridden elements yet allow for customization with overridden elements.

You can also copy over CSS (Cascading Style Sheet) files and then list them in the `barnettechetJLB.yml` file. The copies of the CSS files in your subtheme will override the styles in the base theme's CSS files with the same filename. To override any CSS files, you'll need to have it look as follows:

```
# Override a CSS file:
stylesheets-override:
  - css/color.css
```

In this case I'm overriding the `color.css` file from the Bartik base theme with the contents of the `color.css` file in the `barnettechetJLB/css/color.css` file.

To add new CSS files to the subtheme, I can add them to the lists in the `barnettechetJLB.libraries.yml` file. The `libraries.yml` file described here allows you to add assets like CSS files to a theme. (For more information, see the `drupal.org` documentation: `www.drupal.org/theme-guide/8/assets`.)

For the barnettechetJLB subtheme, I copied over some templates for later use, as stated earlier, but I did not yet modify them (`https://github.com/barnettech/drupal8_book/tree/subtheme`). I also copied over some CSS files, which I did modify. I added a background image to every page of the site to add some color, to liven up the theme a bit (see Figure 13-3).

Figure 13-3. The `barnettechetJLB.info.yml` file marked up to show the changes I needed to make to the copied `bartik.info.yml` file I copied over from the `...core/themes/bartik` folder while I was creating the `barnettechetJLB` subtheme

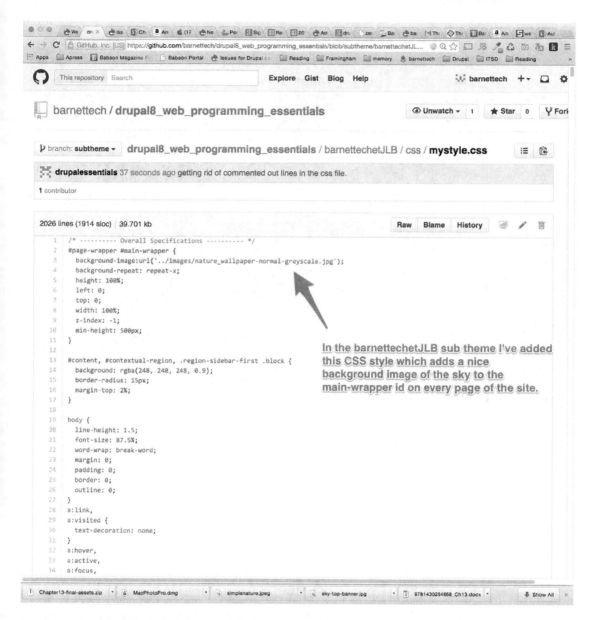

Figure 13-4. The CSS file that I changed in the barnettechetJLB theme, making the new subtheme VERY unique!

I also added a background image to the header id in the colors.css file, as shown in Figure 13-5.

```
#header {
  #background-image:url('../images/sky-top-banner.jpg');
  background-image:url('../images/nature_wallpaper-normal-
  greyscale.jpg');
  background-repeat: repeat-x;
}
```

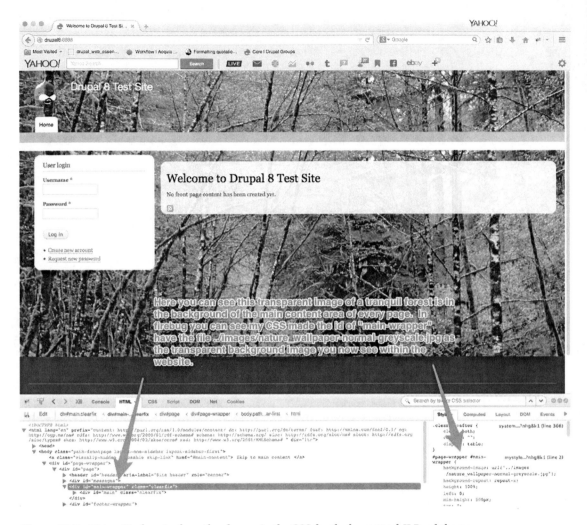

Figure 13-5. *Using Firebug to show the change in the CSS for the barnettechJLB subtheme*

The id `"main-wrapper"` now has a background image, and the background image's file is `../images/css-background-image-sky.jpg`.

It's possible, of course, to continue customizing the barnettechJLB theme, and eventually it could look much different from the base Bartik theme. By using a base theme that you like, you get to use Drupal again to provide much of the look and feel you like, and then the subtheme allows you to tailor the theme to better fit your needs and tastes.

Now that this section has laid the groundwork, you should be able to create and customize a new subtheme (using any base theme) without limiting your creativity.

Creating a New Base Theme

Creating a new base theme is similar to creating a new subtheme—assuming you choose to start by copying an existing base theme. By copying another base theme, you really are jumpstarting your efforts because you can use an existing theme as boilerplate code (as a template). Then, just as with a subtheme, you can customize it as you wish. The only difference is that you will not be overriding templates, CSS, and so on. Instead, your new base theme will become the primary code for the theme. Of course, you can still choose to create subthemes off of your own base theme if you like. The primary bit of code that decides if a theme is a base theme or a subtheme is within the `themename.info.yml` file. Figure 13-6 shows the Bartik theme's `bartik.info.yml` file.

```
bartik.info.yml (~/Sites/drupal8/drupal/core/themes/bartik) - VIM2
name: Bartik
type: theme
base theme: classy
description: 'A flexible, recolorable theme with many regions and a responsive, mobile-first layout.'
package: Core
version: VERSION
core: 8.x
libraries:
  - bartik/global-styling
ckeditor_stylesheets:
  - css/ckeditor-iframe.css
regions:
  header: Header
  primary_menu: 'Primary menu'
  secondary_menu: 'Secondary menu'
  help: Help
  page_top: 'Page top'
  page_bottom: 'Page bottom'
  highlighted: Highlighted
  featured: Featured
  content: Content
  sidebar_first: 'Sidebar first'
  sidebar_second: 'Sidebar second'
  triptych_first: 'Triptych first'
  triptych_middle: 'Triptych middle'
  triptych_last: 'Triptych last'
  footer_firstcolumn: 'Footer first column'
  footer_secondcolumn: 'Footer second column'
  footer_thirdcolumn: 'Footer third column'
  footer_fourthcolumn: 'Footer fourth column'
  footer: Footer
```
```
"bartik.info.yml" 31L, 868C
```

Figure 13-6. *The* `bartik.info.yml` *file shown in the MVIM editor (my favorite code editor on a MAC; it's not user friendly, but it's very developer friendly)*

By comparison, Figure 13-7 shows the extra line in the `barnettechetJLB.info.yml` file:

```
base theme: classy
```

```
barnettechetJLB.info.yml (~/Sites/drupal8/drupal/modules/custom/drupal8_web_programming_essentials/barnettechetJ...
name: BarnettechetJLB
type: theme
base theme: classy
description: 'A JLB Version of a flexible, recolorable theme with many regions and a responsive, mobile-
first layout.'
package: Core                    The line declaring the theme as a base them
version: VERSION
core: 8.x
libraries:
  - barnettechetJLB/global-styling
# Override a CSS file:
stylesheets-override:
  - css/color.css
ckeditor_stylesheets:
  - css/ckeditor-iframe.css
regions:
  header: Header
  primary_menu: 'Primary menu'
  secondary_menu: 'Secondary menu'
  help: Help
  page_top: 'Page top'
  page_bottom: 'Page bottom'
  highlighted: Highlighted
  featured: Featured
  content: Content
  sidebar_first: 'Sidebar first'
  sidebar_second: 'Sidebar second'
  triptych_first: 'Triptych first'
  triptych_middle: 'Triptych middle'
  triptych_last: 'Triptych last'
  footer_firstcolumn: 'Footer first column'
  footer_secondcolumn: 'Footer second column'
  footer_thirdcolumn: 'Footer third column'
  footer_fourthcolumn: 'Footer fourth column'
  footer: Footer
```

Figure 13-7. The barnettechetJLB.info.yml *file with the extra line declaring itself a subtheme of Bartik*

This one line tells Drupal to look to "classy" to be the base theme, which then makes the "barnettechetJLB" a subtheme of the base theme. (Remember that Bartik also uses Classy as its base theme; Bartik is itself just a subtheme of Classy.)

So far, this chapter has explained the mysteries of theming in Drupal. You've learned about base themes and subthemes. Just knowing about creating themes can take you quite far on your road toward creating a great-looking web site. The next section speaks about what theme functions are and how to override them.

Overriding Existing Theme Functions

Now that you have your own custom subtheme, we can continue with the discussion about overriding theme functions. Overriding theme functions is usually done within the theme, and because you don't want to hack a base theme, it's better to start overriding theme functions in a subtheme that you've created. You created your own theme function in Chapter 12, which others can override without having to hack your module when they would like to customize the look of your module's output.

Drupal core ships with lots of theme functions, and community-contributed modules (known as contrib modules in Drupal circles) typically have theme functions. How do we override them? You will first learn to override a theme function in your theme's your_theme_name.theme file (in Drupal 7 and prior versions this was the template.php file).

■ **Note** The template.php file is no longer in Drupal 8; it is now the your_theme_name.theme file. For all intents and purposes, it works exactly the same; only the filename is different.

All you do is make a function in your your_theme_name.theme file. But instead of saying theme_username($variable), which is the original name of the username theme function (as you can see defined here: https://api.drupal.org/api/drupal/core%21modules%21user%21user.module/function/theme_username/8), you name your function instead in your your_theme_name.theme file: your_theme_name_username($variables).

You will have the same $variables available to you, but you can override the look of usernames throughout your site in this manner (remember, we are overriding theme_username). So go and find your custom subtheme within the ...sites/all/themes directory or themes directory. I'll continue to use the bartikJLB subtheme I created earlier in this chapter. Within the bartikJLB subtheme, I find my bartikJLB.theme file. Go to the bottom of the bartikJLB.theme file and paste in the following code:

```
use Drupal\Component\Utility\String;
use Drupal\Component\Utility\Xss;
use Drupal\Core\Template\Attribute;
use Drupal\Core\Url;

function barnettechetJLB_username($variables) {
  if (isset($variables['link_path'])) {
    // We have a link path, so we should generate a link
    // using l().
    // Additional classes may be added as array elements like
    // $variables['link_options']['attributes']['class'][] =
'myclass';
    $output = \Drupal::l($variables['name'] . ' is awesome ' .
$variables['extra'], Url::fromUri('base://' . $variables
['link_path']));
  }
  else {
    // Modules may have added important attributes so they must
    // be included in the output. Additional classes may be
    // added as array elements like
```

```
    // $variables['attributes']['class'][] = 'myclass';
    $output = '<span' . new Attribute($variables['attributes']) .
'>' . $variables['name'] . $variables['extra'] . '</span>';
  }
  return $output;
}
```

Notice this is the same code as you find on the drupal.org page documenting theme_username (see Figure 13-8): https://api.drupal.org/api/drupal/core%21modules%21user%21user.module/function/theme_username/8. This code is actually defined in your Drupal installation in the user module. The only difference is I've added the "is awesome" text, so every user is declared as awesome anytime his or her username shows in the web site.

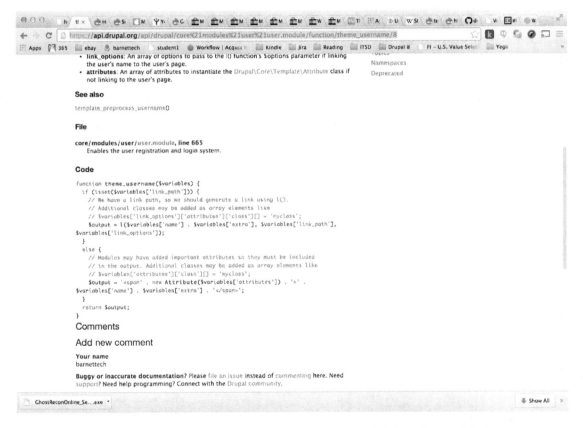

Figure 13-8. *Documentation on drupal.org for theme_username. I copied the code from this drupal.org page into the barnettechetJLB.theme file and modified it a tiny bit*

■ **Note** This is a simplistic example, but in real life knowing how to override theme_username can prove very useful. In a current site I'm working on, for example, we've overridden theme_username to show a chat bubble next to everyone's name. We also have some great JavaScript from the strophe.js JavaScript library and we use the jabber module (which I've written) helping us to show if a user is online or offline in Google's gtalk service.

So now with the new barnettechetJLB_username function in the barnettechetJLB.theme file, the page of a node I just created looks like Figure 13-9. You can see that every time a username is printed to the screen, it instead adds that the user "is awesome"!

Figure 13-9. With the customized theme_username *function, the output of all usernames on the page is altered with "is awesome"*

You can find a list of theme functions in Drupal 8: https://api.drupal.org/api/drupal/core%21modules%21system%21theme.api.php/group/themeable/8. Remember, every downloaded contrib module will likely have its own theme functions as well. I encourage you to *not* hack modules and Drupal core but to instead override theme functions in your custom theme or subtheme, whenever possible. I find it almost never necessary, and it is not encouraged because you will find yourself overwriting your hacks when you update your modules and Drupal core. If you do need to hack Drupal and you're absolutely sure it's necessary, others may find the same problem you have. When that's the case, you should submit your "hack" as a patch to drupal.org as a suggested update for all to enjoy (www.drupal.org/patch).

Exploring Other Options for Overriding Theme Functions

Another thing you often might do to override the output of another module's theme function is to copy the template file from that module's directory, if there is one, into your own theme's templates directory. By making the copy of the template in your templates directory, your copy in your theme will now take precedence over the template file in the downloaded contrib module that came as the default.

Also, you can override a theme function in a module. Many prefer to override a theme function in a module so that the theme file (in my case, barnettechetJLB.theme) doesn't get enormous. To override a theme function in a module, you will need to use the hook_theme_registry_alter function, as defined at https://api.drupal.org/api/drupal/core%21modules%21system%21system.api.php/function/hook_theme_registry_alter/8) and shown in Figure 13-10.

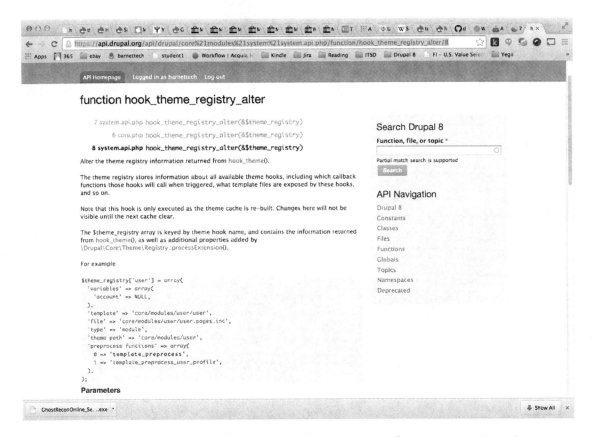

Figure 13-10. *Documentation on drupal.org for* hook_theme_registry_alter *to override theme functions from other modules in your own custom module*

At Babson College we have some code that uses that function to override the theming of the forums, which is a centerpiece of one of our web sites. We basically throw out the theme function that ships with a module, and we completely replace it with the look and feel that our faculty and students prefer. You can see the code in Figure 13-11, which I'll soon be porting over to Drupal 8 from Drupal 7.

```
}
/**
 * access argument only show for site admins.
 */
function babson_forums_add_forum_tab_visibility_admin() {
  global $user;
  if (in_array('administrator', array_values($user->roles))) {
    return TRUE;
  }
  else {
    return FALSE;
  }
}

function babson_forums_theme_registry_alter(&$theme_registry) {
  $path = drupal_get_path('module', 'babson_forums');
  $theme_registry['sts_commons_forum_view_topic']['theme path'] = $path;
  $theme_registry['sts_commons_forum_view_topic']['function'] =
    'babson_forums_hold_the_bloat';
  $theme_registry['sts_commons_forum_group_landing_page']['theme path'] = $path;
  $theme_registry['sts_commons_forum_group_landing_page']['function'] =
    'babson_forums_forum_list_page';
}

function babson_forums_forum_list_page() {
  module_load_include('inc', 'forum_list', 'forum_list.page');
  $content = forum_list_page();
  return $content;
}


function babson_forums_hold_the_bloat($node = '', $course_nid = '') {
  global $user;
  $start_count = 1;
  $comments_per_page = variable_get('comment_default_per_page_forum', 50);
  // get comments per page setting for forum topic node type
  $start = $start_count * $comments_per_page;

  if (module_exists('og_context')) {
    $group = og_context();
  }
  else {
    $group = "";
  }
}
```

Figure 13-11. *The* `hook_theme_registry_alter` *function in use in a site at Babson College*

The `babson_forums_theme_registry_alter` function you see in Figure 13-11 overrides the theme function `sts_commons_forum_view_topic`. It first tells the system the path to find the new theme function being used instead.

```
$path = drupal_get_path('module', 'babson_forums');
$theme_registry['sts_commons_forum_view_topic']['theme path'] =
$path;
```

Then, the next bit of code defines the theme function that will be called instead of the one that shipped with the module.

```
$theme_registry['sts_commons_forum_view_topic']['function'] =
    'babson_forums_hold_the_bloat';
```

The function name that will be called instead to form the output of this theme function will be `babson_forums_hold_the_bloat`. The function has a funny name because at the time the code was created, this one page on our site was loading up very slowly in a browser. This function was created to override the default one that came with the module. The new function was called "hold the bloat" to try to right the wrongs of the overridden code, which had a lot of bloat and was causing major slowdowns to the site.

Overriding theme functions can be essential in succeeding to make your employer or client happy, and it can mean the difference between having just a canned Drupal site and having a site that really is tailored to the site audience's needs and makes for a really great user experience (UX).

Summary

This chapter showed you how to create a custom theme and how to create a subtheme in Drupal. The drupal.org community recommends creating subthemes rather than hacking any existing downloaded theme, and it holds the same for overriding module code. Doing things the right way means that when you update Drupal or a module or theme within Drupal your changes won't be overwritten. You'll be able to customize and extend Drupal to your heart's content, without missing out on the new great updates to code you've been enjoying through drupal.org.

This chapter also spoke about creating your own base theme. After establishing how to create a theme or subtheme, I showed you how to override theme functions. Overriding theme functions in your theme or in a custom module is the proper way to override the output from a module to make it your own, to customize the look and feel, and to get things exactly as you need them to create a great user experience.

## CHAPTER 14

Working with Forms and Creating Custom Forms

To be really, really good in your role as a Drupal programmer, you'll need some tricks up your sleeve. You'll need to be able to programmatically create nodes, alter forms, and create custom forms. This chapter is dedicated to these subjects so you can really give your customers what they want.

Using the Form API

Let's start with forms and Form API. The Form API is a reference to the code needed to create forms programmatically in Drupal. The Form API itself is much the same as it was in Drupal 7, but all the code needs to be contained within the new object-oriented framework. This means that the Form API functions end up in a class. So, again, the scaffolding matters, and this means using a directory structure similar to the one you've already seen with blocks.

Note Let's take a look at the new scaffolding needed to create a form in Drupal 8. We're going to again be adding to the hello_world module to make things easier.

You can find the files for this code on Github: https://github.com/barnettech/drupal8_book/tree/master/hello_world.

The first file in the hello_world module that needs to change is the hello_world.routing.yml file. This is how the file should now look.

```
hello_world_settings:
  path: '/hello/world'
  defaults:
    _content: '\Drupal\hello_world\Controller\HelloWorldController::myCallbackMethod'
  requirements:
    _permission: 'access content'
first.form:
  path: '/first/form'
  defaults:
    _form: '\Drupal\hello_world\Form\FirstForm'
  requirements:
    _permission: 'access content'
```

You'll notice that the new code starts at the line beginning with `first.form`. You set the path where your form will load; in this case the form will load on its own page at the URL (uniform resource locator) `/first/form`. So, for example, if my Drupal site is within my local development environment at URL `http://localhost:8888`, then the form will load at `http://localhost:8888/first/form`.

Next you need to create a new directory, called `Form`, within the `lib/Drupal/hello_world` directory of your module. And then within the `Form` directory, you need to create a new file called `FirstForm.php`. Following is the code that will live in this new `FirstForm.php` file:

```php
<?php

/**
 * @file
 * Contains \Drupal\hello_world\Form\FirstForm.
 */

namespace Drupal\hello_world\Form;

use Drupal\Core\Form\FormInterface;

/**
 * Provides a simple example form.
 */
class FirstForm implements FormInterface {

  /**
   * Implements \Drupal\Core\Form\FormInterface::getFormID().
   */
  public function getFormID() {
    return 'first_form';
  }

  /**
   * Implements \Drupal\Core\Form\FormInterface::buildForm().
   */
  public function buildForm(array $form, array &$form_state) {
    // Use the Form API to define form elements.
    drupal_set_title('First Form');
    $form['user_search'] = array(
    '#type' => 'textfield',
    '#title' => '',
    '#size' => 40,
    '#maxlength' => 60,
    );
    $form['submit'] = array(
      '#type' => 'submit',
      '#value' => t('Search'),
    );
    return $form;
  }
```

```
/**
 * Implements \Drupal\Core\Form\FormInterface::validateForm().
 */
public function validateForm(array &$form, array &$form_state) {
  // Validate the form values.
}

/**
 * Implements \Drupal\Core\Form\FormInterface::submitForm().
 */
public function submitForm(array &$form, array &$form_state) {
  // Do something useful.
    drupal_set_message('thanks for submitting the form!');

}

}
```

Consider the preceding code to be boilerplate code that you can copy and adapt. If you're a Drupal veteran you'll notice the same basic functions you're used to seeing in Drupal to create a form. The first function, buildForm, is where you put all of the form_api array items, which construct the actual form. This corresponds to the old Drupal 7 hook_form function; the validateForm function in Drupal 8 corresponds to the function hook_validate in Drupal 7.

Within the validate function you would place your code to validate that the user submitted valid data. In the submit function you would add your code to process the data, perhaps saving the data to the database, creating a new node with the data submitted, or sending an e-mail. The submitForm function you see for Drupal 8 corresponds to the Drupal 7 hook_form_submit.

For those of you new to Drupal 8, who don't know how forms were created in Drupal 7, no worries. Basically, in Drupal 8 there is more boilerplate code and scaffolding necessary than there was in Drupal 7, but it is essentially the same code now placed within an object-oriented coding structure. However, you will use what I have in FirstForm.php and you'll make your modifications. In the buildForm function in FirstForm.php (shown in context in the preceding chunk of code), I have created two form elements: a text field and a submit button. The text field is created with the array element.

```
$form['user_search'] = array(
    '#type' => 'textfield',
    '#title' => '',
    '#size' => 40,
    '#maxlength' => 60,
    );
```

By adding to the $form array, you can add elements to your form (see the example following this paragraph, which shows how to add a check box element to the form). The Form API and how to construct a form haven't changed much from Drupal 7, and the web page https://api.drupal.org/api/drupal/developer!topics!forms_api_reference.html/8 will look familiar to Drupal veteran developers. This drupal.org documentation page lists all the different types of form elements you can add to a form. As an example, the drupal.org documentation shows this test code for implementing check boxes—adding this element to the form array adds a check box field to the form.

207

```php
<?php
$form['high_school']['tests_taken'] = array(
  '#type' => 'checkboxes',
  '#options' => drupal_map_assoc(array(t('SAT'), t('ACT'))),
  '#title' => t('What standardized tests did you take?'),
...
),
?>
```

To make your own check boxes, you would edit this example code to fit your needs. To create a password field, the drupal.org documentation page gives the following example code (adding this to the $form array adds a password field to the form):

```php
$form['pass'] = array(
  '#type' => 'password',
  '#title' => t('Password'),
  '#maxlength' => 64,
  '#size' => 15,
);
```

You can add to your buildForm function in FirstForm.php to construct the form to your liking. It is definitely worth your time to look through the Form API documentation page to look at what's available to you to construct your form.

■ **Note** Up to this point, this form doesn't do anything. However, it will display in your browser at the URL .../first/form.

Next, let's add to the code so that the form does something when the user submits it. Take a look at this version of FirstForm.php, which validates what is entered into the text field to make sure only letters (no numbers) are typed into the text field. Then, upon submission, if the validateForm function does not throw an error, the form is submitted successfully and a message is displayed to the screen showing successful submission.

```php
<?php

/**
 * @file
 * Contains \Drupal\hello_world\Form\FirstForm.
 */

namespace Drupal\hello_world\Form;

use Drupal\Core\Form\FormInterface;

/**
 * Provides a simple example form.
 */
```

```
class FirstForm implements FormInterface {

  /**
   * Implements \Drupal\Core\Form\FormInterface::getFormID().
   */
  public function getFormID() {
    return 'first_form';
  }

  /**
   * Implements \Drupal\Core\Form\FormInterface::buildForm().
   */
  public function buildForm(array $form, array &$form_state) {
    // Use the Form API to define form elements.
    drupal_set_title('First Form');
    $form['author'] = array(
    '#type' => 'textfield',
    '#title' => t('Author'),
    '#description' => t('Choose who the node should appear written by'),
    '#size' => 40,
    '#maxlength' => 60,
    );
    $form['submit'] = array(
      '#type' => 'submit',
      '#value' => t('Search'),
    );
    return $form;
  }

  /**
   * Implements \Drupal\Core\Form\FormInterface::validateForm().
   */
  public function validateForm(array &$form, FormStateInterface $form_state) {
    // Validate the form values.
    $author = $form_state->getValue('author');
    if (preg_match('#[\d]#', $author)) {
      $form_state->setErrorByName('author', 'You need to submit a name,
      a name does not contain numbers');
      return FALSE;
    }
    else {
      return TRUE;
    }
}

  /**
   * Implements \Drupal\Core\Form\FormInterface::submitForm().
   */
```

```php
  public function submitForm(array &$form, FormStateInterface $form_state) {
    // Do something useful.
    $author = $form_state->getValue('author');
    drupal_set_message('Your form was submitted successfully, you typed
    in the following in the user search field ' . $user_search_value);
  }
}
```

First notice the following line:

```php
$author = $form_state->getValue('author');
```

This line grabs the value the author submitted through the form and puts the value into the newly created $author variable. Now you can use the value placed in the $author variable later in the function for further processing. Notice the line in the validateForm function. The method setErrorByName takes as its first element the form element that you are checking for a problem and is causing the error to be triggered. The second argument is the message to actually display on the screen. Of course, with the setErrorByName method, you, as the programmer, are wrapping this method with an if statement like the one shown earlier.

```php
if (preg_match('#[\d]#', $author)) { }
```

This determines that the form did not pass validation and no system error has occurred, so the web page won't crash. This is the method to display to users, in red text on the screen, that they had a form validation error and now need to check their errors and resubmit the form.

What you've learned here—to create forms and to validate and submit data—is very useful in helping your customers to accomplish many tasks. You can collect customer information, create custom forms and send e-mails, or create nodes. It is very useful to be able to create custom forms with the Form API. In the next section you'll take the information from your custom-created form and create a node using the submitted data.

Creating a Node Programmatically Using a Custom Form

Let's add to the form and create a node programmatically using our own form. Later you're going to put this form into a block, which I often find is a useful thing to know how to do, and it's something customers often want.

First, you create the form and fix the validation; then you verify on submission that you're able to process the values the user submitted. Here are the contents of the new FirstForm.php file. It doesn't yet create a node, but after this step, you're only one more step away from doing so.

```php
<?php

/**
 * @file
 * Contains \Drupal\hello_world\Form\FirstForm.
 */

namespace Drupal\hello_world\Form;

use Drupal\Core\Form\FormInterface;
use Drupal\Core\Form\FormBuilder;
```

```php
/**
 * Provides a simple example form.
 */
class FirstForm implements FormInterface {

  /**
   * Implements \Drupal\Core\Form\FormInterface::getFormID().
   */
  public function getFormID() {
    return 'first_form';
  }

  /**
   * Implements \Drupal\Core\Form\FormInterface::buildForm().
   */
  public function buildForm(array $form, array &$form_state) {
    // Use the Form API to define form elements.
    drupal_set_title('Programmatically create a node with our own form');
    $form['title'] = array(
      '#title' => t('Title'),
      '#type' => 'textfield',
      '#maxlength' => 120,
    );
    $form['body'] = array(
      '#title' => t('Body'),
      '#type' => 'textarea',
    );
    $form['author'] = array(
      '#type' => 'textfield',
      '#title' => t('Author'),
      '#description' => t('Choose who the node should appear written by'),
      '#size' => 40,
      '#maxlength' => 60,
    );
    $form['submit'] = array(
      '#type' => 'submit',
      '#value' => t('Submit'),
    );
    return $form;
  }

  /**
   * Implements \Drupal\Core\Form\FormInterface::validateForm().
   */
  public function validateForm(array &$form, FormStateInterface $form_state) {
    // Validate the form values.
    $author = $form_state->getValue('author');
    if (preg_match('#[\d]#', $author)) {
      $form_state->setErrorByName('author', 'You need to submit a name,
      a name does not contain numbers');
      return FALSE;
    }
```

```
      else {
        return TRUE;
      }
}

  /**
   * Implements \Drupal\Core\Form\FormInterface::submitForm().
   */
  public function submitForm(array &$form, FormStateInterface $form_state) {
    // Do something useful.
    $title = $form_state->getValue('title');
    $body = $form_state->getValue('body');
    $author = $form_state->getValue('author');
    drupal_set_message('Your form was submitted successfully, you typed in
    the title ' . $title);
    drupal_set_message('Your form was submitted successfully, you typed in
    the body ' . $body);
    drupal_set_message('Your form was submitted successfully, you typed in
    the name ' . $author);
  }
}
```

In the preceding code you added to your buildForm function by including a text field so the user can enter the title of his or her new node with the following code:

```
$form['title'] = array(
    '#title' => t('Title'),
    '#type' => 'textfield',
    '#maxlength' => 120,
);
```

Next, you added a text area so the user can enter the body of the new node.

```
$form['body'] = array(
    '#title' => t('Body'),
    '#type' => 'textarea',
);
```

Figure 14-1 shows what the form now looks like at the URL .../first/form. On my local machine, my Drupal URL is http://drupal8:8888/first/form because my base URL to get to my Drupal home page is http://drupal8:8888 (I'm using MAMP) usually for development on my own computer (my local machine).

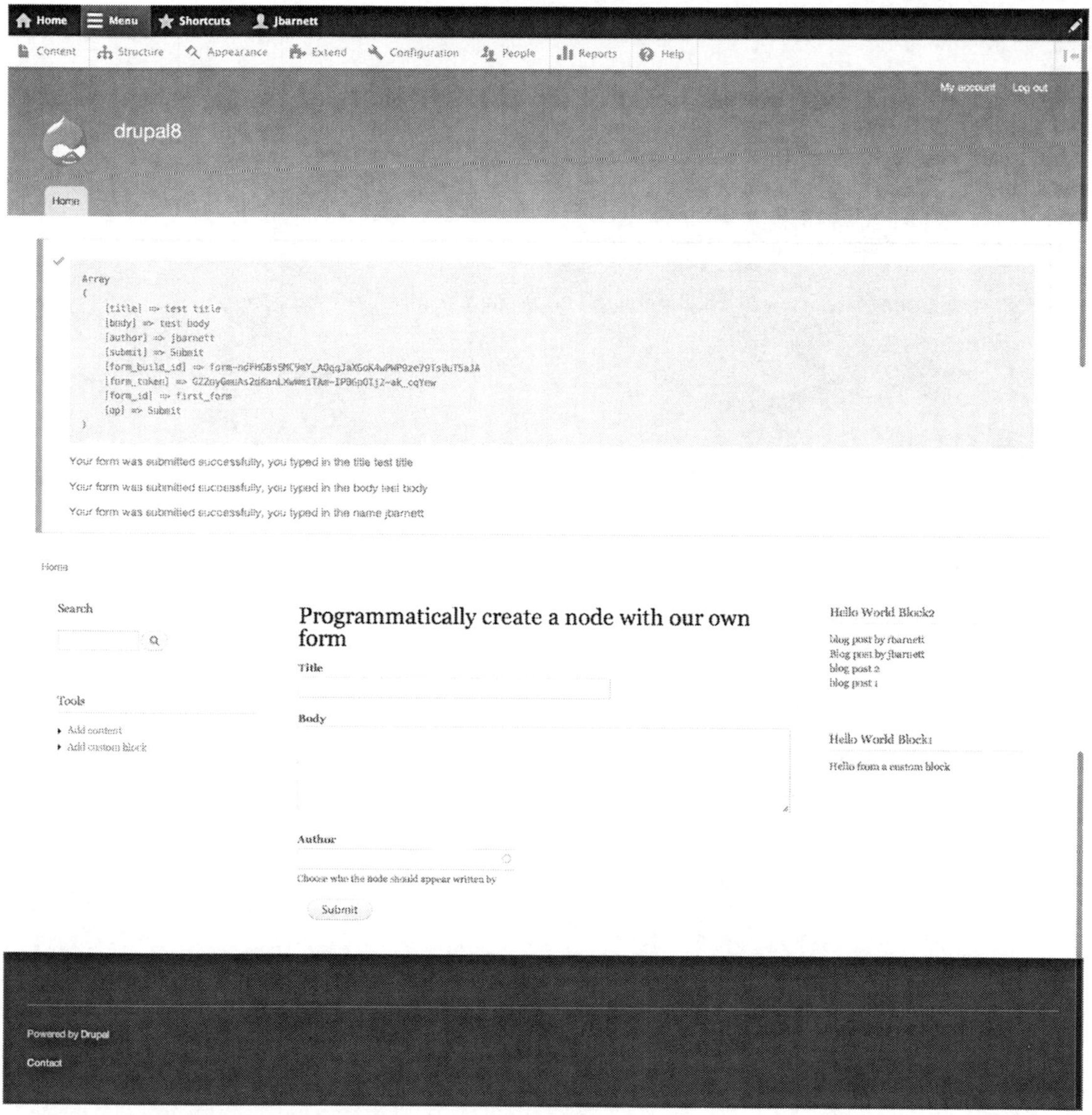

Figure 14-1. *The custom form to create nodes programmatically*

Notice, you added the following lines to grab the rest of the values submitted in the form, the title, and the body:

```
$title = $form_state->getValue('title');
$body = $form_state->getValue('body');
$author = $form_state->getValue('author');
```

Then the following code is there to print out to the screen, upon form submittal, the values that were entered into the form:

```
drupal_set_message('Your form was submitted successfully, you typed in
the title ' . $title);
drupal_set_message('Your form was submitted successfully, you typed in
the body ' . $body);
drupal_set_message('Your form was submitted successfully, you typed in
the name ' . $author);
```

Following is the code that will actually create a node after the form's submission:

```php
<?php

/**
 * @file
 * Contains \Drupal\hello_world\Form\FirstForm.
 */

namespace Drupal\hello_world\Form;

use Drupal\Core\Form\FormInterface;
use Drupal\Core\Form\FormBuilder;

use Drupal\Core\Entity\EntityInterface;
use Drupal\entity\Entity\EntityDisplay;
use Drupal\node\NodeInterface;
use Drupal\rest\Tests\RESTTestBase;

/**
 * Provides a simple example form.
 */
class FirstForm implements FormInterface {

  /**
   * Implements \Drupal\Core\Form\FormInterface::getFormID().
   */
  public function getFormID() {
    return 'first_form';
  }

  /**
   * Implements \Drupal\Core\Form\FormInterface::buildForm().
   */
  public function buildForm(array $form, array &$form_state) {
    // Use the Form API to define form elements.
    drupal_set_title('Programmatically create a node with our own form');
    $form['title'] = array(
      '#title' => t('Title'),
      '#type' => 'textfield',
      '#maxlength' => 120,
    );
```

```
    $form['body'] = array(
      '#title' => t('Body'),
      '#type' => 'textarea',
    );
    $form['author'] = array(
    '#type' => 'textfield',
    '#title' => t('Author'),
    '#description' => t('Choose who the node should appear written by'),
    '#size' => 40,
    '#maxlength' => 60,
    );
    $form['submit'] = array(
      '#type' => 'submit',
      '#value' => t('Submit'),
    );
    return $form;
}

/**
 * Implements \Drupal\Core\Form\FormInterface::validateForm().
 */
public function validateForm(array &$form, array &$form_state) {
  // Validate the form values.
  if (preg_match('#[\d]#', $form_state->getValue('author'))) {
    form_set_error('author', 'You need to submit a name, a name does
    not contain numbers');
    return FALSE;
  }
  else {
    return TRUE;
  }
}

/**
 * Implements \Drupal\Core\Form\FormInterface::submitForm().
 */
public function submitForm(array &$form, array &$form_state) {
  // Do something useful.
  drupal_set_message('Your form was submitted successfully, you typed in
  the title ' . $form_state->getValue('title'));
  drupal_set_message('Your form was submitted successfully, you typed in
  the body ' . $form_state->getValue('body'));
  drupal_set_message('Your form was submitted successfully, you typed in
  the name ' . $form_state->getValue('author'));
  $uid = db_query('SELECT uid from users where name = :name', array('name'
  => $form_state->getValue('author'))->fetchField();
  drupal_set_message('the users uid is ' . $uid);
```

```
    $node = entity_create('node', array(
      'type' => 'article',
      'title' => $form_state->getValue('title'),
      'body' => array(
        'value' => $form_state->getValue('body'),
        'format' => 'basic_html',
      ),
      'uid' => $uid,
    ));
    $node->save();
  }
}
```

Notice the key lines are

```
$node = entity_create('node', array(
    'type' => 'article',
    'title' => $form_state->getValue('title'),
    'body' => array(
      'value' => $form_state->getValue('body'),
      'format' => 'basic_html',
    ),
    'uid' => $uid,
  ));
  $node->save();
```

First, you declared $node as an entity. All nodes are entities at a more base level, just like all dogs are animals. In objected-oriented structure, it's common to have a more base way of dealing with certain objects. Without getting too much deeper into entities at this time, just know that all nodes are also actually entities, and there is a certain way programmatically to handle entities.

Next, you set the type (the content type) to be article. Then you set the title and the body, and you set the uid (the author of the node) to be the value you looked up with the following query:

```
$uid = db_query('SELECT uid from users_field_data where name = :name',
array('name' =>
$form_state->getValue('author')))->fetchField();
```

When programming, it's common to use the unique user id rather than the username. In this case you assigned the node a uid to associate with it the author of this piece of content.

Now the new node has been created. You can find it by clicking the Content tab in the menu bar (see Figure 14-2).

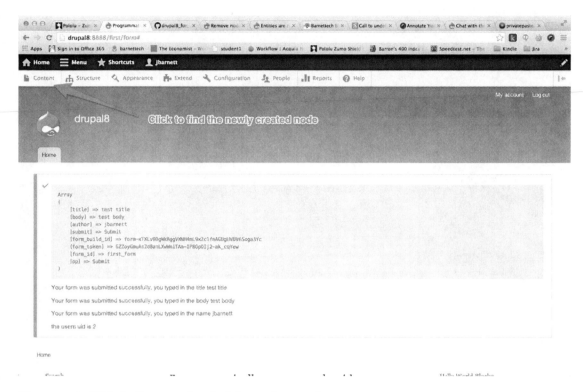

Figure 14-2. *Click the Content tab to find the newly created content*

After you click the Content tab, you'll see the full list of content items. The newest content displays at the top of the list (see Figure 14-3).

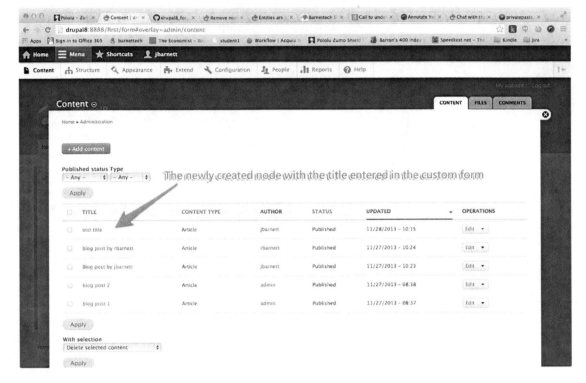

Figure 14-3. *The content list with the node of type Article and the title of "test title"*

You can now click the newly created node title or click the Edit button to the right of the newly created node to view or edit the new node.

At this point, it would be nice to add one more line of code.

```
drupal_set_message('Your new node has been created and can be viewed by
clicking the following url ' . l('Click here to view your node', 'node/' .
$node->id()));
```

By adding the line of code $node->save();, the user will receive a message that his or her node has been created. Also, there will be a link to the new node that the user can click to go right to the new piece of content. Figures 14-4, 14-5, and 14-6 show examples of the finished form and the node that is created programmatically by using the custom form.

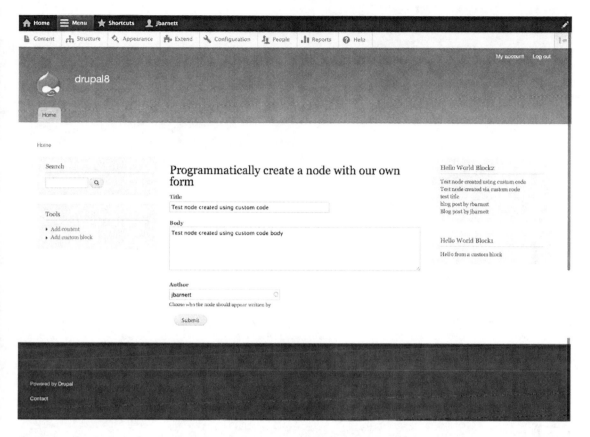

Figure 14-4. *The completed custom form, ready to create a node programmatically*

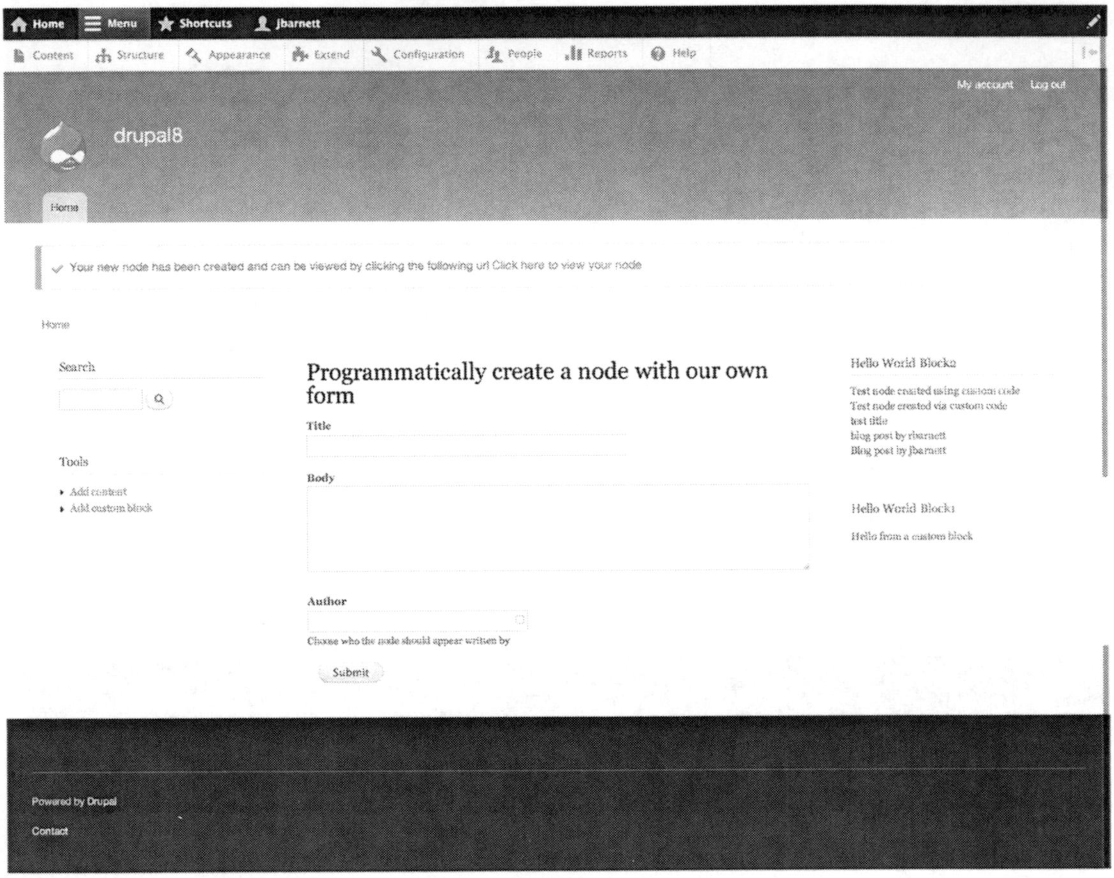

Figure 14-5. *The custom form after being submitted, showing users a friendly message with a link to their newly created content*

Figure 14-6. *The newly created node, which we created programmatically using Drupal's Form API and* $node->save();

> ■ **Note**   You can find the entire code file on Github: `https://github.com/barnettech/drupal8_book/blob/` `programmatically_creating_nodes_part2/hello_world/lib/Drupal/hello_world/Form/FirstForm.php`.

At this point, you have learned how to create forms. Now that you have that under your belt, it's time to look at how to include a form in a Drupal block.

Showing a Custom Form in a Block

The last topic this chapter covers is how to display your custom form, which programmatically can create a node, in a block. In one of my current projects, we use the organic groups module, and we need to use this code to programmatically create an organic group. An *organic group* is just a node to Drupal programmatically, but with some extra attributes added to the node to specify that it's a group node. This approach can be useful when users want to create their own social group—say "The College Gardening Club" or maybe the "Rock Climbing Club" or "Chess Club." Users could—on their own—start making social groups. They could also use the Drupal installation we set up for them to self organize, socialize, and create a better community for the college.

Let's take a look at the block code and see how to put the finished custom form inside the block.

> ■ **Note**   You can find the code on Github: `https://github.com/barnettech/drupal8_book/blob/` `programmatically_creating_nodes_part3/hello_world/lib/Drupal/hello_world/Plugin/Block/` `HelloWorldBlock3.php`.

Here is what the `HelloWorldBlock3.php` file looks like now.

```php
<?php

/**
 * @file
 * Contains \Drupal\hello_world\Plugin\Block\HelloWorldBlock3
 */

namespace Drupal\hello_world\Plugin\Block;

use Drupal\Core\Block\BlockBase;
use Drupal\block\Annotation\Block;
use Drupal\Core\Annotation\Translation;
use Drupal\hello_world\Form\FirstForm;

/**
 * Provides a simple block.
 *
 * @Block(
 *   id = "hello_world_block",
 *   admin_label = @Translation("Hello World Block3"),
 *   module = "hello_world"
 * )
 */
```

```
class HelloWorldBlock3 extends BlockBase {

  /**
   * Implements \Drupal\block\BlockBase::blockBuild().
   */
  public function build() {
    $this->configuration['label'] = t('Create a Node Programmatically
    from within a Block');
    $theForm = drupal_get_form(new FirstForm());
    return array(
      '#children' => drupal_render($theForm),
      //'#children' => 'hello',
    );
  }
}
```

Here is the newly introduced code.

```
$theForm = drupal_get_form(new FirstForm());
```

Then, consider the following line:

```
'#markup' => drupal_render($theForm),   // This line actually renders
(prints out) the form.
```

The drupal_get_form function was also the function used in Drupal 7 to put a form anywhere via a function call. The only difference is that, in Drupal 8, instead of the form name being the argument that the function takes, you instantiate the form using the syntax new FirstForm(), where FirstForm is the name of your form. In this case you named the form FirstForm, as you can see in the file FirstForm.php (https://github.com/barnettech/drupal8_book/blob/programmatically_creating_nodes_part3/ hello_world/lib/Drupal/hello_world/Form/FirstForm.php). You can see in the filename, or in the top of this file, that FirstForm is the form name:

```
/**
 * @file
 * Contains \Drupal\hello_world\Form\FirstForm.
 */
and also in that file the class name created is FirstForm:
/**
 * Provides a simple example form.
 */
class FirstForm implements FormInterface {
```

Once you set the variable to $theForm to contain the results after calling the drupal_get_form function, you then wrap the $theForm variable in the drupal_render function to put the form's output in your block. Without the drupal_render function, it would just be a giant array with no formatting for output. In this case drupal_get_form does all this work for us and produces the correctly formatted renderable array.

As you can see in the Drupal API documentation (https://api.drupal.org/api/drupal/ core!includes!common.inc/function/drupal_render/8), drupal_render takes a "renderable array" as an argument. What this basically means is that the array has to be formed correctly, with all the correct elements, so you can render it.

Figure 14-7 shows what the form looks like in a block, using the code showcased.

Figure 14-7. *The Drupal site featuring a custom form in a block to programmatically create a node*

Of course, if you fill out the form in the custom block, you'll generate the new node. And a `drupal_set_message` command in your code will display a link to the newly created page after the form is submitted.

Summary

In this chapter you covered a lot of ground and learned to do some pretty high-level tasks to wow potential customers with some great customization of Drupal. You first took a look at how to create forms in Drupal, reviewed the Form API, and saw how things have changed in Drupal 8 with regard to rendering custom forms for a site. The basic functions needed are almost the same as in Drupal 7, but the scaffolding and files and directory structure needed to set up a custom form have changed in order to accommodate the new more object-oriented structure of Drupal. This chapter also covered how to create blocks programmatically, and you reviewed how to place blocks in regions in your site. You learned how to use some data retrieved from the database in output displayed back to the end user. This chapter taught you to execute some pretty advanced functions, which should really help you to stand out as a Drupal programmer.

■ ■ ■

## CHAPTER 15

Using Git to Manage Your Source Code

This chapter introduces you to using Git. Git is the most amazing source control versioning system (a source control system allows you to track the various versions and edits of all your code files) for files that I've ever used, and it's the source control system the Drupal community has favored for a number of years. (drupal.org previously used svn and prior to that cvs.) In this chapter you're also going to be looking at using github.com. Github is a vendor that hosts Git repositories. It is free for shared code (code that is made public to the world), but Git charges a fee for private repositories. As you probably know by now, the code for this book is kept at Github: https://github.com/barnettech/drupal8_book. You'll practice managing your files using Github, and you'll also learn several useful Git commands for working with your files.

Introducing Git

Git allows folks to work on the same project (code base) by managing versions of each file, including any conflicts that occur when users co-author a file.

Git allows you to easily create branches (versions of the code, essentially). That means you can safely set up a branch for development work, a branch for experimental coding and projects, a branch for production, and a branch for anything else you can think of. When you're done developing a piece of code, you can merge it from the development branch into the production branch. Or maybe you also have a staging branch—when finished you can merge your code into that staging branch for your quality assurance (QA) team to evaluate the code to make sure there aren't any bugs, to make sure your new feature is ready to rock in production. Then, once the QA team gives the green light to the code in your staging branch, you can merge the code into the production branch.

Once there's a new version of the production branch ready to show on your live site, you can create a tag in Git, which is a non-editable snapshot of your code at that point in time. No commits (changes to the code) can be deleted or added to a tag. You will need to create a new tag to make any changes, and then the new tag can be put into place for the live web site to serve up pages.

There are lots of workflows on moving code from development to production utilizing Git as the center to manage files and keep your files versioned and backed up safely. I've seen many shops that have developers create a new temporary branch for each ticket they are working on; then, when they are done, they merge their branch back into the primary development branch.

Installing Git

First you'll need to install Git on your machine. This chapter has installation instructions for Git on every platform: http://git-scm.com/book/en/Getting-Started-Installing-Git.

Installing Git on a Mac

Figure 15-1 shows the instructions for installing Git on a Mac. Basically, you can just go to https://code.google.com/p/git-osx-installer/ and download the OSX installer. Figure 15-1 shows the official Git documentation online e-book, which is really good and contains detailed instructions. I recommend looking at this free e-book for in-depth information about using Git.

Installing on Mac

There are two easy ways to install Git on a Mac. The easiest is to use the graphical Git installer, which you can download from the Google Code page (see Figure 1-7):

    http://code.google.com/p/git-osx-installer

Figure 1-7. Git OS X installer.

The other major way is to install Git via MacPorts (http://www.macports.org). If you have MacPorts installed, install Git via

    $ sudo port install git-core +svn +doc +bash_completion +gitweb

You don't have to add all the extras, but you'll probably want to include +svn in case you ever have to use Git with Subversion repositories (see Chapter 8).

Figure 15-1. *Installing Git on a Mac from http://git-scm.com/book/en/Getting-Started-Installing-Git*

Installing Git for Windows

Figure 15-2 shows instructions for installing Git on Windows, again from the official Git e-book. This chapter gives you the fast-track tour to getting up to speed in using Git for source control, but the e-book is great and serves as another great recourse to continue learning Git.

Installing on Windows

Installing Git on Windows is very easy. The msysGit project has one of the easier installation procedures. Simply download the installer exe file from the GitHub page, and run it:

http://msysgit.github.com/

After it's installed, you have both a command-line version (including an SSH client that will come in handy later) and the standard GUI.

Note on Windows usage: you should use Git with the provided msysGit shell (Unix style), it allows to use the complex lines of command given in this book. If you need, for some reason, to use the native Windows shell / command line console, you have to use double quotes instead of simple quotes (for parameters with spaces in them) and you must quote the parameters ending with the circumflex accent (^) if they are last on the line, as it is a continuation symbol in Windows.

prev | next

Figure 15-2. *Installing Git on Windows from http://git-scm.com/book/en/Getting-Started-Installing-Git*

The installation process is straightforward—go to http://msysgit.github.com and download the installer. Note, however, that installing Git on Windows is a bit trickier than installing it on a Mac. On a Mac you install Git and then it's ready to use in a Terminal window, but on Windows, Git will not be available from your regular command prompt. Follow these steps to get a command prompt in Windows that will accept Git commands (see Figure 15-3):

1. Click Start and then click All Programs. Click Git Bash.

2. Once the Git Bash program opens, use Linux commands to cd into the Drupal root directory.

   ```
   cd Sites/acquia-drupal/modules
   ```

Figure 15-3. *Getting a command prompt in Windows to issue Git commands*

Although the Git Bash program command window is small in Figure 15-3, basically, once you have the Git Bash command window open, you can enter Linux commands as usual. Now you'll also be able to type in Git commands as well, and they will be accepted just as all the other basic Linux commands are (i.e., `git status`, `git commit`, `git update`).

Now you're ready to create your `custom` and `contrib` directories (see the next section on downloading the book's code). Please note that in the rest of the chapter if you're running Windows you will need to be within this Git Bash program to issue your Git commands.

Installing Git with Linux

There are also instructions on `http://git-scm.com/book/en/Getting-Started-Installing-Git` to install Git on a non-OSX Linux box (see Figure 15-4). The following URL (uniform resource locator) has the files needed to install Git on non-OSX Linux machines: `http://git-scm.com/download/linux`:

Installing on Linux

If you want to install Git on Linux via a binary installer, you can generally do so through the basic package-management tool that comes with your distribution. If you're on Fedora, you can use yum:

```
$ yum install git-core
```

Or if you're on a Debian-based distribution like Ubuntu, try apt-get:

```
$ apt-get install git
```

Figure 15-4. *Installing Git on a non-OSX Linux box*

Now that you've successfully installed Git on your machine, you're ready to create an account on Github.

Creating an Account on Github and Downloading the Book's Code

Once you have Git installed, create an account on https://github.com/. Then complete the following steps to use Git to download this book's code onto your local machine:

■ **Note** I recently became aware of Bitbucket (https://bitbucket.org), which is a Git hosting service offered by Atlassian. Atlassian also makes Jira, which many developers use as an issue/project-tracking tool.

---

1. Go to the root of your Drupal code. On my Mac, my Drupal 8 test installation root folder is located at /Users/jbarnett/Sites/drupal8/.

2. Next, type the following:

   ```
   cd modules
   ```

3. If you already have a custom and contrib directory within this modules directory, then you're ready to proceed to step 4. Otherwise create these two directories now by typing

   ```
   mkdir custom
   mkdir contrib
   ```

4. Change directories to go into the custom directory.

   ```
   cd custom
   ```

5. Type the following, making sure to include the ending period:

   ```
   git clone https://github.com/barnettech/drupal8_book.
   ```

The preceding command will create the hello_world directory from the examples in the custom directory. If you just type in the command without the period (.) at the end, the drupal8_book directory will be created in your custom directory, and then within that directory, you'll see the hello_world module directory. Now go poke around—you'll see you have all the files from the book.

You've now cloned (copied) the repository I've made for this book, called drupal8_for_absolute_ beginners. A clone of a repository allows you to view all the source code within the repository, and it allows you—if you have the proper permissions—to add edit and add to the repository.

Now take a look at all the branches in this repository. I've used branches in this repository not to separate development, staging, and production code but to separate the code into different versions of the code as needed for different sections of this book. You can use branches for anything you deem fit. Take a look at Figure 15-5 and you can see in Github, which has a great interface for browsing Git repositories, all the different branches that currently exist for this repository.

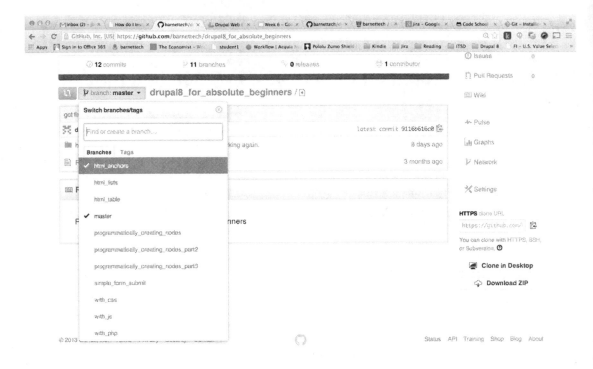

Figure 15-5. *Github showing the different branches of code available for this book's code repository*

The master branch is usually the base branch, and I've seen many people use it as their development branch. drupal.org does not use the master branch for any project because there is always a different version of Drupal like Drupal 6, Drupal 7, or Drupal 8, so using the master branch would have been confusing; it wouldn't signify which branch (version) of Drupal you were in within Git.

■ **Note** In drupal.org there are rules to how to name your branches. The page https://drupal.org/empty-git-master goes over why we don't use the master branch in Drupal projects.

In the repository I've set up for this book, I've made the branch names to be relatively telling of what the code covers. The with_js branch is the Hello World module but with the addition of showing how to add JavaScript to the module, the with_css branch is the basic Hello World module but with some basic code to show how to add CSS to the module, and so on.

So, at your command-line prompt where you did your clone of this book's repository, type the following:

```
git branch
```

Now Git will tell you what branch you're on by showing all the branches available on your local machine, including the current branch. The branch that is currently present in your directory will show with a little asterisk next to it (see Figure 15-6).

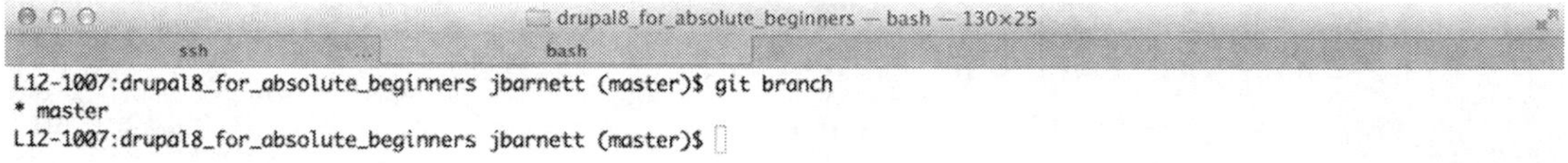

```
L12-1007:drupal8_for_absolute_beginners jbarnett (master)$ git branch
* master
L12-1007:drupal8_for_absolute_beginners jbarnett (master)$ 
```

Figure 15-6. The git branch *command showing the current branch. Notice the* master *branch has an asterisk (*) next to it*

This is a list of all the branches currently in your local Git drupal8_for_absolute_beginners repository. Git is a decentralized system, which means your local repository could actually, if you chose it to, become the new primary "origin" which all other users check their code into. This is a central difference between Git and previous source control systems. The decentralized nature of Git means it's easy to fork (split off projects). That means developers can share projects and fork projects to go in a different direction and create their own versions of the code.

If you type in

```
git remote show origin
```

you can see what the primary Git repository URL is, which is known as the "origin." When you add to the code base, you will push (upload) your changes to the "origin" so that your co-developers can pull (download) your changes. This makes it so that you can collaborate on the project using the "origin" as the place where everyone shares his or her changes. Also, after running the command git remote show origin, you can see all the branches available on the "origin." These branches didn't show up when you did a git branch command in your machine's file system.

Now let's say I want to check out the code for branch with_css. I would type in the following:

```
git checkout with_css
```

Then when I type in git branch again. I will see two branches listed, both master and the with_css branch—but now the with_css branch has the asterisk next to it, meaning my current code reflects what's in the with_css branch.

If you now poke around the hello_world directory on your local machine, you'll see the code within the directory has changed. It now has the version of the Hello World module that demonstrates adding CSS to the module. See Figure 15-7 to see what this looks like in a Terminal window.

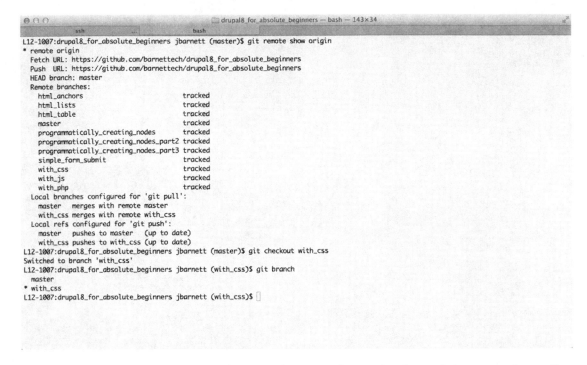

```
● ● ○                         drupal8_for_absolute_beginners — bash — 143×34
       ssh              ..              bash
L12-1007:drupal8_for_absolute_beginners jbarnett (master)$ git remote show origin
* remote origin
  Fetch URL: https://github.com/barnettech/drupal8_for_absolute_beginners
  Push  URL: https://github.com/barnettech/drupal8_for_absolute_beginners
  HEAD branch: master
  Remote branches:
    html_anchors                         tracked
    html_lists                           tracked
    html_table                           tracked
    master                               tracked
    programmatically_creating_nodes      tracked
    programmatically_creating_nodes_part2 tracked
    programmatically_creating_nodes_part3 tracked
    simple_form_submit                   tracked
    with_css                             tracked
    with_js                              tracked
    with_php                             tracked
  Local branches configured for 'git pull':
    master    merges with remote master
    with_css  merges with remote with_css
  Local refs configured for 'git push':
    master    pushes to master   (up to date)
    with_css  pushes to with_css (up to date)
L12-1007:drupal8_for_absolute_beginners jbarnett (master)$ git checkout with_css
Switched to branch 'with_css'
L12-1007:drupal8_for_absolute_beginners jbarnett (with_css)$ git branch
  master
* with_css
L12-1007:drupal8_for_absolute_beginners jbarnett (with_css)$ ▯
```

Figure 15-7. *A screenshot of my Terminal window showing a* git remote show origin *command, as well as the commands* git checkout *and* git branch

Now that you've created a Github account and learned to navigate the various branches of this book's code repository, let's take a look at how to create a Github repository and make changes to your code.

Using Git to Contribute to a Project

In this section we'll cover how to edit code or add new code and add it or update the git repository both on your local machine and then also at the "origin" where you can push your code to and everyone can share changes to jointly collaborate on a project. Take a few minutes to work through the following exercise, which will walk you through the steps of creating your first Github repository and show you how to navigate through the various files and branches of the repository.

Creating a Github Repository

Before you can create a Github repository, you need to log in to your Github account. Then, complete the following steps:

1. Click the New repository button (see Figure 15-8).

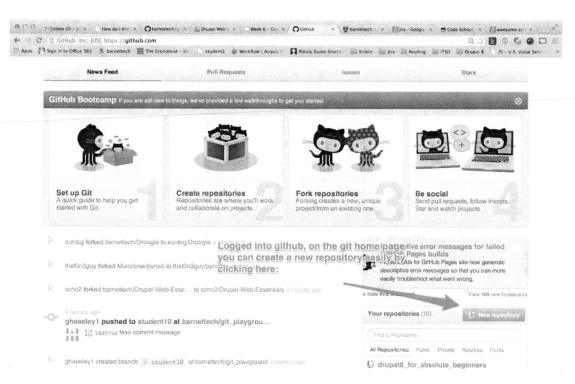

Figure 15-8. *Creating a new Github repository*

2. Clone the repository to your local machine by typing in the following command. I called my new repository git_playgound so on my local machine I typed the following (see Figure 15-9):

```
git clone https://github.com/barnettech/git_playground
```

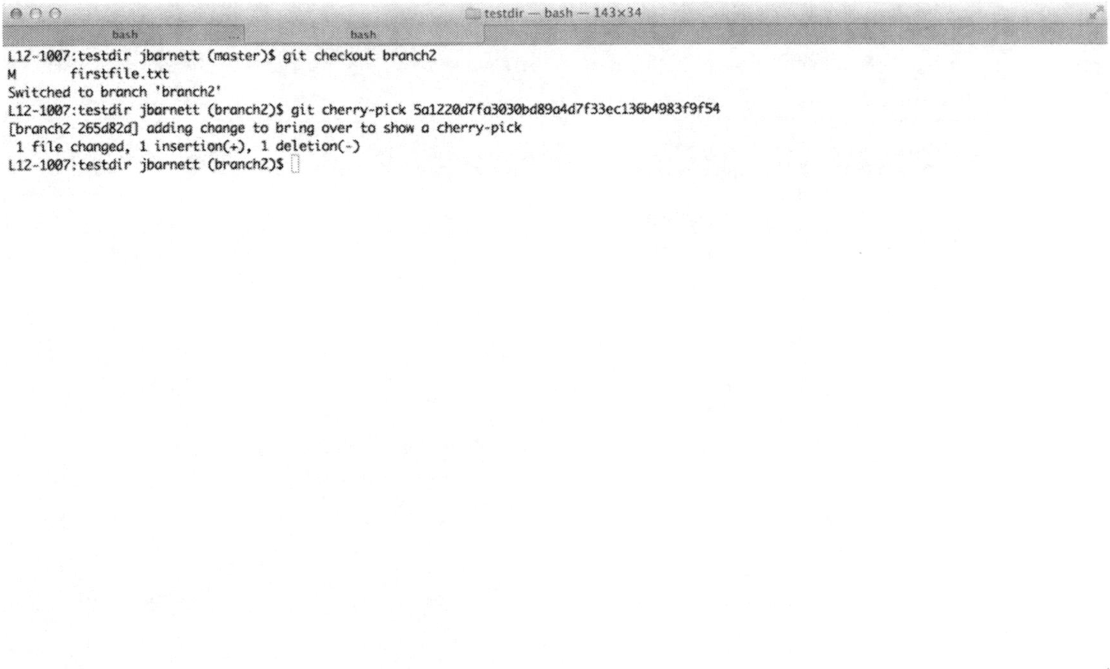

```
● ○ ○                                      testdir — bash — 143×34
            bash                                    bash
L12-1007:testdir jbarnett (master)$ git checkout branch2
M       firstfile.txt
Switched to branch 'branch2'
L12-1007:testdir jbarnett (branch2)$ git cherry-pick 5a1220d7fa3030bd89a4d7f33ec136b4983f9f54
[branch2 265d82d] adding change to bring over to show a cherry-pick
 1 file changed, 1 insertion(+), 1 deletion(-)
L12-1007:testdir jbarnett (branch2)$ ▯
```

Figure 15-9. *Clone of the repository* `git_playgound` *from my Github account*

3. Type in `git branch`. You'll see you're on the `master` branch (the asterisk is next to the word "master"). We haven't added any branches yet.

4. To create a new branch based on the `master`, type

    `git checkout -b testbranch`

This will create a new branch called `testbranch`. Initially, it will be identical to the branch you were within when you issued the command, in this case the `master` branch.

5. Now type `git branch`. You'll see the two branches: `master` and `testbranch`. Notice that `testbranch` now has the asterisk next to it. When you create a branch this way, it automatically switches you to the newly created branch.

6. Switch back to the `master` branch:

    `git checkout master`

7. Create a new file called `firstfile.txt` and add to the file whatever text you like with vi or your favorite text editor.

8. Add the following file to your local Git repository:

    `git add firstfile.txt`

9. Now type in

    `git status`

The `git status` command will show which files have been added or modified and are ready to commit (ready to save to the Git repository) (see Figure 15-10).

```
L12-1007:testdir jbarnett (branch2)$ git diff .
diff --git a/testdir/testfile_abcde.txt b/testdir/testfile_abcde.txt
index c1d8f90..37b3ec1 100644
--- a/testdir/testfile_abcde.txt
+++ b/testdir/testfile_abcde.txt
@@ -1 +1 @@
-abcde  fghij
+abcde  fghij klmnop
L12-1007:testdir jbarnett (branch2)$
```

Figure 15-10. *The Git status showing I've modified* `firstfile.txt`

I did this Git status after modifying `firstfile.txt`. If I had done it right after first issuing the command `git add firstfile.txt`, it would have reported `new file: firstfile.txt`. The `git status` command can show you what files are ready to commit, or maybe if you were just experimenting, it can be a warning to you to be careful not to commit these experiments.

Now the file is a part of the repo (repository).

Navigating Your Github Repository

Earlier you staged the content you wanted to add to the repository with the Git `add` command. Now you'll type in the Git `commit` command to actually record the snapshot of the changes to the repository. The `commit` command will record (save) any files added to the repo and/or any changes made to existing files in the repo.

```
git commit -m "this is my first commit, I am adding
firstfile.txt to the repo" firstfile.txt
```

Now you've added `firstfile.txt` to the repository and you added a commit log message with the –m argument. If you omit the –m argument, you will be prompted to add a commit log message, which you can then do. Afterward the commit will finish and succeed. Figure 15-11 shows the Git commit.

Figure 15-11. *What a Git commit looks like in the Terminal window*

Now when you go to Github, the file `firstfile.txt` will *not* be in the list of files. The file still exists only on your local machine, in your local Git instance of the `git_playground` repository.

1. To "push" the file to the "origin" machine, which in this case is a machine at Github, type the following:

```
git push origin master
```

This command will push all changes committed in the local repository you're within, from master to the origin. If you were within another branch, like `testbranch`, you would have typed `git push origin testbranch`, which would push your changes to `testbranch` up to origin. At the origin (source), other developers will also be pushing files. Now when you go to Github, the file `firstfile.txt` will be there, as seen in Figure 15-12.

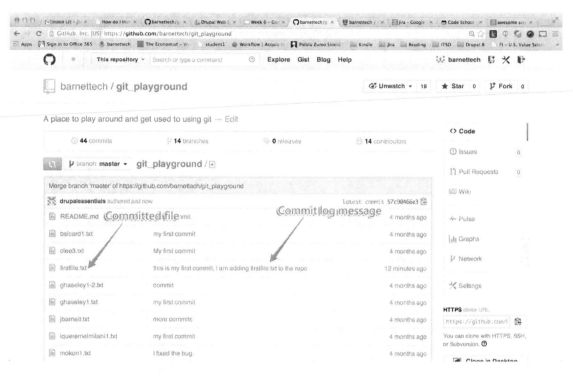

Figure 15-12. *The newly added file showing in the remote repository (at Github)*

In my example, you'll notice that others committed to this test repository as well. You can see their commits in Figure 15-12.

2. In order to get changes and additions that others make to the repository on the command line where you cloned the repository, type the following:

```
git pull
```

After issuing this command, all the files changed (by other people) will be updated on your local machine and all new files added to the repo at Github will be brought into the local repository on your local machine.

If there are any merge conflicts (conflicts with what another developer committed to the repository) that cannot be resolved by the computer, you will be alerted to the conflict. At this point, you would need to resolve any merge conflicts.

▓ **Note**   Github has some great documentation on how to resolve merge conflicts: `https://help.github.com/articles/resolving-a-merge-conflict-from-the-command-line`.

---

3. After you've safely committed all your new files to the "origin" computer (the remote computer—which in this case is at Github), you can actually within your repository type in

```
rm *
```

■ **Caution** Make sure you are in the correct directory when you do perform this action.

This action will delete all files in the present directory.

Ok, so you just deleted all your files in your local repository. But fear not. Everything is safely stored and versioned in the Git repository.

4. To reset and bring all your files back to the most recent state with the latest commits, type

```
git reset -hard head
```

Now if you issue the command ls to list the files in your directory, they will all be there. You forced a reset of the repository back to "head," which is what you call the "tip" of the branch you are on with the latest changes (the latest commits).

5. To create a tag, which is an unmodifiable snapshot of your code, type

```
git tag tagname
```

To push your tag to origin, you could type git push -tags, which would push up all new tags to origin (to Github in this case), which you created in your local repository.

Often a production Drupal site is running off the code in a tag. It is safer to run production off a tag, because no one can modify it by mistake. And even if a new tag is put in place with changed code, you can always revert to using the old tag if there's a problem. You can be safe in knowing that the old tag is there, unmodified, and can be used at any time.

Now that you've worked through quite a few of the essential Git commands, you're well on your way to being well versed in Git usage. In the next section, I'm going to introduce you to some bonus commands that I find extremely useful.

More Great Git Commands

This section will introduce you to some other great Git commands I wouldn't want to do without. First, trying typing in

```
git log
```

This command will show all of your previous commits as well as others' commits (see Figure 15-13). The commits made to the system are listed in chronological order, with the newest commits listed first. When you see the colon (:), that means you can press the spacebar to see more commits.

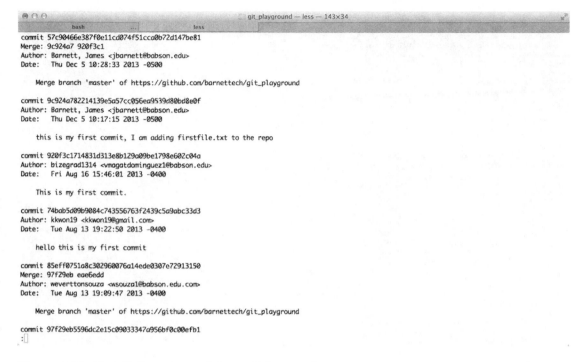

Figure 15-13. The `git log` *command shows all the commits*

Notice that each commit shows the commit, the commit unique id known as the "sha," the author, and the date, followed by the commit log message. So in the commit shown in Figure 15-13 you see

```
commit 9c924a782214139e5a57cc056ea9539d80bd8e0f
Author: Barnett, James <jbarnett@babson.edu>
Date:   Thu Dec 5 10:17:15 2013 -0500
```

The sha in this case is the really long string of letters and numbers: 9c924a782214139e5a57cc056ea9539d 80bd8e0f. You can do a lot knowing this sha. For example, type in the following:

```
git show 9c924a782214139e5a57cc056ea9539d80bd8e0f
```

This command shows you what exactly has changed in this particular commit (see Figure 15-14).

```
L12-1007:git_playground jbarnett (master)$ git show 9c924a782214139e5a57cc056ea9539d80bd8e0f
commit 9c924a782214139e5a57cc056ea9539d80bd8e0f
Author: Barnett, James <jbarnett@babson.edu>
Date:   Thu Dec 5 10:17:15 2013 -0500

    this is my first commit, I am adding firstfile.txt to the repo

diff --git a/firstfile.txt b/firstfile.txt
new file mode 100644
index 0000000..8bc2b4d
--- /dev/null
+++ b/firstfile.txt
@@ -0,0 +1 @@
+This is a first file to test adding to the repository.
L12-1007:git_playground jbarnett (master)$
```

Figure 15-14. *The results of a* `git show` *command*

You'll notice that the results in Figure 15-13 are really a "diff" of what has changed in this commit versus the previous version. A diff is just what it sounds like—a list of differences of what has changed.

Notice the "+" sign next to the text "This is a first file to test adding to the repository." The "+" sign signifies this line as been added in this version. A "-" sign would indicate that the line had been deleted in this commit.

The `git show` command can be very useful in tracking down what changed, in what commit, and who made the change, so you can consult the individual on any problems that may have occurred after his or her commit. Or maybe you just have questions for whoever made the commit.

You can also revert a commit (reverse the commit) if you know the sha. You can type

```
git revert 9c924a782214139e5a57cc056ea9539d80bd8e0f
```

The preceding command would remove the changes made within this Git's sha. This makes it easy to revert problems with a given commit (remove the problematic commit).

You can also create a branch based on that particular commit using the sha. Say a commit is a day old and you want to create a branch based on that old sha. You would type in

```
git checkout sha-of-commit -b new-branch-name
```

So let's say we have two branches and I've made a commit in master but also want to bring the branch over to the second branch, which I've called branch2. First I grab the sha of the commit while still in the master branch by typing in git log. Then I see the following:

```
commit 5a1220d7fa3030bd89a4d7f33ec136b4983f9f54
Author: Barnett, James <jbarnett@babson.edu>
Date:   Thu Dec 5 11:49:22 2013 -0500

    adding change to bring over to show a cherry-pick
```

So I see that the sha of this commit is 5a1220d7fa3030bd89a4d7f33ec136b4983f9f54. Then I switch over to branch2 by typing in git checkout branch2 (see Figure 15-15).

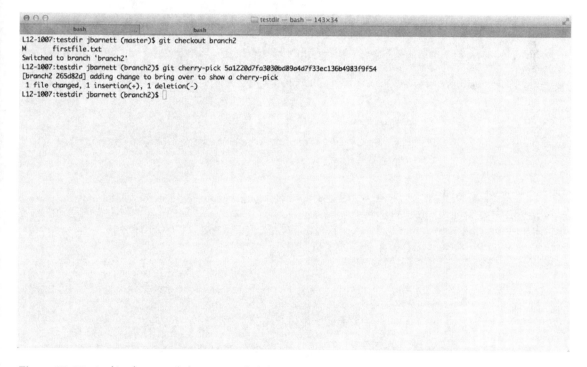

Figure 15-15. A git cherry-pick moves code between branches

Then, knowing the sha of the commit I want to bring over into branch2, I type in

git cherry-pick 5a1220d7fa3030bd89a4d7f33ec136b4983f9f54

Figure 15-15 shows the result.
Then the change is in my local repository, and I can proceed to do a

git push origin branch2

to push the changes to Github to be shared with my other coworkers (other developers on my project). For others to see your commits, remember you need to push them to the remote repository; if you don't they'll just be on your local machine. In this case the git push origin branch2 command pushes your changes to branch2 to the remote server for your coworkers to then be able to pull your changes, so they then can continue to modify the code, or they can just view what you've done. If you do a Git log in branch2, you'll see the first log message is the same as it is in the master branch now.

```
commit 265d82d6f381540a8a672bb8c7ff77066e5cd3ef
Author: Barnett, James <jbarnett@babson.edu>
Date:   Thu Dec 5 11:49:22 2013 -0500

    adding change to bring over to show a cherry-pick
```

You can also move over a file or directory to another branch by using the checkout command. So if I'm in branch2 and I do an ls, I can see the testdir directory. If I want to bring over the testdir directory from master to overwrite what I have in the branch2 directory I can, within the branch2 branch, type in

```
git checkout master testdir
```

This will overwrite what I have in the testdir directory. If I then do a cd testdir, I will now be able to see that the files are the same as they are in the master branch. I can now, if I choose, commit this directory by going to the directory just above the testdir directory.

```
git commit testdir
```

This will commit the changes to the testdir directory to the local branch2 branch. Then I can type

```
git push origin branch2
```

This will push up my changes to Github. In the same way you can check out a whole directory, you can also just check out an individual file from another branch. So if I do an ls and see the file testfile_abcde.txt and want the version from master to overwrite the one in the branch2 branch I can type in

```
git checkout master testfile_abcde.txt
```

This technique is different from cherry-pick in that it pulls in a whole directory or whole file, and that file or directory may have a whole bunch of commits that differ from the branch's version of the directory or file I'm overwriting. I find this useful sometimes to quickly bring over changes and I want to make sure the file on one branch matches the other branch. Although you do lose the commit log message when you do this, you can always refer back to the master branch where the original development and changes occurred to see the Git log history of how these changes were committed.

Checking Differences Between Branches and HEAD

It's often useful to use commands to see the difference between files on one branch or another, or maybe just to check exactly what changes you've made before you commit them. I often use the following command:

```
git diff .
```

This command will show all changes made within the present directory and all subdirectories (see Figure 15-16).

```
L12-1007:testdir jbarnett (branch2)$ git diff .
diff --git a/testdir/testfile_abcde.txt b/testdir/testfile_abcde.txt
index c1d8f90..37b3ec1 100644
--- a/testdir/testfile_abcde.txt
+++ b/testdir/testfile_abcde.txt
@@ -1 +1 @@
-abcde  fghij
+abcde  fghij klmnop
L12-1007:testdir jbarnett (branch2)$
```

Figure 15-16. The `git diff .` *command shows changes I've made that haven't yet been committed*

Unlike a `git status` command, which just shows a list of files that have been added or modified, this command shows what files changed and the exact changes made. So in this case, there's a `-abcde  fghij`, which means this line is now gone, but then there's a `+abcde  fghij klmnop`, which shows this line was added in its stead. This command can be very useful to make sure you're committing exactly what you think you want to commit and not some other experiments you meant to delete before doing a `git push` and forcing others to share your code, which may not be ready for prime time.

To compare two branches you can type

```
git diff --name-status master branch2
```

You can see the output in Figure 15-17, which shows that compared to `master`, `branch2` has added a file, `hello.txt`. In the line `A testdir/hello.txt`, the `A` denotes that a file was added. You can also see `M testdir/testfile_abcde.txt`. The `M` denotes that the file was modified. In this case we modified `testfile_abcde.txt`.

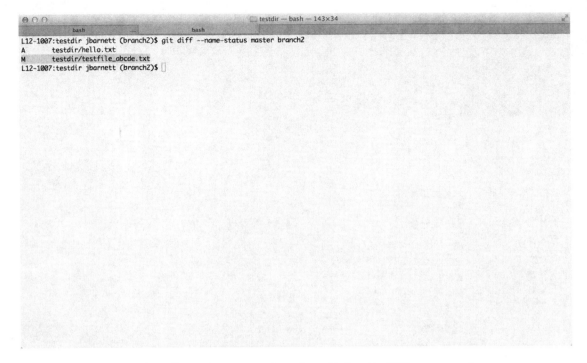

Figure 15-17. *Showing the difference between two branches with the* `git diff .` *command*

You can `diff` one single file between the present branch and another branch with a command, as follows (see Figure 15-18):

```
git diff master -- testfile_abcde.txt
```

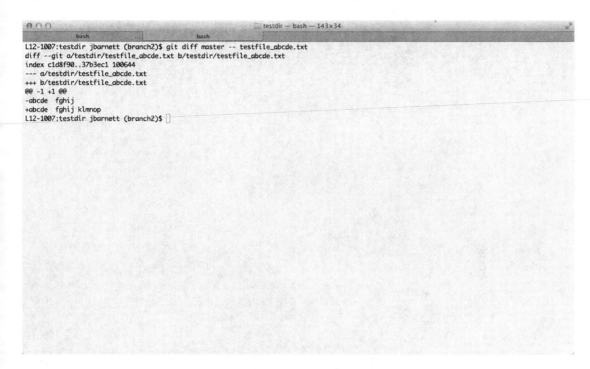

```
000                               testdir — bash — 143×34
            bash                    bash
L12-1007:testdir jbarnett (branch2)$ git diff master -- testfile_abcde.txt
diff --git a/testdir/testfile_abcde.txt b/testdir/testfile_abcde.txt
index c1d8f90..37b3ec1 100644
--- a/testdir/testfile_abcde.txt
+++ b/testdir/testfile_abcde.txt
@@ -1 +1 @@
-abcde  fghij
+abcde  fghij klmnop
L12-1007:testdir jbarnett (branch2)$
```

Figure 15-18. *Using* diff *to show the difference between branches for one single file*

If I'm in the branch2 branch and run the preceding command, it will show the difference between my present branch and master for file testfile_abcde.txt.

This section has gone over quite a few of the commands needed for working effectively with Git. There are also a few graphical user interfaces for using Git. The next section introduces you to my favorite tool.

Using a GUI for Git

There are several graphical user interfaces (GUIs) for Git, and my current favorite is Sourcetree, which is made by Atlassian (www.atlassian.com/software/sourcetree/overview?_mid=e6152f8f6dcf6b760e8265 6a0d7bde7a&gclid=CIvzrfvVmbsCFTRo7AodUyMAfA). Sourcetree allows you to visually look at Git commits in your different branches (see Figure 15-19). It even allows you to do Git pulls, make branches, make commits, and so on. I still prefer to use the command line for writing to the repository and doing anything complex, but for browsing commits and getting a bird's-eye view of everything going on in the repository, this is a great tool.

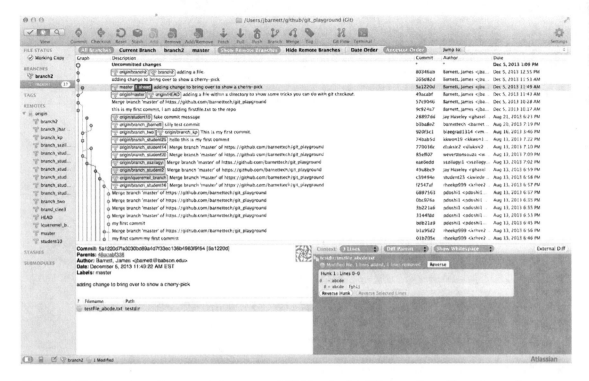

Figure 15-19. *Sourcetree allows you to have a great GUI for viewing Git commits and branches and interacting with your Git repository*

I think Sourcetree or another tool like it is a must-have for tech leads or managers of a bunch of developers so they can get to know what all the developers are up to. Even for an individual developer, it can help you keep up with the changes being made to the repository that you will have to integrate with.

Summary

In this chapter you learned how to use Git to manage your code. Git is a code repository that allows for versioning of your code; it ends up backing up your code and all different iterations of it. Git allows you to safely collaborate on the same code base, and it merges changes to the same file. If there is a conflict the computer can't figure out, Git will point you to the conflict for you to manually merge and resolve the conflict. We also learned about Git branches and how one branch might be for development work and another branch—"stage," for instance—might be where your finished code goes when it is ready for the QA team to look at. We learned about tags, which, unlike a branch, are a snapshot of your code that cannot be altered. Often a tag will be what your production site will point to serve up files. With a version control system like Git, you can easily revert code, share code, and collaborate. drupal.org has thousands of developers, and Git helps us manage this collaboration with a lot of grace.

■ ■ ■

## CHAPTER 16

Advanced MySQL Primer

Chapter 11 covered doing basic select statements (reads) from the MySQL database. This chapter covers the other essential functions encapsulated in the acronym CRUD—Create, Read, Update, and Delete. We'll cover some more complicated selects as well as creating records, updating records, and deleting records; how to create tables; and more. Often, when installing Drupal (not using Acquia Dev Desktop), you'll need to create a MYSQL database first. There are other times you'll need to look in the database to check the data directly to see if there's some problem. This chapter will round out your basic MYSQL skills so you can field more of the common issues you may face.

Creating a New Database

As part of our advanced coverage of MySQL, first we'll cover how to create a new database. Most install instructions for Drupal require you to manually create a MySQL database. After you create the database, you can play around with the new database—looking at how to edit and add records, for example. Recall that Chapter 11 covered using phpMyAdmin. You'll use phpMyAdmin to create the new database, and you'll look at how to create a new database from the command line.

Using phpMyAdmin to Create a Database

To begin, open PhpMyAdmin and click the Databases tab (see Figure 16-1).

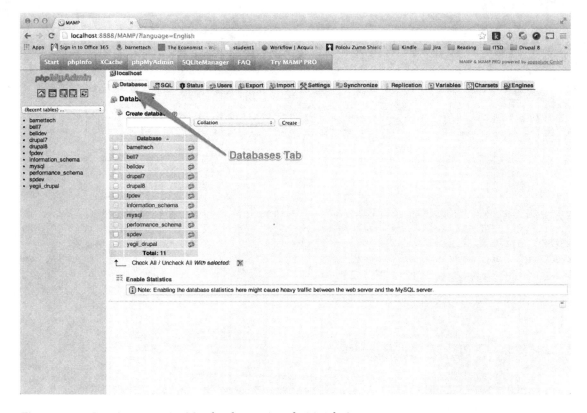

Figure 16-1. *Creating a new MySQL database using phpMyAdmin*

On this screen fill out the Create database text field with the name (see Figure 16-1), your new database will show in the list of databases. Click the name of your newly created database.

That's all there is to it. To see how to create a database from the command line, read the next section. To continue your database work with phpMyAdmin, skip to the section "Creating Tables."

Using the Command Line to Create a Database

Creating a database using phpMyAdmin is just one way to create a database. Alternatively, to create a database from the command line, you would connect to MySQL and then type the following:

```
create database mysqlPlayground;
```

To connect to MySQL from the command line on a Mac or another version of Linux, simply type

```
mysql -u username -ppassword
```

Notice that the -p argument has no space before the password, but the -u argument does have a space before the username.

Once you've created your database, you will need to type

```
use mysqlPlayground;
```

After typing this, you will be using the newly created database called "mysqlPlayground." Now, all SQL statements that you issue will run against this database.

To switch to another database, you can issue the same command.

```
use database_name;
```

To show a list of all available databases, you can issue the following command:

```
show databases;
```

Now that you have successfully created your database, in the next section you'll practice adding a new table to it.

Creating Tables

Now that you have your newly created database, you will create a new table (a table is the basic structure used to store data in the database). First, you'll create a table using phpMyAdmin, and then you'll create a table from the command line using a create statement.

Whenever you define a table, you must designate a primary key (which has a unique value). The primary key column for each row cannot be NULL (empty). Often the primary key will be an integer that autoincrements every time you insert a new row into the table.

Using phpMyAdmin to Create a Table

Again in phpMyAdmin, the process of creating a table easy. At the top of the page showing your new database, there is a Table name field to input the name of the new table you wish to create. You can also specify how many columns you would like your new table to have. After you name your table and specify the number of columns, you'll see the screen in Figure 16-2.

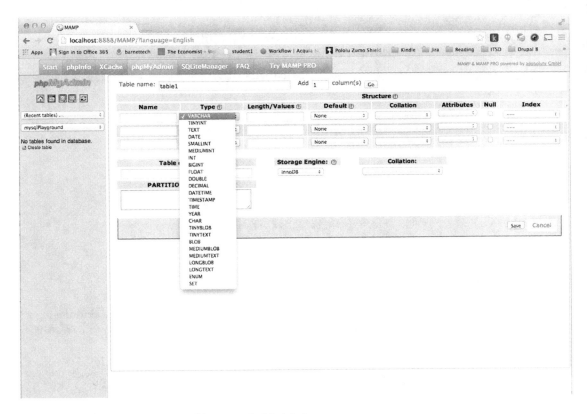

Figure 16-2. *Creating a MySQL table using phpMyAdmin*

You'll notice in Figure 16-2 that I've clicked the Type column. Each column can be defined to contain many different types of data. The primary types you'll see used are INT, which is an integer; VARCHAR, which is a string; DATE, DATETIME, or TIMESTAMP, which are all date types; and LONGTEXT, which is a really long string.

Using the Command Line to Create a Table

Here is an example create statement that you could run from the command line to create a new table. (Alternatively, you can run straight SQL from within the phpMyAdmin tool by clicking on the SQL tab.)

```
CREATE TABLE users
(
ID int NOT NULL AUTO_INCREMENT,
LastName varchar(255) NOT NULL,
FirstName varchar(255),
Address varchar(255),
City varchar(255),
PRIMARY KEY (ID)
);
```

After running the preceding create table SQL code, the users table is now created in the new database (see Figure 16-3). The number in parentheses—for example, the number 255 in the line FirstName varchar(255)—specifies how many characters are allowed in the varchar. (Remember that varchar is just a string.) The line PRIMARY KEY (ID) specifies the ID column as this table's primary key. The primary key in a table uniquely identifies each row in a table. It can be a single column or multiple columns whose values can uniquely identify a row in the table. The primary key is a primary idex for cataloging and searching a table and greatly improves database performance as it's easier to identify data being sought.

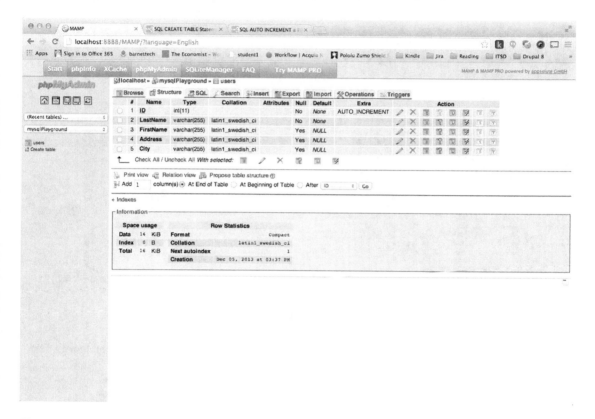

Figure 16-3. *The users table which we just created using a SQL create statement*

If you want to look at the structure of a table on the MySQL command line, you can use the following SQL command:

```
describe table users;
```

Looking at the structure of a table is useful if you're wondering what type of data your table is expecting so then you can write PHP code to correctly insert into the table. Or perhaps you've encountered a problem with inserting into the table and you want to look at the database table structure to identify if the length of a column is too short. There are plenty of great reasons to describe a table, for a closer look at how it's constructed.

In Figure 16-4 you can see the series of commands issued to use the new database and then finally to describe the newly created users table.

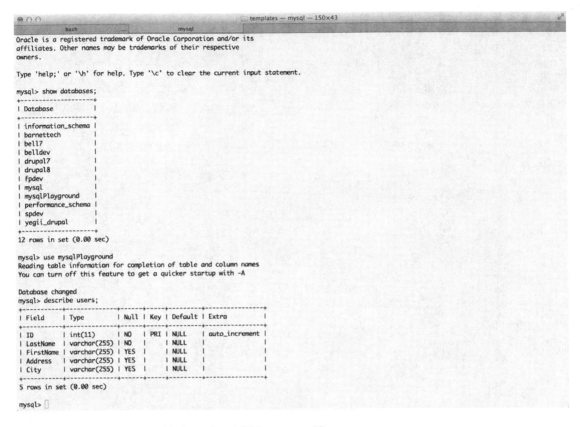

Figure 16-4. Describing a table from the MySQL command line

With the table now created and the primary key designated, we can focus on filling that table with data.

Inserting Data into a Table

Inserting data into our table in phpMyAdmin is fairly straightforward. You just click the Insert tab and then fill out the form (see Figure 16-5). Note you don't need to fill out the ID column. It will get its value automatically because we defined it as a primary key with autoincrement. As such it will just take on the next available integer value.

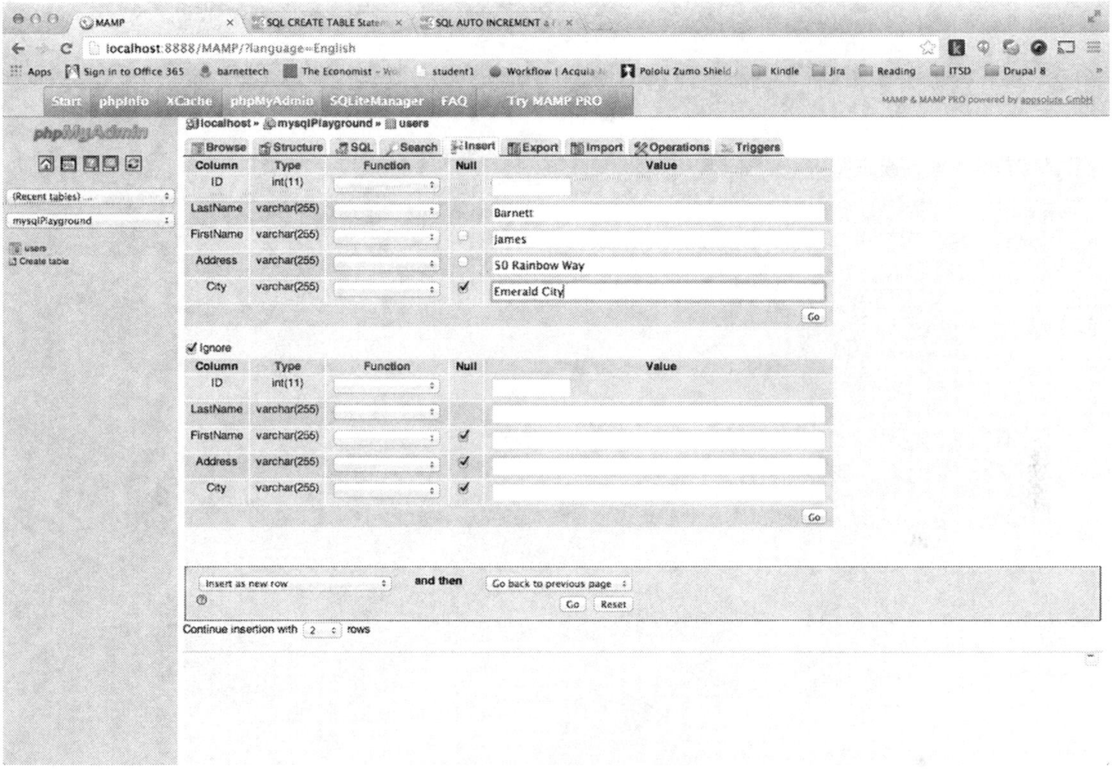

Figure 16-5. *Inserting a row in our users table using phpMyAdmin*

To insert a row using just the command line, we would issue the following SQL command:

```
INSERT INTO users (LastName, FirstName, Address, City) VALUES ('Barnett',
'Jiminy', '50 Rainbow Way', 'Ruby City');
```

You could also write the same INSERT statement as follows:

```
INSERT INTO users ('Barnett', 'Jiminy', '50 Rainbow Way', 'Ruby City');
```

Again, notice in both of the preceding lines of code that we ignore the id column because that will automatically get set because it's an autoincrement column.

After we insert these two rows into our table, we can browse our table using phpMyAdmin (see Figure 16-6).

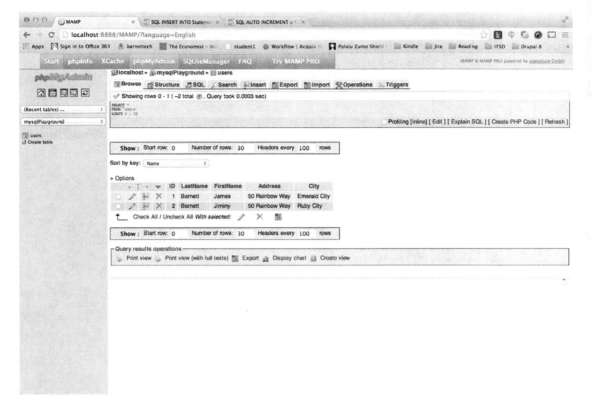

Figure 16-6. *Viewing our newly created rows of data in phpMyAdmin*

We could also view our newly created rows on the command line by just issuing the command

```
SELECT * from users;
```

The output on the command line will look like the output shown in Figure 16-7.

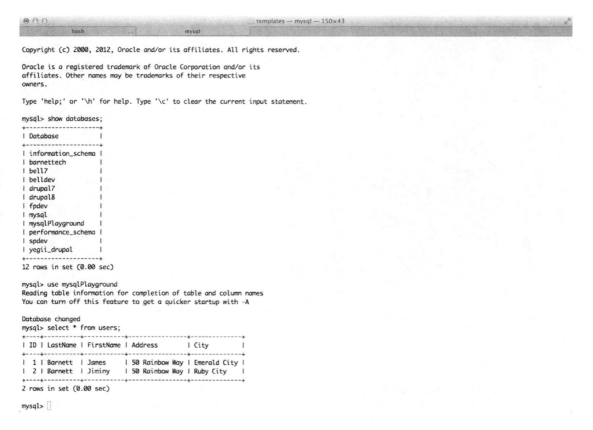

```
Copyright (c) 2000, 2012, Oracle and/or its affiliates. All rights reserved.

Oracle is a registered trademark of Oracle Corporation and/or its
affiliates. Other names may be trademarks of their respective
owners.

Type 'help;' or '\h' for help. Type '\c' to clear the current input statement.

mysql> show databases;
+--------------------+
| Database           |
+--------------------+
| information_schema |
| barnettech         |
| bell7              |
| belldev            |
| drupal7            |
| drupal8            |
| fpdev              |
| mysql              |
| mysqlPlayground    |
| performance_schema |
| spdev              |
| yegii_drupal       |
+--------------------+
12 rows in set (0.00 sec)

mysql> use mysqlPlayground
Reading table information for completion of table and column names
You can turn off this feature to get a quicker startup with -A

Database changed
mysql> select * from users;
+----+----------+-----------+---------------+--------------+
| ID | LastName | FirstName | Address       | City         |
+----+----------+-----------+---------------+--------------+
|  1 | Barnett  | James     | 50 Rainbow Way | Emerald City |
|  2 | Barnett  | Jiminy    | 50 Rainbow Way | Ruby City    |
+----+----------+-----------+---------------+--------------+
2 rows in set (0.00 sec)

mysql>
```

Figure 16-7. *Viewing our data on the command line with the SQL* `select * from users;`

After you've created a table and filled it with data, you may find that you need to update it. You'll do that next.

Updating Tables

To update a table row, you would write a SQL statement like the following, using phpMyAdmin:

To update a table from the command line, it would look as follows:

```
update users set FirstName = 'Barney' where id = 1;
```

In this case in the users table, the FirstName column will be updated to the value of Barney where the value of the id column is 1. This SQL statement will update the value of exactly one row (see Figure 16-8).

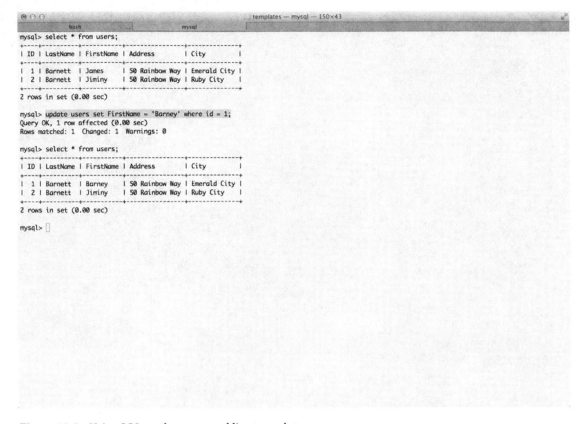

Figure 16-8. *Using SQL on the command line to update a row*

If you had omitted the WHERE clause, where id = 1, then all rows would have been updated with the FirstName column being Barney.

You can also easily update rows using phpMyAdmin, as seen in Figures 16-9 and 16-10. Simply click the pencil icon to edit a row.

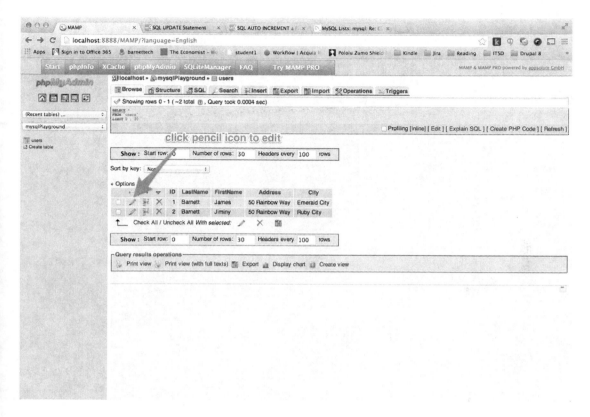

Figure 16-9. *To update a row in phpMyAdmin, click a pencil icon next to the row you'd like to edit*

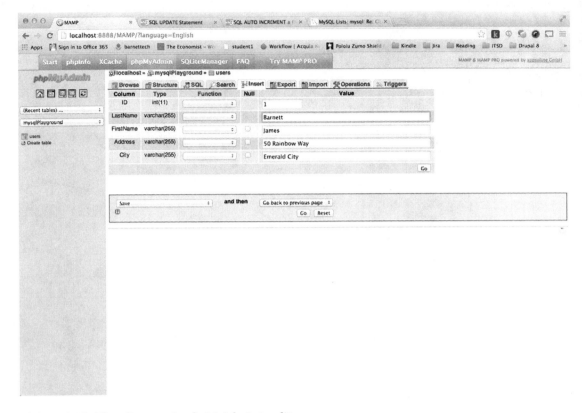

Figure 16-10. *The edit screen in phpMyAdmin to edit a row*

In addition to editing your table data, you might have to delete data, when it is no longer needed. To find out how, read on.

Deleting Data

Using phpMyAdmin you can very easily delete data, as seen in in Figure 16-11. To do so, you can click the red X in the row you want to delete. Alternatively, you can select the row or rows you want to delete and then click the red X located under the table rows.

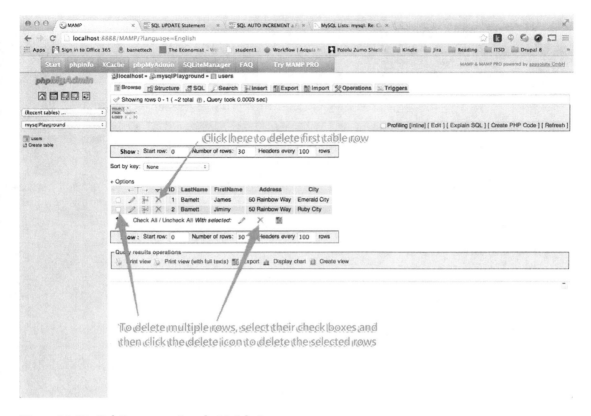

Figure 16-11. *Deleting rows using phpMyAdmin*

To delete data from the table, you can issue a statement like the following:

```
delete from users where id = 3;
```

Just as you would guess, the row of the table with the id of 3 would be deleted. But if you were to omit the WHERE clause, where id =3, then all rows would be deleted from the table.

Now that you've seen how to work with tables directly in MySQL, the next section looks at how to add and work with tables in Drupal modules.

Creating and Editing Tables in Drupal

To create tables in Drupal, the process is a bit different. You will be defining your tables in a your_module_name.install file, where if your module's name was "hello_world," then the file for your module would be hello_world.install. The MySQL tables you create will be created with your module upon installation of the module.

■ **Note** You can find a copy of the hello_world.install file at https://github.com/barnettech/drupal8_book/blob/with_install_file/hello_world/hello_world.install in the branch of the repository called with_install_file.

Creating the Table in the Drupal Module

The following code, which is found within the hello_world.install file, creates a table called hello_world for the Hello World module. Recall that the Hello World module was first introduced in Chapter 4; you'll be adding to that module in this chapter.

```php
<?php

/**
 * @file
 * Install, update and uninstall functions for the dblog module.
 */

/**
 * Implements hook_schema().
 */
function hello_world_schema() {
  $schema['hello_world'] = array(
    'description' => 'Table that contains information for the hello world
    module.',
    'fields' => array(
      'hid' => array(
        'type' => 'serial',
        'not null' => TRUE,
        'description' => 'Primary Key: Unique hello world event ID.',
      ),
      'uid' => array(
        'type' => 'int',
        'unsigned' => TRUE,
        'not null' => TRUE,
        'default' => 0,
        'description' => 'The {users}.uid of the user who entered the data.',
      ),
      'message' => array(
        'type' => 'text',
        'not null' => TRUE,
        'size' => 'big',
        'description' => 'Text of log message to be passed into the t() function.',
      ),
      'timestamp' => array(
        'type' => 'int',
        'not null' => TRUE,
        'default' => 0,
        'description' => 'Unix timestamp of when event occurred.',
      ),
    ),
    'primary key' => array('hid'),
  );

  return $schema;
}
```

This code in the hello_world.install file creates a table that looks like the one shown in Figure 16-12. I've used the command describe hello_world; within the MySQL command line.

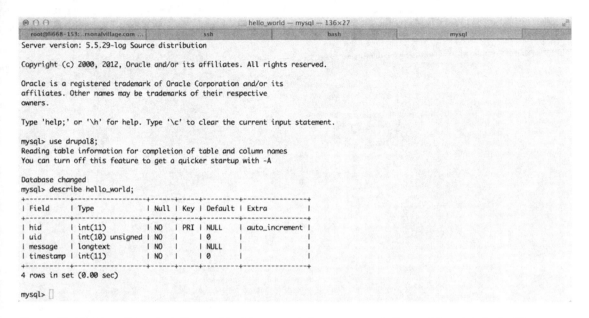

Figure 16-12. *Describing the hello_world table we create in our custom hello_world module in the file* hello_world.install

In this section you created a custom table within your Hello World module. In the next section, you'll interact with the table by doing some inserts, updates, and deletes.

Inserting Data in a Drupal Table

In this section you're going to update the form you created in Chapter 14, which created nodes, so that you can instead create entries in the hello_world table. Next, you'll select from the hello_world table to print output on the screen. Finally, you'll put your custom form into a block. Essentially, you're going to pull together all the skills you've learned so far to create this functionality.

Figure 16-13 shows the end result of what you're going to create. You enter a message into the custom form that lives in a custom block, which you've put into a region on the right-hand side of the screen. Then, upon submission of the form in the custom block, you've created a new row in the hello_world table. The custom page then shows the output of what's in the hello_world table, listing the contents of each row.

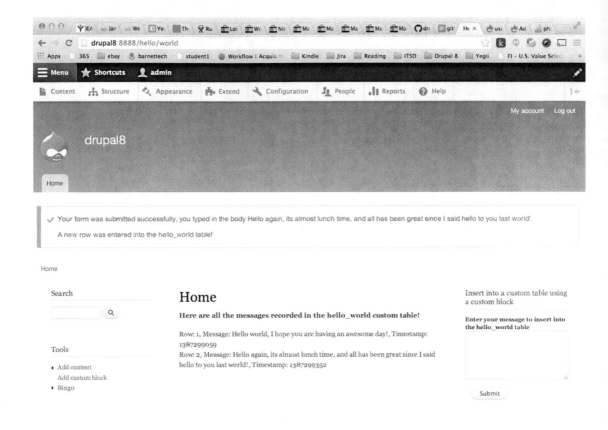

Figure 16-13. *A custom block, with a custom form within it, to submit data to our custom* hello_world *table, and displaying the contents of the* hello_world *table in our custom page*

To have this code work in your browser, you need to have the with_install_file branch checked out and active in your modules/custom directory (or anywhere under the modules directory will do). You need to have the hello_world module enabled, and you need to place Hello World Block3 in the second sidebar. (Chapter 2 covered how to enable and place blocks within your Drupal site.)

Now, let's go over the code that was needed to create what you saw in Figure 16-13.

■ **Note** The code is available in the with_install_file branch at https://github.com/barnettech/drupal8_book/tree/with_install_file. You'll see that your custom page at .../hello/world had you modify your controller file, which is located here: https://github.com/barnettech/drupal8_book/blob/with_install_file/hello_world/src/Controller/HelloWorldController.php.

Recall that the controller file is in the hello_world/src/Controller directory. Notice the controller now has a db_query statement to do a simple select from the hello_world table. Then in a foreach statement, we loop through the results and add them to the $content variable. Finally, the $content variable's contents become the output to the screen.

```php
<?php
/**
 * @file
 * Contains \Drupal\hello_world\HelloWorldController.
 */

namespace Drupal\hello_world\Controller;

/**
 * Provides route responses for the hello world page example.
 */
class HelloWorldController {
  /**
   * Returns a simple hello world page.
   *
   * @return array
   *    A very simple renderable array is returned.
   */
  public function myCallbackMethod() {
    $content = '<p><b>Here are all the messages recorded in the hello_world
      custom table! </b></p>';
    $results = db_query('SELECT * from hello_world');
    foreach($results as $row) {
      $content .= 'Row: ' . $row->hid . ', Message: ' . $row->message . ',
      Timestamp: ' . $row->timestamp . '</br>';
    }

    $element = array(
      '#markup' => $content,
    );
    return $element;
  }
}
```

Then I also changed the form in the FirstForm.php file, which lives here in Github: https://github.com/barnettech/drupal8_book/blob/master/hello_world/src/Form/FirstForm.php.

Remember, the custom form lives within the hello_world/src/Form directory within our hello_world module. The form just needs one text field to input the message that will be inserted into the hello_world custom table. Then I also modified the submit function public function submitForm to do a submit into the hello_world table with the result values we collect from the custom form.

```php
<?php

/**
 * @file
 * Contains \Drupal\hello_world\Form\FirstForm.
 */

namespace Drupal\hello_world\Form;

use Drupal\Core\Form\FormBase;
use Drupal\Core\Form\FormStateInterface;

class FirstForm extends FormBase {

  /**
   * {@inheritdoc}
   */
  public function getFormId() {
    return 'first_form';
  }

  /**
   * {@inheritdoc}
   *
   * @param \Symfony\Component\HttpFoundation\Request $request
   *   The request object.
   */
  public function buildForm(array $form, FormStateInterface $form_state) {
    // Use the Form API to define form elements.
    // This array element will collect the message
    // to put into the message column of the
    // hello_world table in the database.
    $form['message'] = array(
      '#title' => t('Enter your message to insert into the hello_world table'),
      '#type' => 'textarea',
    );
    // This array element will create the submit button on the form.
    $form['submit'] = array(
      '#type' => 'submit',
      '#value' => t('Submit'),
    );
    return $form;
  }

  /**
   * {@inheritdoc}
   */
  public function validateForm(array &$form, FormStateInterface $form_state) {
    // Validate the form values.
  }
```

```
/**
 * {@inheritdoc}
 */
public function submitForm(array &$form, FormStateInterface $form_state) {
    // This line gets the currently logged in user's information, we'll
    // put this user's uid into the hello_world table in the uid column
    // along with whatever he or she enters within the form on the
    // /first/form page.
    $account = \Drupal::currentUser();
    // This line actually inserts the data submitted in the form
    // on the /first/form page into the hello_world table in the database.
    db_query("INSERT INTO hello_world (uid, message, timestamp) values
    (:uid, :message, :timestamp)", array(':uid' => $account->id(), ':message' =>
    $form_state->getValue('message'), ':timestamp' => time())));
    // The lines below just display a message to the user that their
    // form was submitted successfully.
    drupal_set_message('Your form was submitted successfully, you typed in
    the body ' . $form_state->getValue('message'));
    drupal_set_message('A new row was entered into the hello_world table! ');
  }

}
```

You've also put your modified custom form into your custom block.

▓ **Note**   You can find the custom block code on Github: https://github.com/barnettech/drupal8_book/blob/master/hello_world/src/Plugin/Block/HelloWorldBlock3.php.

Remember, the blocks are within the /hello_world/src/Plugin/Block directory within the hello_world module. I just modified some text in this file that made more sense for the current example. Here are the contents of the HelloWorldBlock3.php file. Please note that even the code in the PHP comments, between the /** **/ comment markers, is essential to get a Drupal block working. This code is not just PHP comments; it is, in fact, used by the system to identify the block id, admin label, and module name this block belongs to.

```
<?php

/**
 * @file
 * Contains \Drupal\hello_world\Plugin\Block\HelloWorldBlock3
 */

namespace Drupal\hello_world\Plugin\Block;

use Drupal\Core\Block\BlockBase;
use Drupal\block\Annotation\Block;
use Drupal\Core\Annotation\Translation;
use Drupal\hello_world\Form\FirstForm;
```

267

```
/**
 * Provides a simple block.
 *
 * @Block(
 *   id = "hello_world_block",
 *   admin_label = @Translation("Hello World Block3"),
 *   module = "hello_world"
 * )
 */
class HelloWorldBlock3 extends BlockBase {

  /**
   * Implements \Drupal\block\BlockBase::blockBuild().
   */
  public function build() {
    $this->configuration['label'] = t('Autocomplete Form Example');
    // This line below actually puts the new form we created in the
    // $theForm variable.
    $theForm = \Drupal::formBuilder()->getForm('Drupal\hello_world\Form\FirstForm');
    // We actually render the form in the code below.
    return array(
      '#markup' => drupal_render($theForm),
    );
  }
}
```

Figure 16-14 shows you that the inserts made it into the custom hello_world table.

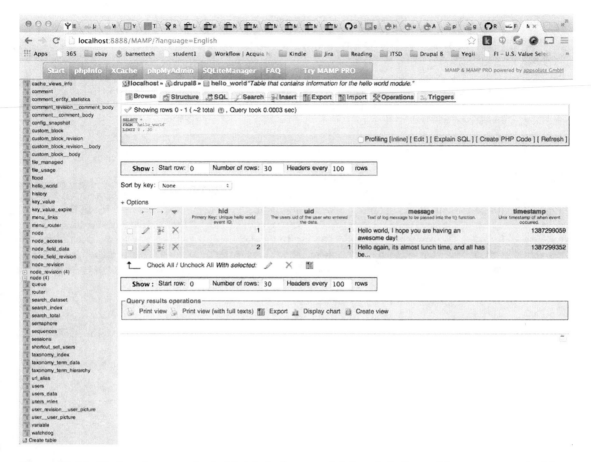

Figure 16-14. *The inserts, as seen in phpMyAdmin, have made it into the hello_world custom-created table, from the Drupal form you created*

And there you have it—a custom form, within a custom block, using a custom table, created in a
.install file, and the contents of the custom table spat out as output in the custom page at the URL
.../hello/world.

If you've come this far, you have learned a lot and are really becoming a proficient Drupal 8 programmer.
Next, you'll continue to dive deep in your understanding of how to use MySQL within Drupal. You'll learn
how to update and delete records within Drupal module code.

Updating and Deleting in Drupal

Following is an example of what an UPDATE statement would look like in Drupal:

```
db_query("UPDATE {hello_world} SET message = 'goodbye world' WHERE uid = :uid",
array(':uid' => 1));
```

This example, which you can adapt to your needs, would set all rows in the hello_world table to have
the message column be "goodbye world" where the uid row is equal to 1.

Following is an example of what a DELETE statement would look like in Drupal:

```
db_query('DELETE FROM {hello_world} where uid = :uid',
    array(':uid' => 5));
```

This example DELETE statement, which you could put in your Drupal custom code if you found it appropriate, deletes all entries in the hello_world table where the uid is equal to 5. You can obviously adapt this SQL to fit your needs.

Summary

In this chapter you created and edited a basic table, and you learned about basic insert statements, update statements, and delete statements in MySQL. Then you practiced how to create a custom table in Drupal 8 using a .install file. You then used this new table in your custom Hello World module and saw how to put your custom form into a custom block. Finally, you inserted data (via the newly created form) into the new Drupal table you created yourself in your module's .install file. After that exercise, you took a brief look at inserts, updates, and deletes within Drupal coding. This chapter really pulled together lot of techniques you've learned so far and showed off some great Drupal 8 programming skills.

■ ■ ■

## CHAPTER 17

Linux

Drupal is usually found within a LAMP (Linux, Apache, MySQL, and PHP) stack. This chapter is dedicated to helping you understand Linux, and it has lots of tips and tricks so you can get comfortable with navigating around your Linux box. My personal machine is a Mac running OSX, which is a Linux flavor. I also like Ubuntu for my production computers, which house the development, stage, and production environments for my projects. Ubuntu is another popular Linux flavor. This chapter will focus on these two flavors of Linux—OSX and Ubuntu—but once you learn one flavor of Linux, it's not difficult to pick up other Linux variants. Most of the commands are identical.

■ **Note** If you're using Mac OSX from the command line, then you already know some basic Linux. Macs use a Linux core as the base of the operating system, which is the reason many developers love having a Mac. Many of us know the rivalry between Macs and PCs; there is also a friendly rivalry between Linux and PC-based computing in the world of professional computing. In any case Drupal has traditionally been a LAMP-based technology, and the "L" in LAMP stands for Linux. Recently Microsoft has been courting the Drupal community. It has sponsored getting Drush to work in Windows, and it has been trying to jump into the hot open source space. And anything that helps open source, well, I wish them much luck.

Let's now look at some Linux basics. We'll begin by accessing a Linux prompt from both a Mac and a Windows machine.

Introduction to Linux on a Mac

With a Mac all you need to do to get to a Linux command-line prompt is open your Terminal program. You can go to Spotlight (the magnifying glass that helps you find things on a Mac), type "terminal," and click the Terminal program that pops up. You can also go to your Applications list and then into the Utilities folder; you'll find the Terminal icon there as well. If you wish, you can drag the Terminal icon to your dock for easier access, as I have done (see Figure 17-1).

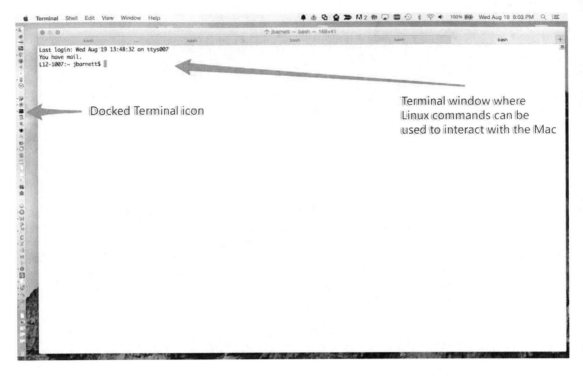

Figure 17-1. The Terminal program on a Mac

Once the Terminal program on a Mac is open, you can start typing in Linux commands. (The section "Getting to Know Some Common Linux Commands" later in this chapter covers some of the most common Linux commands and tasks.) You'll notice in Figure 17-1 that I have multiple tabs open with multiple Terminal windows in use (one per each tab). To open the first new tab, you click Shell in the Terminal menu bar and then click New Tab. You can open additional new tabs by clicking to the right of the word "bash" in the upper part of the tab furthest to the right. It can be very useful to have multiple tabs open at the same time.

■ **Note**   You can get your own Linux box to connect to by opening an account with Amazon, Rackspace, Linode, Digital Ocean, or countless other vendors that offer cloud computing at a price.

Connecting to Ubuntu

Ubuntu is the other Linux flavor I use almost every day. This section shows you how to connect to Ubuntu via the Mac and Windows interfaces.

Connecting to Ubuntu from a Mac

Typically, you would connect to a Linux box from a Mac through the Terminal program. If you needed to connect to a Linux box, you would type a command similar to the following—my Linux box is called drupalessentials.babson.edu; your name would differ:

```
ssh drupalessentials.babson.edu
```

Then you would be prompted to type your username, followed by another prompt for your password. You could also type the following command, replacing jbarnett and the Linux box name with your own information:

```
ssh jbarnett@drupalessentials.babson.edu
```

In this case, you would be prompted to type your password, because you provided the username in the initial command to connect to your Linux box. You can see in Figure 17-2 I've successfully connected to my Ubuntu Linux box with the domain name drupalessentials.babson.edu.

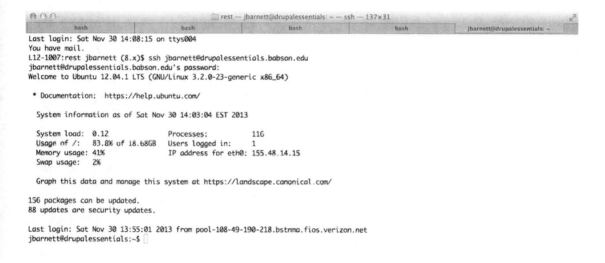

Figure 17-2. *Connecting successfully from a Mac to an Ubuntu box that exists out on the Internet*

Connecting to Ubuntu from Windows

To connect to an Ubuntu box from Windows, first you will need to download a tool called Putty (www.putty.org/). Once you install Putty on Windows, consider leaving the Putty icon on your desktop for easy access to it.

When you double-click the Putty icon, Putty will open. You'll see the Putty terminal, which is ready for you to input the connection information to your Linux box (see Figure 17-3).

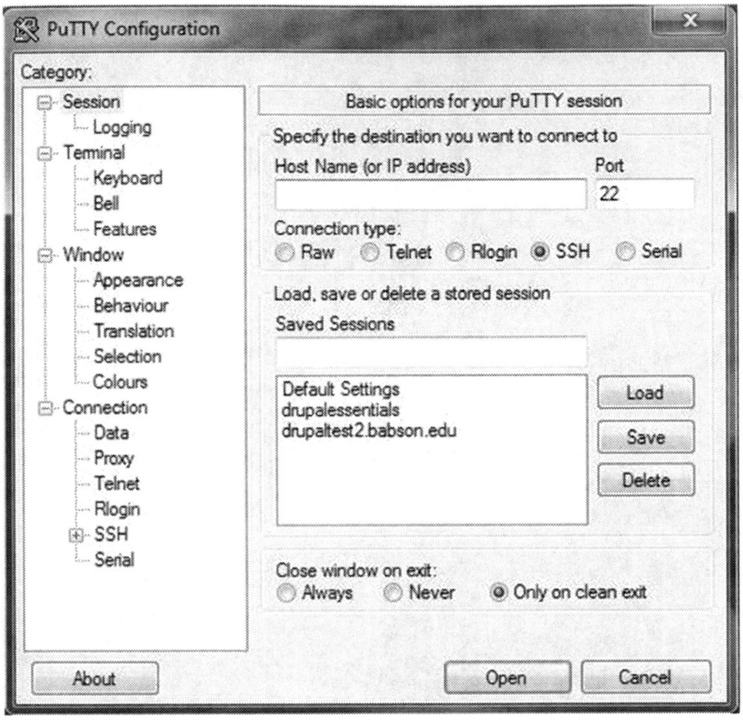

Figure 17-3. *Putty in Windows*

You can connect to a Linux box by IP (Internet protocol) (four groups of numbers separated by dots that uniquely identify a computer on the Internet) or by its domain name. I usually connect by the domain name. In Figure 17-4 I'm connecting to the Ubuntu Linux box `drupalessentials.babson.edu`, so for the hostname I type `drupalessentials.babson.edu` and I make sure that the SSH connection type is selected.

Figure 17-4. *Inputting connection info into Putty to connect to the Linux box*

You can see in Figure 17-4 that I've input my username and password. In Figure 17-5 you can see what it looks like after I click Open within Putty. Doing so connects me to the drupalessentials.babson.edu Linux box.

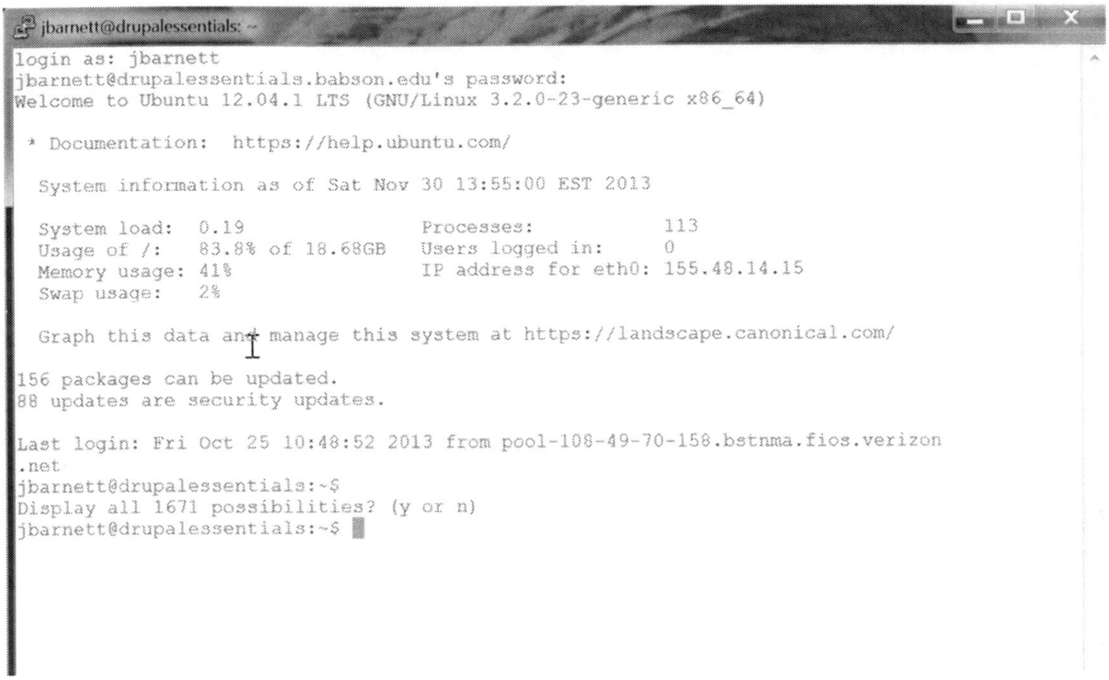

Figure 17-5. *Successfully logged into a Linux box using the Putty program to connect via the SSH prototcol*

Getting to Know Some Common Linux Commands

Now we're going to go through some common commands and things to know in Linux to help you navigate around and be very effective to get things done.

Navigating Among Directories and Managing Files

You can use the following command to show you the current directory you are working in:

pwd

To look at the contents of a directory, type

ls

To look at a "long" listing of a file or files, add the -l option.

ls -l

The ls -l command will give you much more information about a file, such as the current permissions on a file, who owns the file, and which group owns the file. For instance, take the following line (see Figure 17-6):

-rwxrwxrwx 1 jbarnett www-data 0 Dec 1 06:53 filename.txt

```
L12-1007:drupal jbarnett (8.x)$ ls -l filename.txt
-rwxrwxrwx  1 jbarnett  www-data  0 Dec  1 06:53 filename.txt
L12-1007:drupal jbarnett (8.x)$ []
```

Figure 17-6. *A long list (ls -l filename.txt) of filename.txt*

The preceding line displays after issuing the command ls -l filename.txt. The user who owns the file filename.txt is jbarnett, and the group that owns the file is www-data. We'll learn commands to change the owner or group that owns a file shortly.

To look at the contents of a directory in reverse chronological order (I use this command quite often to see what files have changed recently); the files that have changed most recently show at the bottom of the directory listing with the following command:

ls -ltr

To copy a file use

cp

And to copy recursively (all subdirectories and files), use the -r argument to the cp command as follows:

cp -r simple_block /Users/jbarnett/github/Drupal-Web-Essentials

With the preceding command, I copied the simple block directory and all subdirectories and files into the path Users/jbarnett/github/Drupal-Web-Essentials.

To move a file (where you don't leave a copy behind), use

mv

For example,

mv file.txt /home/jbarnett

277

The preceding command will move `file.txt` into the `/home/jbarnett` directory.
To delete a file, use the `rm` command.

```
rm file.txt
```

The period (.) refers to the current directory; the double period (..) refers to the directory above the one you're in. Consider the following:

```
mv filename.txt ..
```

This command moves the `filename.txt` file into the directory above the one you're in currently (i.e., into the parent directory).

Installing LAMP

If you see `apt-get` in any Linux instructions, you're calling the Linux package manager to download some new software for your Linux (or OSX) machine. To get LAMP on an Ubuntu box (a favorite Linux flavor) you have to type the following:

```
sudo apt-get install tasksel
```

This is not the only way to install the full LAMP stack in Ubuntu; I'm just showing you what `apt-get` is in case you use the popular Ubuntu flavor of Linux. Other versions of Linux, OSX as well, have their own package manager. For example, OSX uses `macports` rather than `apt-get`.

Adding Security with Permissions

If you see the sudo command in front of some Linux commands, it means you need "root" access—"root" in the Linux world is the uber admin user on a Linux box. You can be the root user to run commands, but best practice is for your Linux admin to add you as a sudo user, so the system will log who did what using sudo (root) rights. This is a good security precaution. If you sudo to root, this is synonymous with "I switched temporarily to be the root user." You would sudo to root if your regular user account doesn't have enough permissions to complete a particular task.

If you want to simply create a new empty file, you type

```
touch filename.txt
```

This preceding code will create the file `filename.txt`.
To change the permissions of a file, you use the `chmod` command, for example,

```
chmod 771
```

I'll explain what the numbers 771 are. First, do an `ls -l` on a file to view the file's permissions. Alternatively, you can do an `ls -ltr` to see a whole directory's list of files and each file's permissions. Consider the following output:

```
L12-1007:drupal jbarnett (8.x)$ ls -ltr
total 200
-rw-r--r--  1 jbarnett  1321145334  70280 Oct 17 15:42
   composer.lock
```

```
-rw-r--r--    1 jbarnett  1321145334   1156 Oct 17 15:42
   composer.json
-rw-r--r--    1 jbarnett  1321145334   4880 Oct 17 15:42 README.txt
drwxr-xr-x   27 jbarnett  1321145334    918 Oct 17 15:43 core
-rw-r--r--    1 jbarnett  1321145334   4053 Oct 17 15:43 web.config
drwxr-xr-x    3 jbarnett  1321145334    102 Oct 17 15:43 themes
drwxr-xr-x    5 jbarnett  1321145334    170 Oct 17 15:43 sites
-rw-r--r--    1 jbarnett  1321145334   1292 Oct 17 15:43 robots.txt
drwxr-xr-x    3 jbarnett  1321145334    102 Oct 17 15:43 profiles
-rw-r--r--    1 jbarnett  1321145334    564 Oct 17 15:43 index.php
-rw-r--r--    1 jbarnett  1321145334    999 Oct 17 15:43
   example.gitignore
drwxr-xr-x    5 jbarnett  1321145334    170 Oct 17 15:44 modules
```

You can see README.txt has the permissions -rw-r--r-- next to it on the far left. If the first letter is a d, this signifies that it is not in fact a file but a directory; if the first character on the far left is a dash symbol (-), then it is in fact a file. The next three letters define the permissions for the file for the currently logged-in Linux user. The next three letters define permissions for the group. And the final three letters define the permissions for "other"—the rest of the world outside the group that owns the file and he or she who is not the currently logged-in user.

Now for what the numbers mean: 4, 2, 1—these numbers correspond to the permissions for read-write-execute, respectively. The 4 is read (the right to open and read the file), the 2 is write (the permission to write and make changes to the file), and the 1 is execute (if the file is a command, the right to execute the file). If the group has all three permissions, its members have 4+2+1 = 7. So, for example, if I type #chmod 070, the user has no permissions, the group has all permissions possible, and everyone else has no permissions.

There is another system to set permissions as well, which is common, although I use the numbers 4+2+1 myself. You can add read, write, and execute permissions to a file for the user (whoever is currently logged in) with the following:

```
chmod +rwx "filename.txt"
```

You can add just execute permission for the user (whoever is currently logged in) with the following:

```
chmod +x "filename.txt"
```

You can likewise add permissions to the group or all other users by prefixing with g or o, for example,

```
chmod g+wx
```

This would give the group that owns the file both write and execute permissions. If you didn't use the plus sign (+) but typed in chmod g-wx, then this would subtract the write and execute permissions from the group-level permissions.

Take a look at Figure 17-7. You can again see the ls -l command on filename.txt.

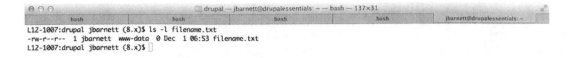

```
L12-1007:drupal jbarnett (8.x)$ ls -l filename.txt
-rw-r--r-- 1 jbarnett www-data  0 Dec  1 06:53 filename.txt
L12-1007:drupal jbarnett (8.x)$
```

Figure 17-7. *The file permissions currently on filename.txt*

Figure 17-8 shows the result if I instead issue the command chmod 777 filename.txt. Notice in the far left the permissions read -rwxrwxrwx since now we've given all permissions to all users at the user level, the group level, and the other (all other users) level.

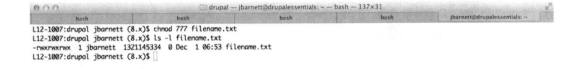

```
L12-1007:drupal jbarnett (8.x)$ chmod 777 filename.txt
L12-1007:drupal jbarnett (8.x)$ ls -l filename.txt
-rwxrwxrwx 1 jbarnett 1321145334  0 Dec  1 06:53 filename.txt
L12-1007:drupal jbarnett (8.x)$
```

Figure 17-8. *The file permissions on filename.txt after running chmod 777 filename.txt*

If I type chmod og-rwx filename.txt to remove read, write, and execute permissions for both the other and group users, the result—after typing ls -l—would look like the display in Figure 17-9.

```
L12-1007:drupal jbarnett (8.x)$ chmod og-rwx filename.txt
L12-1007:drupal jbarnett (8.x)$ ls -l filename.txt
-rwx------  1 jbarnett  1321145334  0 Dec  1 06:53 filename.txt
L12-1007:drupal jbarnett (8.x)$
```

Figure 17-9. *Removing some permissions from a file*

To change the group that owns a file, you would use

```
chgrp www-data filename.txt
```

The preceding command would change the group ownership for filename.txt to be www-data (the name of the group needed to serve up web files on an Apache server without permission errors). If you are a member of a group that has permissions to a file but are not the owner of the file, you will still be able to manage the file depending on what file permissions are given to the file at the group level. If at the group level you have read, write, and execute permissions, then even though you're not the owner of the file you still have full permissions. To add users to a group, if you have root access to the box or sudo access (you're in the list of users with sudo rights—which means you have root/administer level status—you can edit the /etc/group file to add folks to groups.

To change the owner of a file you would use

```
chown student2 filename.txt
```

The preceding code changes the user who owns the file to be student2.

You can search for a file with the following command:

```
find . -name filename.txt
```

The find command can also take wildcard characters.

```
find . -name file*
```

The preceding code would find all files that start with file as the first four letters, like filename.txt, filename.php, filename.html, or filezilla.txt.

Searching for Specific Files

One of my favorite commands, which is really useful, is grep.

```
grep -lri "James" *
```

This command searches all files recursively starting in the present directory for any files that contain the word James in them. You can omit the l in the command and it will list more than just filenames; it will also show you the context of where it found "James" in the file. Also you can omit the i to make the search case sensitive. You can omit the r from the command and the search will no longer be recursive through all files, and all files within subdirectories under the present directory.

These are some of the most basic, most common, and most important Linux commands, and this should take you pretty far in being effective in your work with Linux. There are whole courses available in Linux administration, but you would be surprised how far you can get just with the preceding knowledge.

Creating Shell Scripts

You can also create "shell scripts," which allow you to put a bunch of Linux commands in a series to run one after another. And there are looping structures and other features you find in programming languages available when shell scripting. Here is an example shell script in my Mac Vim editor which loops through all files with the .txt extension and replaces any instances of the word "needle" in the files with the word "haystack" (see Figure 17-10).

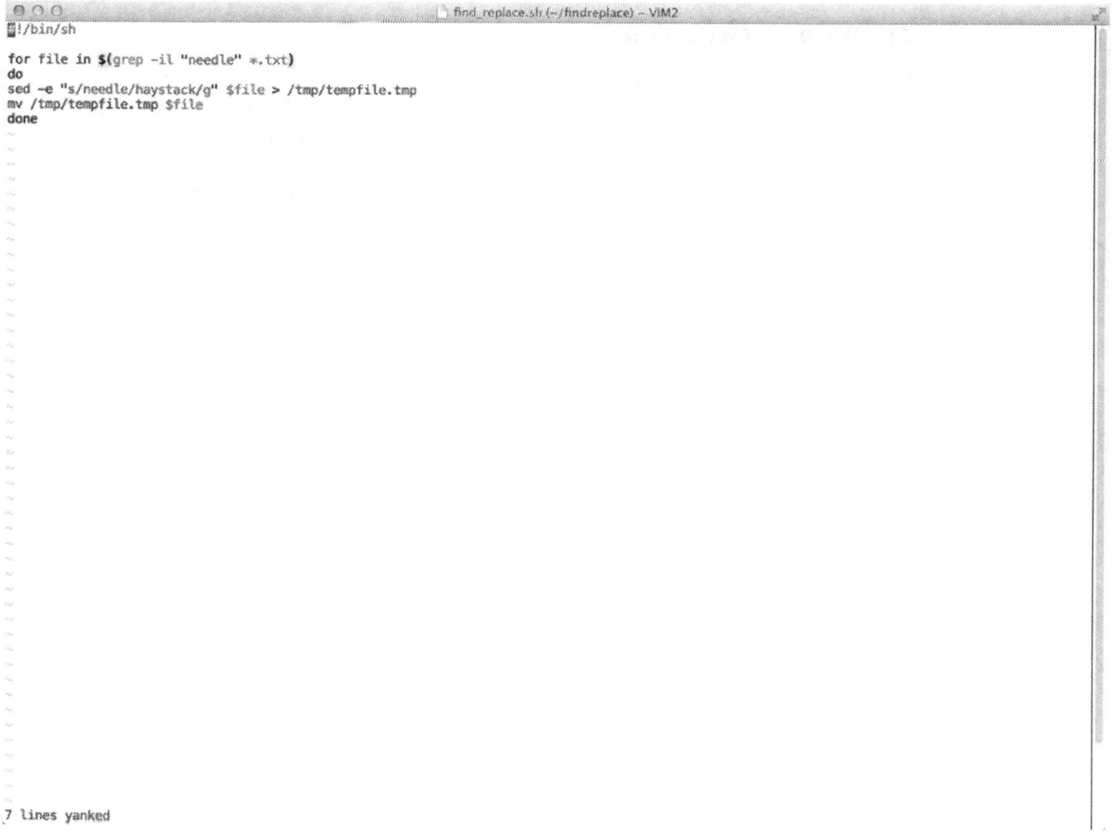

```
#!/bin/sh

for file in $(grep -il "needle" *.txt)
do
sed -e "s/needle/haystack/g" $file > /tmp/tempfile.tmp
mv /tmp/tempfile.tmp $file
done
~
~
~
~
~
~
~
~
~
~
~
~
~
~
~
~
~
~
~
~
~
~
~
~
~
~
~
~
~
~
~
~
~
7 lines yanked
```

Figure 17-10. *A linux shell script*

The name of this shell script file is find_replace.sh. To run this shell script on the command line, type

sh find_replace.sh

You can, of course, call your shell script file anything you like and then just give it the sh extension. To run your script, type

sh filename.sh

You'll notice at the top of my shell scripts I put in the following line:

#!/bin/sh

This code defines which Linux shell to run, as each Linux shell has minor variations on the syntax and commands it takes. Actually, even on the command line, you can switch shells. I usually use the bash shell because if you start typing a command and press the Tab key it will often autocomplete what you're about to type.

Editing Files on a Linux Box

When you want to edit a file on a Linux box, you have a few options. If it's your local Mac, then you can use whatever editor you like. All editors can edit local files quite well. But if your file is on a remote Linux machine, your options are a bit more limited. You can use an editor like Komodo Edit, which allows you to edit remote files (files not located on your own computer), and you can connect via sftp protocol, which some editors support. But you also might find yourself wanting to just make a few quick edits. This section shows you how to do that using Komodo Edit and Vim.

Editing Files with Komodo Edit

If you want to use the Komodo editor to edit local windows, local Mac, or remote Linux files, you would first open up the Komodo editor. You'll see a screen that looks like the one in Figure 17-11.

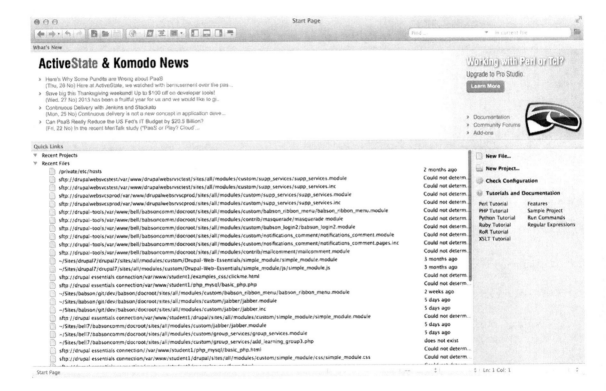

Figure 17-11. *Using Komodo Edit to edit Linux files*

Then once Komodo Edit is open, you'll want to open up the file browser, which you can learn how to do by looking at Figure 17-12.

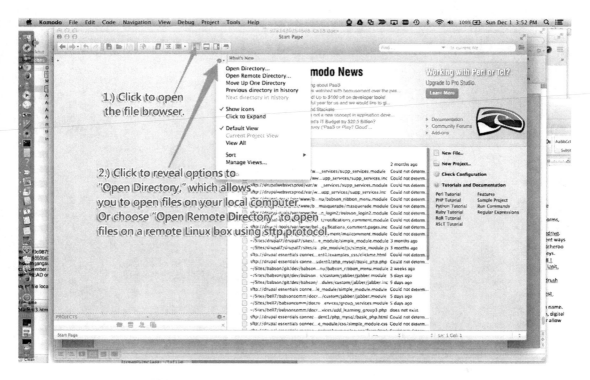

Figure 17-12. Opening a file browser in Komodo Edit to open a local or remote file

Once you have the file browser open, you can click Open Directory and easily browse for a local file on your Mac or Windows machine to edit.

If you want to open a remote file on a Linux box, you need to configure an sftp connection first. Take a look at Figure 17-13 to see how to configure an sftp connection to a remote Linux box.

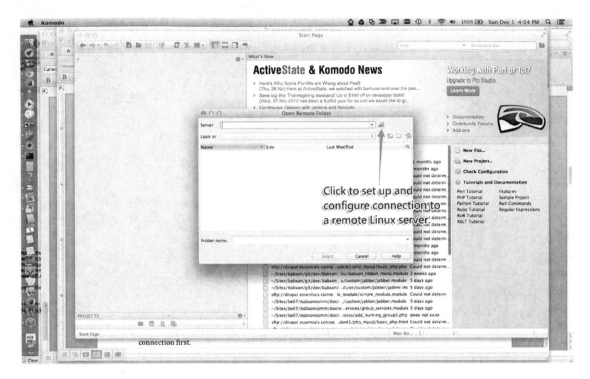

Figure 17-13. *Configuring Komodo Edit to edit a remote file*

Then once you click the icon to configure your sftp connection, you'll see the screen shown in Figure 17-14.

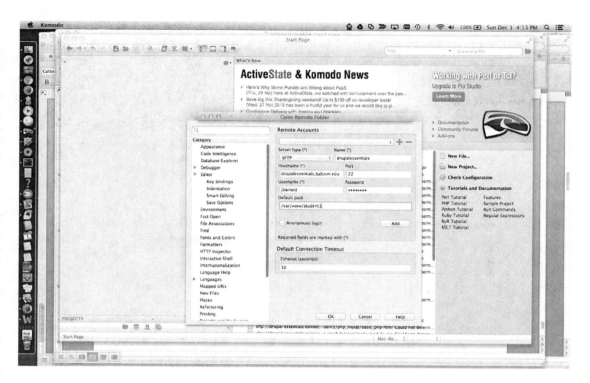

Figure 17-14. *Configuring an sftp connection in Komodo Edit to edit remote Linux files*

You can see I've put in the hostname of my Linux machine, which is `drupalessentials.babson.edu`. I put in 22 as the port, which is the default port for sftp connections. I also provided the username and password to connect with, and I provided the default directory path to open files within, which I put in as `/var/www/student1`. I also put in the name of the connection as `drupalessentials`, because the Komodo editor will save the connection for later use under this name. When you're done, click the Add button so that this connection will be saved for later use. Then choose your new connection, as shown in Figure 17-15.

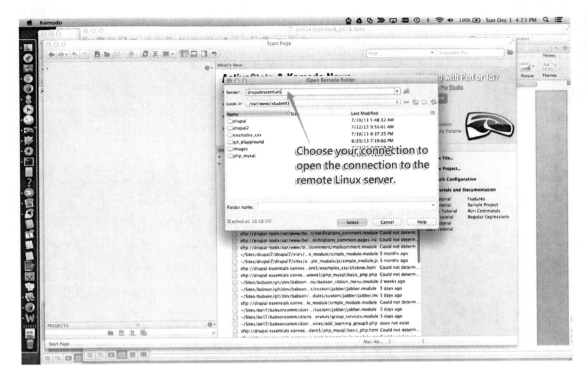

Figure 17-15. *Choosing your already saved, configured remote connection*

Now you'll see the default remote directory you configured to open, in the left pane of your Komodo editor. You can choose files to edit by clicking them in the left pane; the files will open in the main pane of the editor on the right (see Figures 17-16 and 17-17).

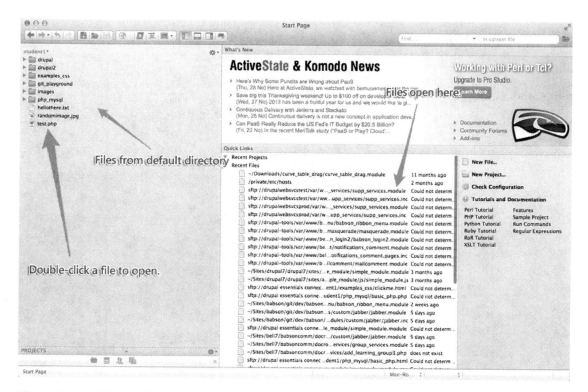

Figure 17-16. *Picking a file to edit from the remote directory, a local file directory will display this way as well and files can be opened in the right pane of the editor in the same manner*

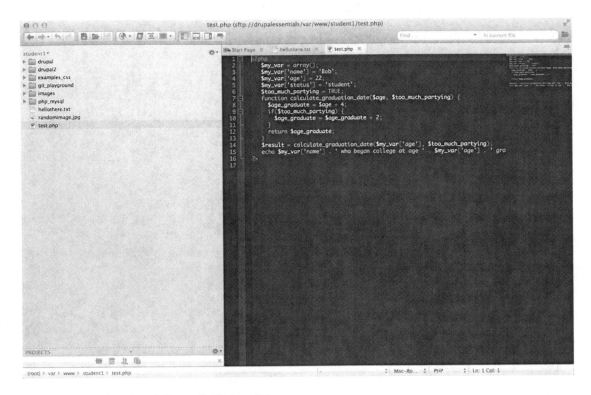

Figure 17-17. *The selected file available for editing*

You can see I've double-clicked the `test.php` file on the left and the file has opened for editing on the right side. You can make your edits and then save your file just as you would in Microsoft Word or any other editor you're used to. The file with your changes will be saved on your local computer or remote computer, depending on where you opened the file from.

Opening Files with VIM

You can also edit files directly on the remote Linux box using a program called vi editor. There a few other choices as well, like emacs, but I favor vi editor. Opening files right on the remote Linux box you've connected to via SSH protocol using Putty or the Mac Terminal can be great for a quick edit, rather than having to hook up your more bulky editor like Komodo Edit.

vi is annoying, geeky, and cool all at the same time! (You can tell hard-core programmers you prefer vi as your editor and they will know you are one of them and are hard core!) I actually use VIM, which is a slightly more graphical and friendly version of vi, over 50% of the time. Once you know it, it is very powerful and you probably won't want to use anything else, but there is a learning curve. I'm going to stick primarily to vi in this tutorial, but you can download vim (or the Mac version mvim) and play around with it.

When you open a file with vim, you type

```
vi filename.txt
```

The file opens for editing, as shown in Figure 17-18.

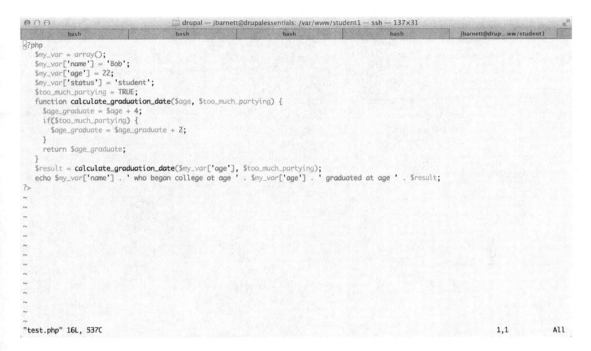

```
[?php
  $my_var = array();
  $my_var['name'] = 'Bob';
  $my_var['age'] = 22;
  $my_var['status'] = 'student';
  $too_much_partying = TRUE;
  function calculate_graduation_date($age, $too_much_partying) {
    $age_graduate = $age + 4;
    if($too_much_partying) {
      $age_graduate = $age_graduate + 2;
    }
    return $age_graduate;
  }
  $result = calculate_graduation_date($my_var['age'], $too_much_partying);
  echo $my_var['name'] . ' who began college at age ' . $my_var['age'] . ' graduated at age ' . $result;
?>
~
~
~
~
~
~
~
~
~
~
~
"test.php" 16L, 537C                                                    1,1          All
```

Figure 17-18. *Opening a file for editing using vi*

Once you've opened a file with the vi editor, you can use the arrow keys on the keyboard to move around the screen. Initially you're in "command mode" and you can press a key like the "i" key (a command) to go into insert mode and begin typing. Then you can press the escape key again to get out of insert mode and back into command mode. You can then press the "x" key to delete a character or "dd" to delete a whole line.

When in command mode—rather than insert mode (you can always press the escape key to make sure you're in command mode)—you can press ":w" to save the file or ":w!" to "force save" if the editor gives you any warnings about saving. You can also type ":q" to quit the file or ":q!" to force quit to avoid any warnings. Or you can combine these two commands and type ":wq" to save (write) the file and then quit right afterward, or you can type ":wq!" to force a write (save of the file) and then quit.

The vi editor is not known for being very user friendly, but it is still loved by many. As I said, for the desktop there is a very popular version of vi called VIM (`www.vim.org/`) and there's also a Mac version called mvim (`https://code.google.com/p/macvim/`). This version of vi is more user friendly and has tons of options and integrations with other libraries and projects to aid with code completion, error checking, integration with Git version control, and so on. I prefer mvim and use it 99% of the time when editing a file. I usually recommend Komodo Edit for newbies but it's a powerful full-featured editor in its own right as well, certainly not second best.

Summary

In this chapter, you learned how to connect remotely to your Linux box using either a Mac or a Windows machine. You then discovered the most important Linux commands so you can find your way around a Linux box. In addition, you learned how to list files and directories, and you worked with permissions, group ownership, and individual ownership of files. Commands like find and grep are essential to help you find what you're looking for and grep in particular is great if you see a word on your web page and need to modify that page where you see that word or words appear. You then can use the grep command to try to figure out what files you need to modify to make the changes you need to make. Finally, you explored the various methods of editing files either directly on the Linux box using vi editor or by connecting with an editor with sftp capabilities like Komodo Edit.

CHAPTER 18

■ ■ ■

Publishing Your Site to a Production Linux Box

Let's imagine you've set up your site locally and it's running great. But now you would like to move your site to a production box in the cloud at Amazon, Rackspace, Linode, Digital Ocean, or any number of other cloud-hosting providers. These vendors will, out in cyberspace (out in the cloud), set up a Linux box for you on which to run your web site. Often to really follow best practices you'll set up at least two Linux boxes and a load balancer to balance traffic between the two (or more) Linux boxes. This setup will also give you redundancy in case one of the Linux servers has any problems.

This chapter shows how to set up Drupal on a Linux (Ubuntu) box, including how to set it up in the cloud, but much of the instruction is applicable to any Ubuntu Linux box. For this chapter you'll be setting up a fictitious site to run on a single Linux box. The single Linux box will run Apache and MySQL. Most smaller sites run using only a single web server. Larger sites often will move the database off of the box running the web server to alleviate competition for resources between the web server and the database.

■ **Note** In this chapter I'll spin up a box out in the cloud using `Linode.com`. The process for setting up a Linux box at Linode is very much like it is at Amazon, Rackspace, or any other cloud-hosting service. Recently I trolled `drupal.org` pages, looking for a better cloud service, and I saw a lot of Drupalers raving about Linode and Digital Ocean. The reviewers were saying these two vendors were dirt cheap, and comparatively this is absolutely true. I've been using Linode for my personal blog for almost a year, and it beats the pants off of a larger, more famous competitor. Going through how to set up a Linux box at Linode should prepare you to understand the process whenever you decide to spin up a Linux box in the cloud. I've had great luck with Linode—it's very reliable, and pretty fast hardware is available for a fraction of the cost.

Setting Up the Linux Box in the Cloud

Before you can begin the setup process, you need to go to `www.linode.com` and create an account. This process is fairly simple.

I already have a Linode account, but for the purposes of this chapter, I'm going to pay for a new Linux box ($20 a month as of the time of this writing for 1 GB of RAM, a pretty good price). As you can see in Figure 18-1 Linode has a few choices of what size Linux box to spin up. I've chosen Linode 1024, which is the cheapest option and comes with 1 GB of memory (1,024 mb) and 48 GB of hard-drive storage.

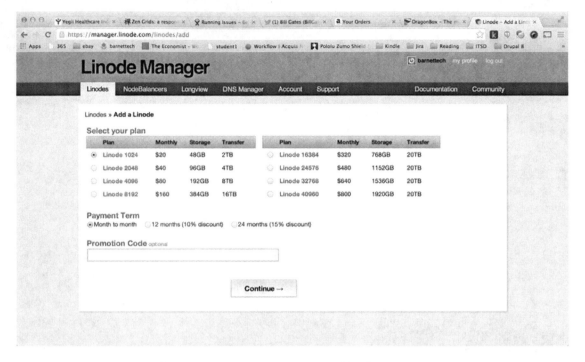

Figure 18-1. *Choosing how large a Linux box to spin up at* www.linode.com

I run my simple blog (www.barnettech.com) using Linode's service. My blog has only one authenticated user (one user who needs to log in); I log in as the admin, and I use a Linode Linux box with 1 GB of ram. It's been pretty speedy, and I've had no performance problems. If you get tons of traffic or have a lot of traffic especially for authenticated users, you will need a beefier box.

After you select your plan, click Continue. You'll then see screens similar to those shown in Figures 18-2 and 18-3.

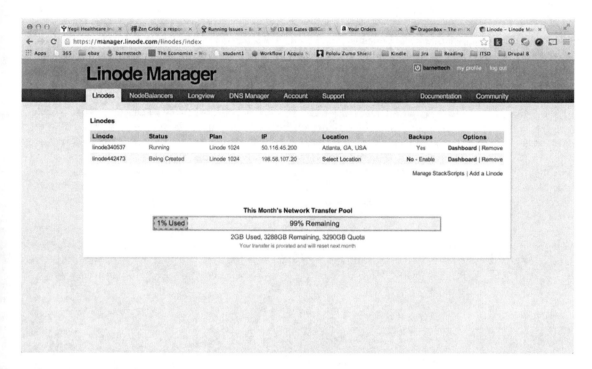

Figure 18-2. *The status of this newly purchased Linux box (Linode box) is "Being Created"*

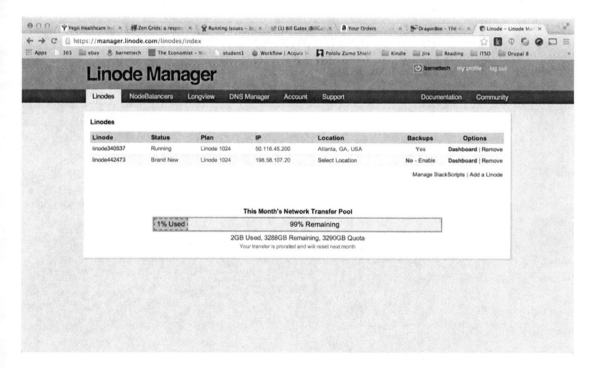

Figure 18-3. *The new Linux box successfully created with "Brand New" status*

In Figure 18-3 you can see the newly created Linux box is in "Brand New" status and there is a link to select a location. I'll pick Atlanta, GA because most of my users are on the East Coast. Actually I've looked at Google Analytics and I get a lot of traffic from California, not surprising with Silicon Valley being such an active technological hub. I've actually heard from expert sources that the infrastructure connecting the East Coast to the West Coast (in the United States) is so good using speed-of-light fiber communications that often you're better off serving the West Coast with a server in an East Coast server farm. I know my Linux box in Atlanta will do fine serving up web pages fast even to Californian visitors to my web site.

As you can also see in Figure 18-3, you can turn on site backups, which I recommend. Although Linode charges an extra $5 a month for its nightly backup service, this is still an excellent price for 1 GB of RAM and a private Linux server; most other services charge much more. One disadvantage, at the time of this writing, is that Linode only accepts support tickets submitted through the Web; Linode doesn't have a phone number, and it doesn't have an instant chat support service, something some other services have (usually the more support you get, the higher the price, understandably). For me this is fine; I'd rather pay less, and I prefer to get paid to support Drupal and Linux rather than pay someone else.

After choosing the location of your Linux box, you'll be prompted with the screen shown in Figure 18-4. You need to choose the Linux flavor to use, and you need to set the root (the primary administrator user on a Linux box is called the root user) password. There are some other options, but you can leave the defaults for most of the fields. In this case I will choose Ubuntu as my Linux flavor, and I'll set my root password.

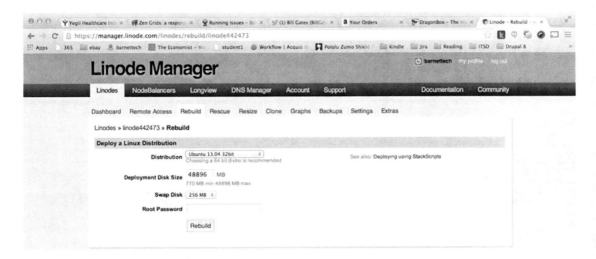

Figure 18-4. *Configuring a Linux box to use Ubuntu and setting the root password*

After you click the Rebuild button, shown in Figure 18-4, the box starts to get built (rebuilt) on the Linux flavor you chose and with the root password you chose.

After the screen shown in Figure 18-4 you'll be taken to your Linode dashboard (see Figure 18-5). Toward the top, on the dashboard, click the Boot button to power on your Linux box. Once the box has booted you'll see graphs on your dashboard and other stats showing the health of the box.

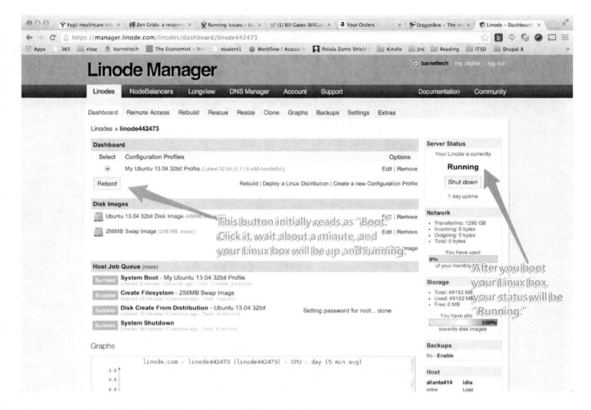

Figure 18-5. *Your Linode dashboard—you'll "boot" the box to turn it on*

With your Linux box now turned on, it's time to focus on how to connect to the Linux box in the cloud via ssh.

Connecting to a New Linux Box Via SSH

In this section you use ssh to connect to the command line of the newly created Linux box. Notice in Figure 18-6 that the Linodes tab lists the IP addresses of your Linux boxes. In this case, my new Linux box has an IP address of 23.92.31.153.

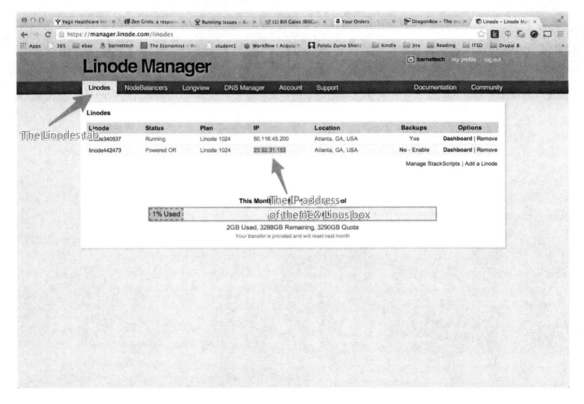

Figure 18-6. Finding the IP address of your Linux box

Using the Terminal application on a Mac or Putty on a Windows machine, locate the command line and ssh to the IP address you located (see Figures 18-7 and 18-8). In this case, I typed ssh root@23.92.31.153.

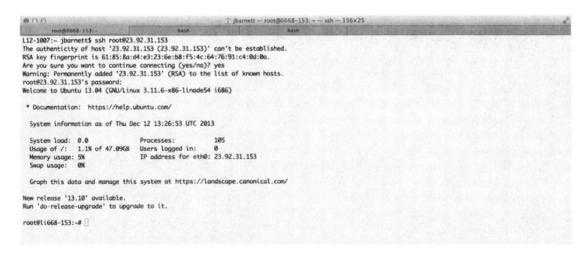

Figure 18-7. Connecting to the Linux box using the IP using the ssh protocol

Figure 18-8. *Using the Putty program—configure as shown and then click Open*

Now that you've learned to connect to a Linux box in the cloud via ssh, in the next section you'll learn to set up the full LAMP stack on your Linux box using commands on the command line.

Setting Up the LAMP Stack on an Ubuntu Linux Box

Once you've connected to the Linux box as root, you can set up the full LAMP stack and install Apache, PHP, and MySQL. Apache will serve up your web pages, MySQL will be your back-end database to store your back-end data, and PHP will be the programming language used in creating your web sites. This is, of course, the basic infrastructure that Drupal uses to function.

To set up Apache, MySQL, and PHP you will need to run each of the commands shown in the following bulleted list, one at a time. Press "Y" for yes to continue at any time when prompted on the command line after running one of these commands. When installing the mysql-server package you'll be prompted to enter the root (primary administrator account) password for MySQL; make sure you remember or write down whatever password you choose here.

- `apt-get update`
- `sudo apt-get install apache2`
- `apt-get install mysql-server`
- `apt-get install php5 libapache2-mod-php5`
- `/etc/init.d/apache2 restart`

Now, open your favorite web browser and type the IP address of your new Linux box. You can buy a domain name and map it to this IP address so you can view your web site via the domain name rather than the corresponding IP address. You can buy a domain name from godaddy.com, dreamhost.com, or any number of other service providers; those vendors will have instructions to map your domain name to you IP address. For now you'll just bring up the web pages using the IP address. You should see a screen similar to the one shown in Figure 18-9, which confirms that Apache is set up and running.

Figure 18-9. *Putting the IP address of your new Linux box in a web browser brings up this default Apache web page, confirming Apache was set up correctly to serve up web pages*

Next, type the following to confirm that the MySQL database installed correctly:

```
mysql -u root -ppassword
```

Use the root password you configured when prompted while installing the mysql-server package. This will connect you to your MySQL database from the Linux command line (see Figure 18-10).

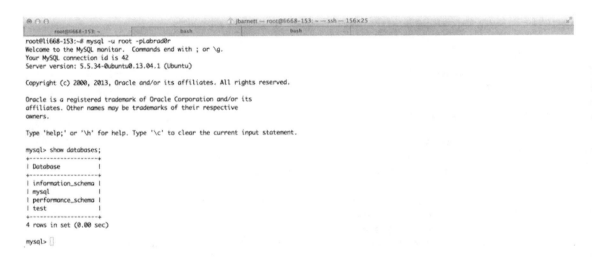

Figure 18-10. *Connecting to the newly installed MySQL database and confirming it's operational*

Installing git for Version Controlling Your Code Base

Installing git is fairly simple. On the Linux command prompt, simply type the following and press the "Y" key to confirm you want to proceed with the installation when prompted:

```
apt-get install git
```

Installing Drush

Now it's time to install Drush on your Ubuntu Linux box. Drush is the Drupal command-line tool which provides many operations to make Drupal much easier to administer and interact with, all from the command line. Drush allows you from the command line to create users, add roles to user accounts, clear the cache, etc. Drush code is managed using Github: `https://github.com/drush-ops/drush/`. The true Drupal geek will, in my opinion, tell you to install Drush by first cloning the git repository. This way you can always easily update to the latest version of git and still check out an older branch of git as well. (This approach can be useful if the latest cutting-edge version is something you want to try but is still buggy and you want to revert later to a more stable version.) Although there are other ways to install Drush, you're going to get the Drush code using git.

Run the following commands in order:

```
cd /usr/share
git clone https://github.com/drush-ops/drush/ drush
cd drush
ln -s /usr/share/drush/drush /usr/bin/drush
```

Now when you go to any directory as root and type `drush`, you can confirm it's working. You'll see a screen that looks like the one shown in Figure 18-11 with the Drush usage information.

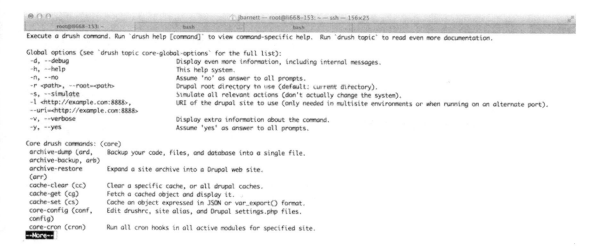

Figure 18-11. *Confirmation that Drush is running*

When I typed `drush | more` and `drush help`, usage information came up, as you can see in Figure 18-11. When you type a Linux command and "pipe" it to `more` (you type in | more), it will paginate the results, so it doesn't scroll off the screen too quickly to read. The | character is called a "pipe," and it allows you to chain Linux commands together to have commands after the pipe character act on the previous pieces of the Linux command.

Now that you've set up your Linux box with LAMP, in the next section you'll take a look at getting your first web pages served up on the Linux server.

Putting Up Your First Web Pages

Now you're ready to put up your first simple web page. Change directories to the Apache root directory, where you put your files to be served up as web pages by Apache, by typing the following:

```
cd /var/www
```

Now type in the `ls` command, and you'll see there's one file in there called `index.html`. Edit this file (using vi or another editor). And, yes, we found the file that Apache serves up by default, showing that Apache is indeed set up correctly (see Figure 18-12).

Figure 18-12. *The `index.html` file that we saw earlier in a web browser saying "It works!"*

This `index.html` file is the HTML code behind what you saw in the browser, as seen earlier in Figure 18-9. So now, play around if you like with changing the text of this `index.html` file. If you bring up the IP address of this Linux box in your browser, you'll see that you've successfully been able to make changes to this web page. I've simply added the text "James Barnett was here in 2013" to the `index.html` file found in the `.../var/www` directory which is the root folder of the Apache web server installation (see Figure 18-13).

Figure 18-13. *I've edited the `index.html` file to show that my changes will also show up in my web browser*

You've now served up your first simple web page. The next section covers setting up Drupal on the Linux server.

Installing Drupal

In this section you'll learn how to install Drupal on your Ubuntu Linux box. This process is definitely more involved than simply using the DAMP installer, which was created specifically to make it much simpler for local development work. Make sure you're still in the `.../var/www` directory—you can type pwd to see what present working directory you're within to confirm it. Then simply type the following:

```
drush dl drupal
```

Now, type `ls`. You should see the directory `drupal-8.24` and, within this new directory, all of your Drupal files. Don't worry if your directory name is slightly different; the `8.24` in the directory name represents the current version of Drupal. The number "8" represents which major version of Drupal it is, and the numbers after the period represent which minor version of Drupal 8 it is.

After Drupal is downloaded by Drush, it's helpful to rename the directory to something meaningful. In this case I'm calling the directory `drupaltest`, so I issue this command:

```
mv drupal-8.24 drupaltest
```

This command allows me to set up other instances of Drupal on this web server without worrying about using Drush to download Drupal and then overwriting my already existing Drupal directory, which would blow away any changes I'd made to the already existing instance of Drupal within its code base. Later you'll rename this directory to match the name of the domain name you'll hook up to this web site.

Now go to the URL (uniform resource locator) `http://23.92.31.153/drupaltest` (your IP address number will vary). You should see the screen shown in Figure 18-14, waiting for you to start the Drupal installation process via the GUI (graphical user interface).

Figure 18-14. *With Drupal downloaded to the Linux box, the installation setup process can begin*

I chose English as my language, and then I chose to set up the "standard" installation profile." Easy so far. But then I get to a screen showing any requirements problems. And as I tell my students, errors or alerts like these are your friends; they make it easy to know what you need to do next to succeed. Take a look at Figure 18-15, and then we'll address each problem to get Drupal up and running.

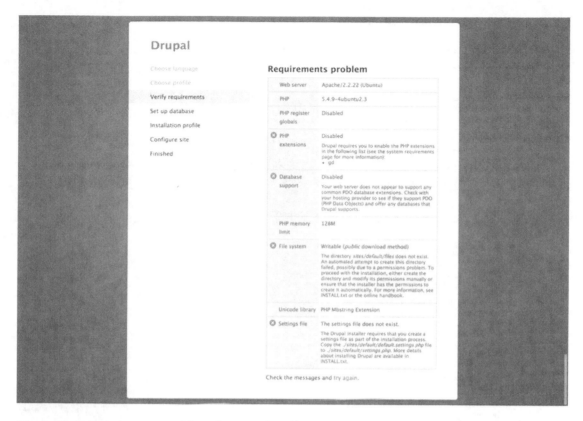

Figure 18-15. *Requirements problems that must be addressed to finish the setup process*

First, next to the alert on missing PHP extensions, it says we need to install the gd library. To do this, type `apt-get install php5-gd` and then press "Y" to confirm you want to install the extension.

Next, type `apt-get install php5-gd php-db php5-mysql` to clear up the error about database support problems. I also edited the `.../etc/php5/apache2/php.ini` file. I found the line `memory_limit = 128M`, and added two lines under it.

```
memory_limit = 128M
extension="pdo.so"
extension="pdo_mysql.so"
```

Then, to solve the last two requirements problems, I first changed directories to the `...site/default` directory in my Drupal installation. I then created a `settings.php` file by copying the `default.settings.php.default` file. Next I created a `files` directory for Drupal to store files within (pictures, attachments to nodes, etc.). And finally I changed the permissions of the `settings.php` and `files` directories.

Run the following commands as described in the order shown:

```
cd /var/www/drupaltest/sites/default
cp default.settings.php settings.php
mkdir files
cd /var/www/drupaltest
chmod a+w sites/default
chmod a+w sites/default/settings.php
chmod a+w sites/default/files
```

Now when you refresh your screen or click "try again" on the web page that showed the requirements problems, you should be able to move on to the next step. You'll see the screen shown in Figure 18-16.

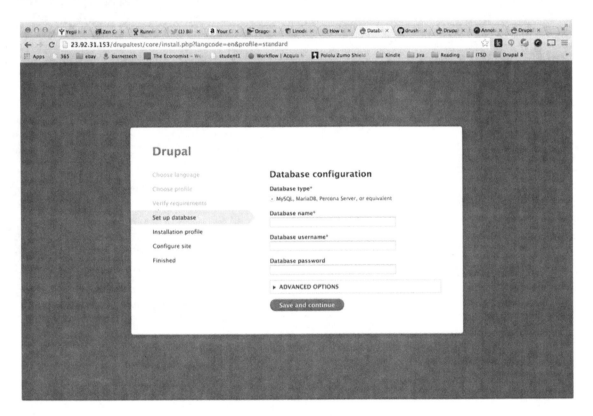

Figure 18-16. *Installing Drupal and configuring which MySQL database to use*

Next you'll need to create a database for Drupal to use. On the command line, log in to MySQL with the command you issued earlier.

```
mysql -u root -ppassword
```

Use the root password you created earlier (notice "password" is the password and is appended right after –p with no space in between when issuing this command). Now, create a new database, which Drupal will use, by typing the following command:

```
create database drupaltest;
```

Then type

```
use drupaltest;
```

You can name your database anything you like; I've named mine drupaltest.

Now you're going to create a new user for MySQL so your Drupal instance doesn't have to connect using the root user account. Issue the following command at the MySQL command prompt:

```
GRANT SELECT, INSERT, UPDATE, DELETE, CREATE, DROP, INDEX, ALTER
on drupaltest.* To drupaluser@localhost IDENTIFIED by
'mypassword';
```

This will create the user named drupaluser, with this user's password set to mypassword. It also grants this user rights to the drupaltest database.

Next, log in as this user to make sure all went well. First type exit, press the Enter key, and then log in again to MySQL with the following command:

```
mysql -u drupaluser -pmypassword
```

Now you are logged in using the drupaluser account. You can make sure this user has access to the drupaltest database by typing the following:

```
use drupaltest;
```

Now you're ready to plug in your database name and database username into the Drupal installation GUI, as seen in Figure 18-17. You don't need to touch anything in the Advanced Options section.

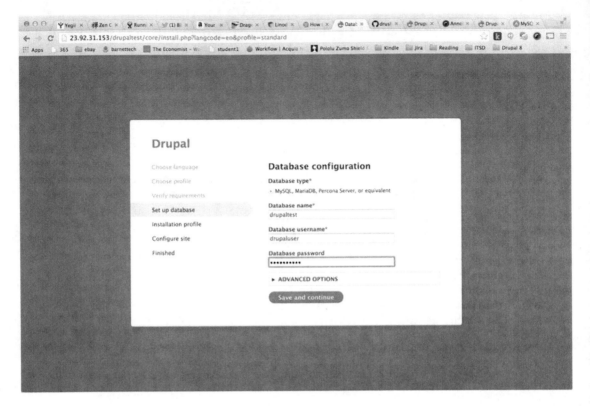

Figure 18-17. *Put the Drupal database name and MySQL username you just created into the GUI to continue the installation process*

Drupal will begin installing itself (see Figure 18-18).

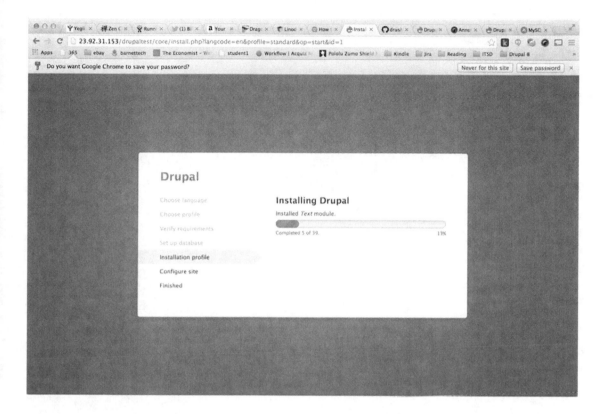

Figure 18-18. *Drupal proceeding to install itself once everything is configured properly*

Figure 18-19 shows you the last page of input needed to complete the configuration of your Drupal installation. You'll input the site name, and you'll set the admin account name and password (make sure to write this down!).

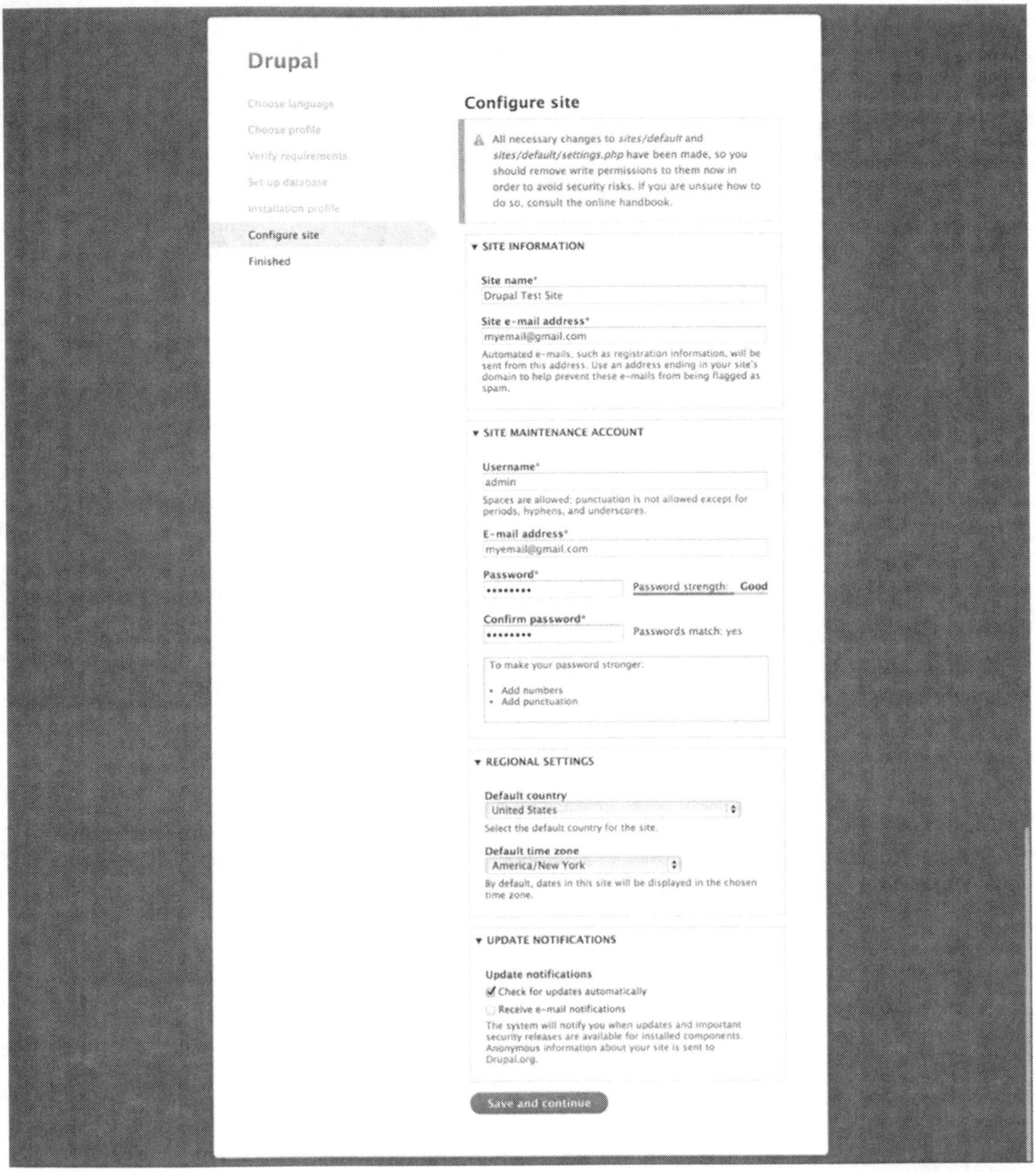

Figure 18-19. *Last installation configuration screen, asking for you to set the name of the site, an admin maintenance password, country settings, etc*

■ **Caution**   For better security, don't choose an admin username of `admin` or `administrator` or anything that someone might guess to try to break into your site. For most sites this isn't much of a worry. Most of us just have to worry more about spammers and annoying marketing firms trying to post links to their clients' products.

Finally, you can click the "Save and continue" button. You should now see the screen shown in Figure 18-20, verifying that installation of Drupal is complete.

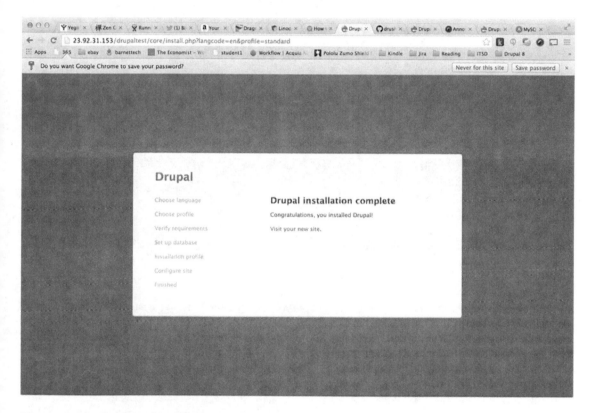

Figure 18-20. *The Drupal installation is now complete*

When you click the "Visit your new site" link, you'll be taken to the front page of your new Drupal site (see Figure 18-21).

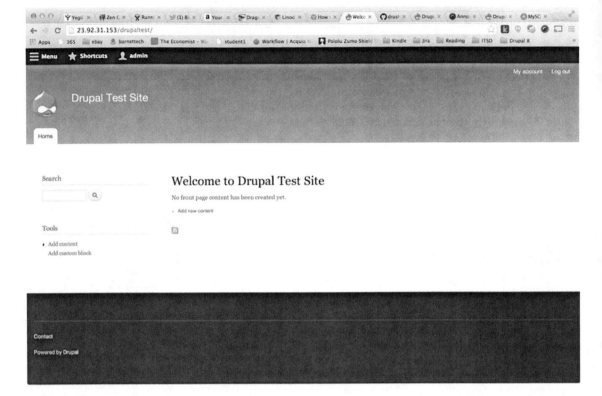

Figure 18-21. The front page of the new Drupal site

Before proceeding, let's secure a few of the files we changed permissions on earlier so that Drupal could install itself. Changing these permissions back to being more secure is an essential security step, so I want to make sure to mention that you should run a few commands before continuing. Run the following commands from the Drupal docroot directory (`.../var/www/drupaltest` in our example site):

```
chmod go-w sites/default
chmod go-w sites/default/settings.php
```

So now you've set up Drupal on a Linux box in the cloud, but there is still a big problem: your URL is currently `http://23.92.31.153/drupaltest/` (your IP address will differ), which isn't very user friendly. To fix this, you'll set up a domain to point to your Drupal installation so folks can visit the site using a nice pretty URL, rather than an IP address followed by the subdirectory where you've put your Drupal files.

Getting a URL for Your New Drupal Site

In order to get a URL for your new Drupal site, you'll need to have a domain. It so happens that I already have a domain (which I haven't had time to build a site for): `www.mypersonalvillage.com`.

■ **Note**   If you want to buy a domain there are plenty of sites that sell them, including godaddy.com and dreamhost.com. If you google "Buy domain name," you'll be inundated with links to vendor sites where you can buy a domain.

Using the domain I set up at DreamHost, www.mypersonalvillage.com, I will show you how to configure that domain to connect to my Linode Linux box out in the cloud, so that my Drupal site will load up not only a visitor who goes to http://23.92.31.153/drupaltest/ but also when the visitor goes to www.mypersonalvillage.com.

When I log in to my DreamHost account, I see the screen shown in Figure 18-22.

Figure 18-22.   *The dashboard at DreamHost*

We're now going to configure the DNS (domain name service) for our domain. (DNS is a mapping service for computers to map domain names to computers and their IP addresses where files are served.) From the DreamHost dashboard, I click Manage Domains. Then on the next screen, I click the DNS link next to the domain I'm interested in—in this case, that domain is http://mypersonalvillage.com.

Then I see the screen in Figure 18-23. I put in the DNS nameservers for Linode, which I researched on its site. They are ns1.linode.com, ns2.linode.com, ns3.linode.com, and ns4.linode.com. (Each site usually has instructions.) At Linode on the dashboard, there's a DNS tab with lots of info; we'll be going to that tab shortly to configure things on the Linode side as well.

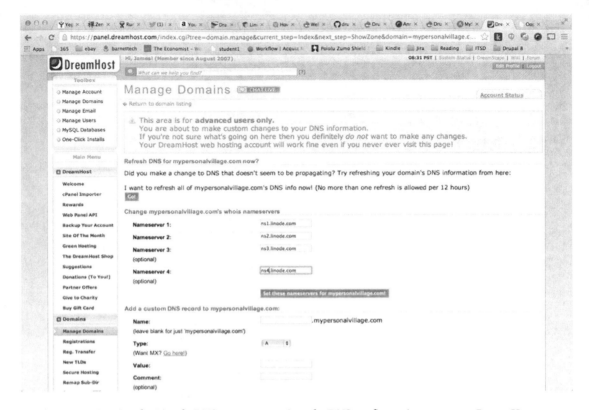

Figure 18-23. *Putting the Linode DNS server names into the DNS configuration screens at DreamHost*

In the `.../etc/apache2/apache2.conf` file, add the following line at the bottom of the file using your IP address for your new Linux box, not mine of course (see Figure 18-24):

```
NameVirtualHost 23.92.31.153:80
```

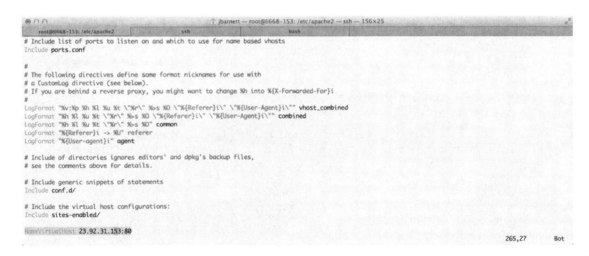

Figure 18-24. *Adding the line* `NameVirtualHost 23.92.31.153:80` *to the end of the* `apache2.conf` *file*

Make sure to put :80 after your IP address in this new line you add to apache2.conf, which sets the system to look at port 80.

Next, change your directory to ...etc/apache2/sites-available. In this directory make a file called mypersonalvillage.com—be sure to replace this domain name with the one you're using. In this file put in the following:

```
<VirtualHost *:80>
  ServerName mypersonalvillage.com
  DocumentRoot /var/www/mypersonalvillage.com
    <Directory /var/www/mypersonalvillage.com\>
       Options +Indexes +FollowSymLinks +ExecCGI
       DirectoryIndex index.php
       AllowOverride All
       Order allow,deny
       Allow from all
    </Directory>
</VirtualHost>

<VirtualHost *:80>
  ServerName www.mypersonalvillage.com
  DocumentRoot /var/www/mypersonalvillage.com
    <Directory /var/www/mypersonalvillage.com\>
       Options +Indexes +FollowSymLinks +ExecCGI
       DirectoryIndex index.php
       AllowOverride All
       Order allow,deny
       Allow from all
    </Directory>
</VirtualHost>
```

Make sure you save the file. You'll notice we pointed the domain to pull files from the directory ...var/www/mypersonalvillage.com, but we named our directory ...var/www/drupaltest originally. I like to name my directory the same as the domain name so I can find it easily, especially if I host more than one domain on a single Linux box (which I often do for development boxes, not production boxes).

Rename this directory ...var/www/drupaltest to ...var/www/mypersonalvillage.com with the following command (modify the command to work with your domain name):

```
mv /var/www/drupaltest /var/www/mypersonalvillage.com
```

Now we will issue the command from within the .../etc/apache2/sites-available directory.

```
a2ensite mypersonalvillage.com
```

After issuing the preceding command, I get the following response from the server:

```
Enabling site mypersonalvillage.com.
```

To activate the new configuration, you need to run:

```
service apache2 reload
```

Next, type

```
service apache2 reload
```

Then, at Linode.com, I go to https://manager.linode.com/dns and see the screen shown in Figure 18-25. Click the "Add a domain zone" link.

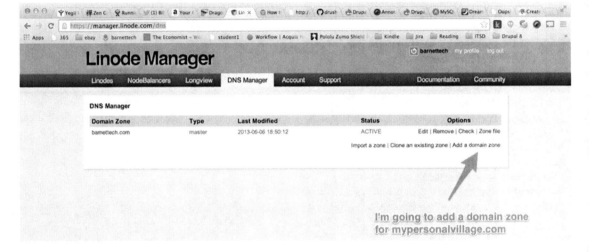

Figure 18-25. *Click to add a domain zone*

Here are the settings for the new domain zone mypersonalvillage.com, which in edit mode looks like Figure 18-26.

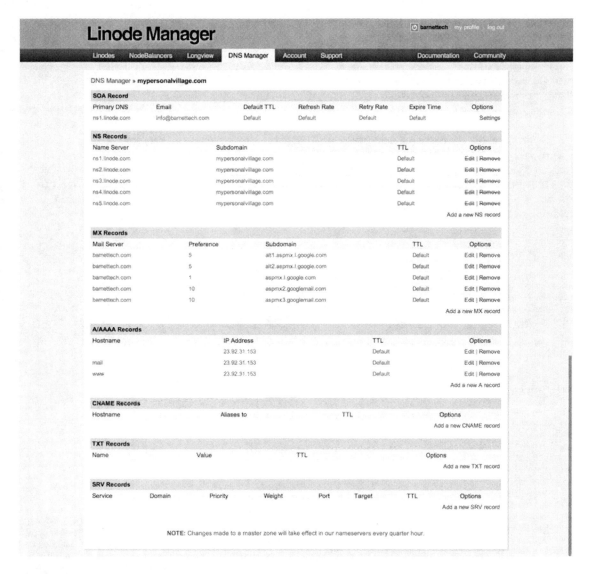

Figure 18-26. *The new domain zone at Linode.com for* mypersonalvillage.com

Whenever you make DNS changes, it can take a half hour or more for the changes to propagate over the Internet, so be patient. At the command prompt. I kept typing

nslookup www.mypersonalvillage.com.

Once the changes were in effect, I received the correct response that the IP address associated with the domain was in fact 23.92.31.153.

```
L12-1007:linode jbarnett$ nslookup mypersonalvillage.com
Server:            192.168.2.1
Address:        192.168.2.1#53

Non-authoritative answer:
Name:    mypersonalvillage.com
Address: 23.92.31.153
```

So now my web site comes up using the pretty URL http://mypersonalvillage.com/ or www.mypersonalvillage.com/. We no longer need to access the site using the IP of the web site at http://23.92.31.153/mypersonalvillage.com/.

In Figure 18-27 you can see the site loading nicely using a normal URL, www.mypersonalvillage.com, the domain name, which you're more used to using to access Internet sites, rather than using a site's IP address.

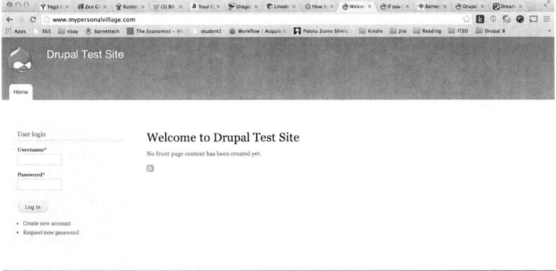

Figure 18-27. *The domain name* www.mypersonalvillage.com *working correctly to bring up the Drupal site*

Summary

This chapter covered a lot of ground with regard to learning how to set up an Ubuntu Linux box in the cloud. You set up the LAMP stack to prepare the box to run Drupal. You then installed all the packages you needed to run the Drupal stack, and you installed and set up MySQL. You created a new MySQL user to have Drupal log in as that user to connect to its MySQL back-end datastore. In MySQL you set up the new database for Drupal to use. You also handled some of the permissions problems that arise when setting up Drupal to be able to access and write to the files it needs (settings.php, for instance). You set up a domain name and configured the DNS on the site where you purchased the domain, and you set up the DNS in the hosting service's GUI where your Linux web server lives in the cloud.

The setup is not simple, but the reward for understanding how this all works is that you have a very valuable skill set. The skills to set up a Drupal site from start to finish in the cloud are considered the work of a system administrator, but I often find Drupal geeks know quite a bit about both the programming side and the system administration side, although certainly there are engineers who develop their career focusing on one side or the other. I would recommend that you know how to set up a Linux box in the cloud, and for highly secure sites, or sites that need performance tuning, let someone who's specialized in sys admin work button down the site for optimal performance and higher security—something beyond the scope of this book.

■ ■ ■

Other Ways to Install Drupal

Another common way of installing Drupal on a Mac, probably more common, is using MAMP. MAMP is a way to set up Apache, MySQL, and PHP on a Mac with one installer. The Mac comes with these items pre-installed, but they're not always up to date. I find that most developers will use MAMP or something just like it (another top developer I know uses something called Homebrew, which is also very good).

I've used the free version of MAMP for years, and it works perfectly even for professional development needs. Installation with MAMP is a bit more complicated than using DAMP, but it is useful to learn to install it this way because on a production Linux box, you won't be able to install Drupal with Acquia Dev Desktop—and setting up Drupal on MAMP is much more like setting up Drupal on a Linux box. You'll need to configure virtual hosts, you'll need to know a bit of how to navigate the Linux command line, and you'll need to manually create a MySQL database. The setup is not exactly the same as on Ubuntu (see Chapter 18), which is a popular Linux distribution for production-grade Drupal sites, but there are many steps in common.

Installing Drupal with MAMP on a Mac

To begin, go to www.mamp.info/en/index.html and download MAMP to your Mac. Then double-click the downloaded file, which will end with .dmg. At this point, run through the installer, accepting the defaults and clicking "Next" until the install is complete. When you have MAMP up and running, you'll see a screen that looks like the one in Figure A-1.

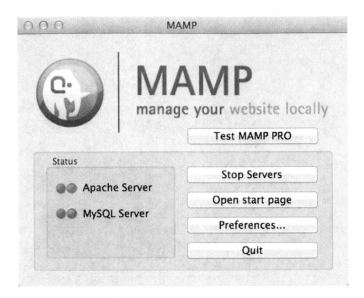

Figure A-1. *MAMP control panel*

If the lights (circles) next to MySQL Server and Apache Server are red, then Apache and MySQL have not been started yet, and the top button on the right will display "Start Servers." You can click this Start Servers button to start Apache and MySQL. After everything starts up successfully, click "Open start page." You'll see a web page pop up that looks like the one shown in Figure A-2.

Figure A-2. *MAMP web page on your localhost with useful links to MAMP tools and info*

Notice that the top tab includes useful links. The link that I use most often is a link to my system's `phpinfo` file, which provides the status of PHP, what libraries are installed for PHP, memory configuration stats for PHP, and more. In addition to the top tabs is a link to phpMyAdmin, which is an easy-to-use admin tool for managing your MySQL database. These are useful links. To bring up this MAMP start page at any given time, you can click "Open start page" from the MAMP control panel, as shown earlier in Figure A-1.

Now that MAMP is installed and PHP and MYSQL are set up, we can continue to get the Drupal install set up using MAMP.

Next we'll create a database. There are two ways to quickly create a MySQL database. First you can do it through the command line. To do this, open a terminal window on your Mac (by going to Launchpad to view all your installed applications and then type "terminal"). Figure A-3 should assist you in opening the terminal from Launchpad.

Figure A-3. *Opening the Mac terminal application*

You can also use the Spotlight on your Mac to find and open the terminal, as shown in Figure A-4.

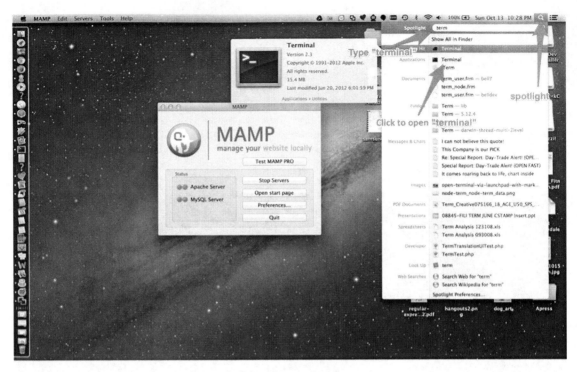

Figure A-4. *Opening the Mac terminal application from Spotlight*

Once you have the terminal open, type mysql -u root -proot at the command prompt, which is the default root password for MySQL in MAMP. (See Figure A-5.) Then once you've logged into MySQL, after typing the previous command, type create database drupal8;. You can call the database anything you like, but this example uses drupal8.

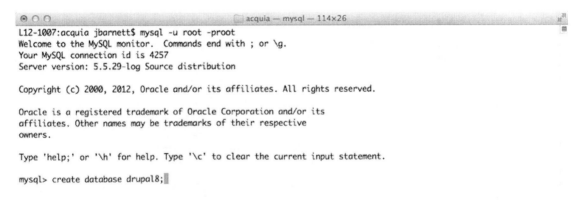

Figure A-5. *Using the Mac terminal application to log in to MySQL and create a database*

You should receive a response from MySQL that the database was created successfully.

The other way to easily create a MySQL database is with phpMyAdmin. Recall that you can open the MAMP welcome page from the MAMP control panel. In the MAMP control panel, click "Open start page." Then along the top tabs, click "phpMyAdmin." Once you click the phpMyAdmin link, you'll see a page that looks like the one in Figure A-6.

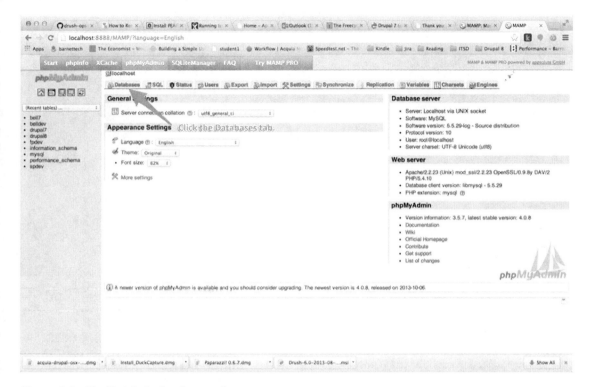

Figure A-6. *PhpMyAdmin databases tab*

Click the Databases tab and you'll see the screen shown in Figure A-7, where you can easily create the database.

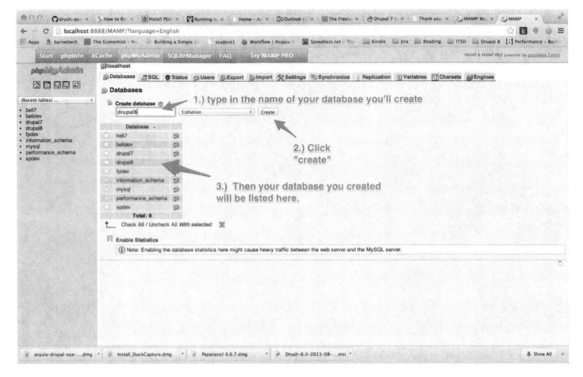

Figure A-7. *Creating a new database with PhpMyAdmin*

As Figure A-7 shows, you'll type the name of your new database and click "create." Then you'll find your database in the list of databases, ready to use.

Next we'll need to set up a virtual host. Basically a virtual host allows you to have multiple web sites all running using the same web server. Each web site will be set up with a domain name and the Apache configuration will tell the system which web files to use to serve up to that web site. Additional configuration files in Drupal will point the web site to the correct database to use.

To begin, we'll need to edit our /etc/hosts file. Because we'll need to use sudo access to edit the file—this means we'll need to edit the file as an administrator—we'll edit the file using vi editor, which comes with all Linux and OS X distributions. In the terminal application, type sudo vi /etc/hosts and type your Mac password (you'll need to be an administrative user of your Mac). You'll see a file that looks similar to the following:

```
##
# Host Database
#
# localhost is used to configure the loopback interface
# when the system is booting. Do not change this entry.
##
127.0.0.1 localhost
```

Just add the following to the bottom of the file: 127.0.0.1 drupal8. You move to the bottom of the screen using the arrow keys. Next, press the "I" key to go into insert mode, and type 127.0.0.1 drupal8. Press the escape key (the "esc" key). Then type :wq. When you pressed the escape key, you left insert mode and went into command mode; then you issued the command after the colon (wq), which stands for "write" and "quit." So you saved/wrote the file to disk and then quit back to the terminal application command prompt. So not only did you edit the file, but you also learned some basic vi editor skills.

Now there is just one more configuration file to edit. Type sudo vi /Applications/MAMP/conf/apache/httpd.conf and again type your Mac user password, if prompted. You'll be editing your MAMP httpd.conf file. At the end of the file add the following:

```
<VirtualHost *:8888>
DocumentRoot "/Users/your-user-name/Sites/drupal8/drupal"
ServerName drupal8
</VirtualHost>
```

The hosts file and httpd.conf file configuration we just entered will make it so that when you go to http://drupal8:8888 in your web browser, you'll be pointing that URL to your new Drupal installation.

Replace your-user-name above with your username on your Mac.

Now you're ready to install Drush and download and install Drupal.

You can find the official instructions to install Drush at http://docs.drush.org/en/master/install/. There's also a video on how to install Drush using Composer: www.youtube.com/watch?v=eAtDaD8xzOQ&feature=youtu.be.

Once Drush is installed on your system, you can go to your /Users/your-user-name/Sites/drupal8/ directory and type drush dl drupal. As an alternative, you can go to drupal.org and manually download the file to your local machine; then unzip it into the drupal8 directory.

Now all the Drupal files will be in place. You can go to the URL you set up in your httpd.conf file—http://drupal8:8888/install—and run through the Drupal installation screens, filling out the installation forms by inputting the Drupal database name you created earlier, the database password, a username for your administrator account, and a password for the administrator account (refer to Chapter 1 for more detailed directions).

Next we'll take a look at installing Drupal on a Windows machine using a LAMP package called XAMPP. Many of the steps are exactly the same as you've seen for installing MAMP.

Installing Drupal with XAMPP on a Windows Machine

To install XAMPP on your Windows machine, go to www.apachefriends.org/index.html and click the link to download XAMPP for Windows. There is an installation package for OS X as well, but my personal preference is to use MAMP on a Mac. Run through the installer for XAMPP once you've downloaded the installer.

Once you've installed XAMPP, go to the Start menu in the lower left of your Windows GUI (graphical user interface), and click to open the XAMPP control panel (see Figure A-8).

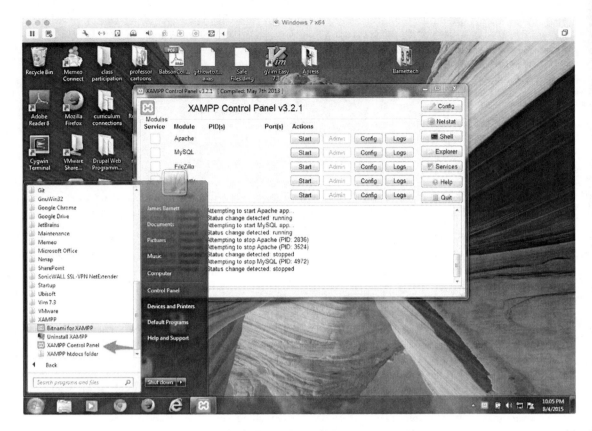

Figure A-8. *Opening the XAMPP control panel*

Once the control panel is open, you'll see the screen shown in Figure A-9. Click the Start button next to Apache and MySQL.

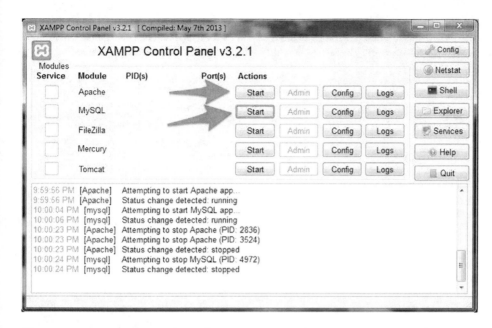

Figure A-9. Starting the Apache and MySQL servers in the XAMPP control panel

Once the two servers are started, click the Admin button next to the Apache Start button you just clicked. You'll be taken to the basic Apache start page, as shown in Figure A-10.

Figure A-10. The XAMPP Apache start page

Now that XAMPP is set up, any web pages that you put in the `c:\xampp\htdocs` directory (the Apache docroot directory—the base directory within Apache to serve up web files from) will be served up by XAMPP's Apache server. Figure A-11 shows a simple PHP script I created and had served up on the web server.

Figure A-11. *The XAMPP Apache server, serving up a simple PHP file placed in the* `c:\xampp\htdocs` *directory*

Now that you have XAMPP running, installing Drupal is as simple as downloading it from `drupal.org` into the `c:\xampp\htdocs` directory. Alternatively, you can install Drush from this URL and install Drupal using Drush: `https://github.com/drush-ops/drush/releases/download/6.0.0/Drush-6.0-2013-08-28-Installer-v1.0.21.msi`. Drush is an easy-to-use Windows installer; it may be slightly out of date but is still usable. You can find the most up-to-date link with instructions to install Drush on Windows at `http://docs.drush.org/en/master/install/#windows-zip-package`.

You'll notice that there's a warning on the `docs.drush.org` page that Drush does work better on a Linux-based system, a Mac, or other Linux installation. In general Drupal is a LAMP-based system, and it will be easier to use on a Linux-based operating system.

Summary

These are just two ways to install Drupal: using MAMP for the Mac or XAMPP for Windows (yes, you can use XAMPP on a Mac; I haven't tried it, but I bet it works quite well). Chapter 1 covered installing Drupal using Acquia Dev Desktop, and Chapter 10 covered installing Drupal in the cloud on an Ubuntu Linux box. If you've followed along, you will be well on your way toward being very adept at installing Drupal in any environment you may encounter.

APPENDIX B

■ ■ ■

Basic Linux Commands

This appendix includes a short and sweet reference of some basic and frequently used Linux commands. Note you that you don't type the # sign, which signifies the command prompt in Linux; you type the command next to the command prompt. The following table describes commands for working with directories, including moving files within various directories. Following the table is a description of the key permissions-related commands you will use frequently.

Command	Descriptions
#pwd	Identifies the present working directory, such as /home/student1. If my username is student1, this is known as my home directory. On my Mac, my home directory is /Users/jbarnett.
#ls	Lists the contents of your directory.
#ls -ltr	Gives the ls command three arguments: l to give a long listing (more verbose output about your files and directories), t to sort by time, and r to sort in reverse chronological order. This is by far the command I use the most.
#cd directory_name	Changes to a given directory. You can use relative and absolute paths.
#mkdir directory_name	Creates a new directory. Specifying a folder name only creates the new directory within the present directory.
#touch filename.txt	Creates the file named filename.txt.
#cp filename.txt /home/student1	Copies the file named filename.txt file into the home directory.
#cp /home/student1/ filename.txt /home/ student2	Copies the file named filename.txt from the student1 directory into the student2 directory.
#mv filename.txt /home/student1	Moves the file named filename.txt into the student1 home directory without leaving behind a copy of the file in the directory it was moved from.
#rm filename.txt	Deletes the file named filename.txt. Warning: Avoid using rm -rf unless you really mean it—it deletes all files and folders from the present directory, as well as all folders and all folders within it.

(continued)

Command	Descriptions
`#cp /home/student1/ filename.txt ..`	Copies the file named `filename.txt` to the parent directory `/home`. The two dots (`..`) signify the parent directory, also referred to as "up one directory." (A single dot signifies the present directory.)
`#mv /home/student1/ filename.txt .`	Copies the file named `filename.txt` to the current directory. If I were in the `/var/www/student1` folder when I typed this command, for example, then `filename.txt` would be in the `/var/www/student1` folder after I entered this command. The single dot (`.`) refers to the current directory.

Now that you are familiar with the essential file- and directory-related Linux commands, it's important to understand how to identify, set, and apply permissions for these files.

The `chmod` command changes the permissions assigned to a file. To view a file's permissions, type `ls -l`.

You can set three types of permissions: user, for the currently logged-in user; group, for the group that owns the file; and other, for everyone else. The numbers 4, 2, and 1 correspond to the permissions for read–write–execute, respectively—so the number 4 is read, 2 is write, and 1 is execute. For example, if you wanted to assign to the group all three permission types (read, write, and execute), the group would have 4+2+1, which is 7. In this case, you would type `#chmod 070`. This commands means that the user has no permissions (the beginning 0), the group has all three permission types possible (7), and everyone else—other—has no permissions (the ending 0).

In some cases you will also want to change ownership for a file. To change the group ownership for `filename.txt` to be `www-data` (the name of the group needed to serve up web files without permission errors), type the following command: `#chgrp www-data filename.txt`. To change the user ownership for `filename.txt` to be student2, type `#chown student2 filename.txt`.

Index

▪ A

Acquia Dev Desktop, 1–2, 5

▪ B

Base theme
  bartik.info.yml file, 197–198
  boilerplate code, 197
Basic Linux commands, 331–332
Blog, creating
  basic page, 12
  blog node
    cck fields, 18
    content types, 18
    Manage fields, 18
  blog post
    authored on, 16
    blog's title/body fields, 14
    icons, 15
  save and
    publish, 13–14, 19
    unpublish, 16–17
  sticky, 13
  test first post, 12

▪ C

Cascading style sheets (CSS) primer, 167
  additional styles creation, 76–78
  backgrounds image, 86
  box model, 88–90
  classes and IDs, 78
  comments, 76
  conflicting styles, 79–80
  element, 81
  external style sheet, 74–75
  fonts and sizes, 83
  HTML, 73–74
  inline styles sheets, 81
  internal style sheets, 80–81
  links, 84
  <div> and <span> tags, 75–76
  positioning, 87
  tables, 84–86
  text, 82–83
CSS primer. *See* Cascading
    style sheets (CSS) primer
Custom Drupal module
  hello_world module, 91
  hello_world.info.yml, 91
  hello_world.permissions.yml file, 91
  hello_world.routing.yml file, 92
  hello_world.routing.yml file, 91
  scribble.jpeg, 95
Custom form
  block code, 222
  Drupal API documentation, 223, 225
  drupal_get_form function, 223
  FirstForm, 223
  helloWorldBlock3.php file, 222–223
  organic groups module, 222

▪ D

DNS. *See* Domain name service (DNS)
Domain name service (DNS), 313–314
Drupal docroot directory, 61–62
Drupal 8
  configuration process
    Drupal 8 site, 5
    final configuration screen, 4
    MySQL database, 4
  installation
    Acquia Dev Desktop, 2
    default settings, 2
    link, 3
  LAMP stack, 5
Drupal module. *See also* MySQL Primer
  bare bones custom, 58
  block layout option, custom block on page, 149
  boilerplate code, 62

Drupal module (*cont.*)
    creation, 262–263
    directory structure, 60
    docroot directory, 57
    Drupal 8 directory structure, 59
    inserting data, 263–265, 267–269
    Github code, 59
    hello_world, 71–72
    HTML, 63–65, 67–71
    MySQL (*see* MySQL queries)
    object-oriented coding, 61
    PHP code, 147–148
    hello_world to hello World Block1, 150
    preceding code, 149
    programmatically created
        custom block, 151–152
    region to place block into on page, 150–151
    syntax, 59
    updating and deleting, 269–270
    YAML, 60
Drupal site
    add user, 9
    authenticated users, 8
    blocks
        basic text/HTML, 21
        block layout, 19–20
        custom block library, 23–24
        regions, 19, 21
    views
        bloglist, 26
        content types, 24, 27–28
        edit view link, 25
        GUI, 29
        site information, 29
        wikis/blogs, 27

■ E

External style sheet
    CSS rule, 75
    HTML file, 74

■ F

Firebug
    CSS, 103–104
    installation, 101–102
    net tab, 102–103
Form API
    hello_world module, 205–206
    URL, 206
Form directory
    drupal.org documentation, 207
    FirstForm.php file, 206–207
    form array, 207

method setErrorByName, 210
object-oriented coding structure, 207
validateForm function, 208
validation error, 210

■ G

Git
    experimental coding and projects, 227
    git cherry-pick, 243
    git diff . command, 245–246
    git log command, 241
    git show command, 242
    graphical user interfaces, 247
    installation
        command prompt, 230
        Git Bash program
          command window, 230
        Linux, 230–231
        Mac, 228
        Windows, 228–229
    production branch, 227
    Sourcetree, 248
Github
    book's code repository, 232
    Drupal code, 231
    git branch command, 233
    git remote show origin command, 234
    hello World module, 232
    repository
        clone, 236
        Github account, 234
        git status command, 237
        navigation, 237–240

■ H

HelloWorldController.php, 170–171
hook_permission() function, 174
HTML. *See* HyperText markup language (HTML)
HyperText Markup Language (HTML)
    adding anchors
        frequently asked question, 48
        href link, 49
        Lorem ipsum generators, 49
        real code, 49
        take me back to the top, 49–50
        Visit Section 5, 48
    adding comments, 44
    CSS, 73–74
    custom module, 62
    elements, 64–66, 68–71
    first web page
        Drupal essentials primer, 41
        Komodo edit, 39–40, 42, 44

nested tags, 42
web browser, 44
wrapped text, 41
forms, creation
all together, 54
drop-downs, 53
elements, 51–52
password fields, 52
radio buttons, 52
submit buttons, 53
text areas, 53
text fields, 52
images, 44, 46
layout elements, 55–56
limitations, 73
lists, creating, 46–47
tables, creating, 47–48

■ I

Inline styles sheets, 81
Internal style sheets, 80–81

■ J, K

JavaScript
console.log message, 123
draggable jQuery library, 122–123
Firebug console, 122
hello_world module, 119
helloWorldController.php file, 121
hello_world.js file, 122
hello_world.module file, 120
hello_world.routing.yml file, 119
JavaScript Primer
code modification, 104–106
events, 109–112
hello World script, 97–99
jQuery l (*see* jQuery library)
programming constructs
arrays, 108
Booleans, 109
integers/numbers, variables, 107
objects, 108–109
strings, 107–108
variables, 106–107
web page, 99–101
jQuery library
accordion affect, 115
events, 116–117
HTML file, 113–114

■ L

Linux
directories and
managing files, 276–278
Mac, 271–272
searching, 282
security, 278–282
shell scripts, 282–283
Linux box
cloud
"Brand New" status, 296
disadvantage, 296
install Drush, 301
IP address, ssh protocol, 297–298
LAMP stack, 299–300
Linode dashboard, 296–297
Putty program, 299
speed-of-light fiber
communications, 296
Ubuntu and root password, 296
www.linode.com, 294
Drupal
configure site, 309–310
creation, database, 307
DAMP installer, 303
database name and
MySQL username, 307–308
DNS, 313
domain zone, Linode.com, 316
DreamHost, 313
drupaltest, 303
front page, 311–312
installation setup process, 304, 309
mypersonalvillage.com, 315–318
MySQL database, 306
NameVirtualHost 23.92.31.153\:80, 314
requirements problems, 305
"save and continue" button, 311
"standard" installation profile", 304
www.mypersonalvillage.com, 313
Komodo edit
configuration, 285–286
Linux files, 284
opening, local/remote file, 284–285
remote directory, 288–289
select file, 288, 290
sftp connection,
configuration, 286–287
VIM, 290–291
web pages, 302

■ M

MAMP
 Drupal installation on Mac
  hosts file and httpd.conf
   file configuration, 327
  LAMP package XAMPP, 327
  Mac terminal application, 323–324
  MAMP control panel, 321–322
  new database creation
   with PhpMyAdmin, 325–326
  PHP and MYSQL set up, 323
  PhpMyAdmin databases tab, 325
  web page on localhost, 322
 Homebrew, 321
 MySQL database, 321
Model, view and controller (MVC)
  design pattern, 63–64
MVC design pattern. *See* Model, view and
  controller (MVC) design pattern
MySQL Primer
 AND and OR keywords, 164
 database, creation, 249–251
 deletion, 260–261
 distinct keyword, 162
 order by, 165
 tables
  command line, 252, 254
  inserting data, 254
  phpMyAdmin, creation, 251–252
  updation, 257, 259–260
  viewing, 255–257
 where keyword, 163–164
 wildcard character in queries, 161–162
MySQL queries
 data display, 157, 159–161
 node and users table within
   Drupal8 database, 153–154
 node_field_data table within
   phpMyAdmin, 154–155
 phpMyAdmin, 152–153
 relational databases, 155
 results of, 152
 running query in phpMyAdmin, 156
 "WHERE" clause, 157

■ N

Node creation
 code, 214, 216
 content list, 218
 content tab, 217
 custom form, 213, 219–220
 Drupal's Form API, 221
 FirstForm.php fil, 210, 212

■ O

Overriding theme functions
 bartikJLB subtheme, 199–200
 Drupal core ships, 199
 drupal.org, 200
 hook_theme_registry_alter function, 202–203
 in module, 202
 theme_username function, 201

■ P, Q, R

PHP code
 hello_world.module file, 143, 145
 web page, 145
phpMyAdmin
 command line, 250–251
 creation, 249–250
PHP Primer, Drupal
 basic codes
  Apache docroot directory, 128–129
  web browser, 130
 functions
  array_keys and array_values, 140
  array_push command, 139
  array_search function, 138–139
  assort, arsort, ksort,
   and krsort commands, 140
  description, 136
 hello World Web Page, 126–127
 if, if else, and else if statements, 133
 installation, 125
 looping structures
  foreach Loop, 130–131
  while Loop, 131–132
 printing to screen, 132
 strings
  strlen, 135
  strpos and stripos
   commands, 135–136
 switch statement, 134

■ S

Shell scripts, 282–283
Site building
 add-on modules
  drush, 35–36
  URL, 37
 site's theme
  copy link address, 34
  drush, 30, 32–33
  file transfer protocol, 30, 34
  secure file transfer protocol, 30, 34
  URL, 34

site users
    anonymous user, 11
    Drupal permissions system, 9
    type of control, 10
title and logo, 7–8
web sites, 7
Subtheme
    barnettechetJLB.info.yml file, 194
    barnettechetJLB subtheme, 191–192
    Bartik (classy) subtheme, 189–191
    CSS files, 193, 195
    Drupal subtheme, 189
    Firebug, 196
    Github, 192
    README.txt file, 190

■ T

Theme functions
    CSS, 167
    helloWorldController.php, 167–168, 170–172
    hello_world.module file, 170
    hello_world.theme.inc, 169–170
    hello world Twig Template, 176–177
    hook_theme, 169
    MVC, 176
    template, 172–176
    theme_hello_world_primary_page, 170
Twig control structures
    for loops, 180
    if statements, 180
Twig functions
    date, 181
    dump, 181
    include, 181
Twig Primer
    blocks, 183
    comments, 181

comparisons, 185
conditional inheritance, 183
control structures (*see* Twig control structures)
dynamic inheritance, 183
escaping characters, 184
extensions, 186
filters, 179–180
functions. Twig functions
hashes, arrays,
        strings and integers, 184
home page, 178
in and not in, 186
in Drupal 8, 187
in PHP, 178
math, 185
null and true/false values, 184
regular expressions, 185
string interpolation, 186
template inheritance, 182–183
tests, 186
variables, 179
Twig's syntax, 176

■ U, V, W

Ubuntu
    Mac, 273
    Windows, 273–276

■ X, Y, Z

XAMPP
    Drupal installation on Windows Machine
        Apache and MySQL servers, 328–329
        Apache start page, 329
        control panel opening, 327–328
        serving up simple PHP file, 330
    LAMP package, 327

Get the eBook for only $5!

Why limit yourself?

Now you can take the weightless companion with you wherever you go and access your content on your PC, phone, tablet, or reader.

Since you've purchased this print book, we're happy to offer you the eBook in all 3 formats for just $5.

Convenient and fully searchable, the PDF version enables you to easily find and copy code—or perform examples by quickly toggling between instructions and applications. The MOBI format is ideal for your Kindle, while the ePUB can be utilized on a variety of mobile devices.

To learn more, go to www.apress.com/companion or contact support@apress.com.

CPSIA information can be obtained at www.ICGtesting.com
Printed in the USA
LVOW09s2238011015

456633LV00005B/30/P